BREAKING NEWS

BREAKING NEWS

Renaissance Journalism and the Birth of the Newspaper

Chris R. Kyle and Jason Peacey

The Folger Shakespeare Library
Washington DC 2008

This volume has been published in conjunction with the exhibition *Breaking News: Renaissance Journalism and the Birth of the Newspaper* presented at the Folger Shakespeare Library, Washington, DC, from September 25, 2008 through January 31, 2009.

Gail Kern Paster, Director

Richard Kuhta, Eric Weinmann Librarian

Elizabeth Walsh, Exhibition Consultant
Virginia Millington, Exhibitions Manager

Julie Ainsworth and Tom Wachs, Photography

This exhibition and the catalog accompanying it have been funded by the The Gladys Krieble Delmas Foundation and The Winton and Carolyn Blount Exhibition Fund of Folger Shakespeare Library.

Printed in the United States.

Distributed by University of Washington Press,
Seattle and London
ISBN 978-0-295-98873-3

ACKNOWLEDGMENTS

The question is often posed: "Is the newspaper dead?" In an age in which information is largely gleaned online or through the television, print journalism threatens to become increasingly irrelevant. Print newspaper subscriptions are declining, the papers are shrinking, and the previously authoritative broadside format is being replaced by smaller, more commuter-friendly sizes. The outlook appears bleak. But ever since the newspaper developed in early modern Europe, papers have evolved in format and content and the role they play in society. While the printed newspaper may be on the wane, public demand for breaking news remains. People are increasingly turning to online sources for information. Unique "hit" counts on newspaper websites are showing dramatic increases and publications have adapted by offering content especially designed for this new medium. The newspaper is once again evolving to meet the insatiable demand for news.

This exhibition began when both of us held fellowships at the Folger Shakespeare Library. Explorations into the Library's holdings revealed the Folger to be a major repository of early newsbooks, newspapers, and periodicals. From that realization sprang the idea of an exhibition on the development of the newspaper in England and colonial America. This exhibition draws attention not merely to the ways in which early newspapers appear very alien to modern news consumers, but also highlights many crucial elements of the modern newspaper which can be traced to their earliest ancestors. The English newspaper in the seventeenth century began as a dry purveyor of translated foreign news, which later evolved into a serial publication that included elements recognizable to readers today: editorials, classified advertisements, illustrations, letters to the editor, and political, partisan commentary. The process of selecting items and objects for inclusion was undertaken with the idea of highlighting these parallels and tracing key developments in the newspaper's evolution.

In tracing this history we have incurred many debts. Both Gail Kern Paster, Director of the Folger Shakespeare Library, and Richard Kuhta, the Eric Weinmann Librarian, showed tremendous enthusiasm for the project from its inception and did much to bring it to fruition. As ever, the Reading Room staff at the Folger has been a wonderful and generous resource, and quickly and with good humor dealt with our never-ending requests for material. Erin Blake, Curator of Art and Special Collections, Heather Wolfe, Curator of Manuscripts, Steven Galbraith, Curator of Books, and Georgianna Ziegler, Head of Reference, all provided their expertise at various stages of the project. Their knowledge of the Folger collections helped to bring this exhibition together as a coherent whole. Of course, none of this would have been possible without the creativity and skill of the Folger conservation department, particularly Frank Mowery, Head of Conservation. His zeal and inventiveness is boundless, and his input has been invaluable. The beauty of the catalogue design is down to the wonderful imagination of Antonio Alcalá of Studio A.

Our greatest debt of gratitude is owed to two people: Virginia Millington, Exhibitions Manager, and Elizabeth Walsh, Head of Reader Services. We have spent countless hours in the vault poring over material, even more in meetings and in hundreds of e-mails, and not once has their enthusiasm or generosity ever flagged. This exhibition simply would not have happened without their tireless work, creative ideas and willingness to join in this enterprise. Our debt to them is immeasurable. We must also express our gratitude to Caryn Lazzuri, who had this whole project thrust upon her at the very last minute. She has quickly learnt the vagaries of exhibition management and contributed greatly to the successful completion of this project.

Finally, we would like to offer a note of personal thanks to colleagues and friends who have spent far more of their lives hearing about seventeenth-century newspapers than they ever imagined. At Syracuse University, Chris would like to thank his colleagues in the History Department for patiently listening to seemingly endless ideas about obscure newspapers and his friends in the Physics Department, particularly Mark Trodden, who all too often had to put away the formation of the very early universe to discuss the formation of very early newspapers. Last, but by no means least, Chris' brilliant wife, Dympna Callaghan, has provided wisdom, energy, wit and intellect throughout this project. Jason would like to express his thanks to colleagues at University College London for their support, and to Annette Bullen, who has never shown any sign of boredom with his many tales from the archives, and who has never complained about the fact that her partner kept abandoning her in London in order to make extended trips to Washington.

Chris R. Kyle and Jason Peacey

Today, the newspaper as we have known it is in mortal danger—threatened by dwindling circulation numbers, falling advertising revenues, and most of all a loss of readership to the explosive proliferation of new digital media. Most Americans do not remember a time when daily newspapers were delivered to homes both morning and evening, and when every major American city had more than one important daily newspaper, contending for public attention and influence over public opinion. We are told frequently that younger Americans tend to receive news on their computers or through broadcast media, expecting instant and apparently unfiltered access to events as they unfold. As we ponder the dwindling influence of the print news in a digital age and the role of print news in delivering information about the world, there has never been a better time for a reminder of the origins of the earliest forms of print journalism in seventeenth-century England and the transformative power of newsprint on government, on social mores, and on the development of public opinion and the public sphere.

"Breaking News: Renaissance Journalism and the Birth of the Newspaper" offers a bracing and informative look at the beginnings of journalism and the myriad material forms in which news of all kinds was delivered to the English reading public. It is perhaps not surprising to learn that the delivery of news in print dates almost from the beginnings of print in England with William Caxton or how early in the history of printing news monarchs and parliaments tried to manipulate the press for their own ends. One of the themes running throughout this exhibition catalog is the perennial tension between the government and the press—a tension expressed in attempts at suppression of "seditious" newsbooks, in censorship and the regulation of the news as a trade, or in official sponsorship of partisan publications. The dissemination of news and the gradual formation of the regular features of the modern newspaper owe a great deal to the unfolding crises of the British Civil Wars. It is little short of miraculous that many of the most popular forms of English newsprint survive, given the ephemerality and fragility of the early corantos, newsletters, broadside ballads (which became a clever way of delivering news by other means), broadsheets, and pamphlets. But the Folger's collection is strong in such rare ephemera, allowing our guest curators Chris R. Kyle and Jason Peacey to document in rich and absorbing detail the intimate involvement and huge impact of early journalism on the unfolding political crises of the seventeenth century. Journalism, they also make clear, was always commercial as well as political—satisfying an apparently perennial public appetite for scandal and sensation; creating niche products for specialized groups of readers; and demonstrating an interest in making news no less than reporting it in matters such as ladies' fashion. The cultural profile of the civilized and amiable English gentleman of the early eighteenth century, familiar to many even today through the anthologized occasional essays of Addison and Steele, was itself largely a creation of influential periodical magazines such as *The Tatler* or *The Spectator.*

I and my colleagues at the Folger are deeply grateful to Chris Kyle and Jason Peacey for their enthusiastic and persuasive proposal for this exhibition and catalog, their painstaking research into a complex and multi-faceted history, and their clear-sighted definition of what materials in the Folger collection could most powerfully convey this explosive and fast-moving story—the birth of modern journalism in the political cauldron of mid-seventeenth century England.

Gail Kern Paster

Detail, figure 6

On May 23, 1618, members of Bohemia's Protestant aristocracy subjected two representatives from the newly elected Catholic King Ferdinand of Bohemia to a mock trial and threw them out of a window in Prague Castle, fifty feet above the ground. Remarkably, the officials survived. In the Catholic version of events, their lives were spared by angels who comforted their fall. The Protestants, on the other hand, claimed that as the representatives landed in a pile of manure, God had shown what he thought of Catholic "heresy." The Defenestration of Prague, as the event came to be known, sparked the Thirty Years' War, which engulfed Europe and created an insatiable demand for news throughout the continent.

In Germany and the Netherlands, the idea of a weekly serial providing reports about the war and other events throughout Europe rapidly developed. Weekly news sheets printed in English were first produced in Amsterdam by an enterprising Dutch publisher, who began exporting these serials to London in December 1620. The enterprise was so successful that it was picked up in England the following year by two publishers of cheap pamphlets, Nicholas Bourne and Nathaniel Butter. But it was not until 1702 that the first daily newspaper was available in England. In the intervening years, government censorship, the British Civil Wars, and the rise of partisan electoral politics all played significant roles in the development of the newspaper industry.

The printing press arrived in England in 1476. Like all his Continental counterparts, William Caxton, the first English printer, concentrated on producing religious works and editions of the classics. But amid this plethora of devotional and legal books and pamphlets, Caxton occasionally printed news items. However, the publication of news was not a deliberate effort to inform the English about affairs on the Continent but rather a bespoke publication by interested parties. For example, in 1483, Caxton printed a series of letters exchanged between Giovanni Mocenigo, Doge of Venice, and Pope Sixtus IV on the peace treaty between the papacy and the Duke of Ferrara. The publication was sponsored by Petrus Carmelianus, a Venetian residing in England, whose motivation was to bolster support for Venice.

It did not take long for the government to realize the value of the printing press in spreading news and information. In 1484, Parliament deliberately encouraged the establishment of presses and the immigration of foreign printers and other workers engaged in the new book trade. The government also moved quickly to use the new technology to disseminate propaganda, beginning in 1486 when a printed proclamation was circulated in England announcing that Pope Innocent VIII had confirmed Henry VII's right to the throne of England. Given Henry's precarious hold on the throne after the Wars of the Roses, assuring the people that he had papal support was a matter of some urgency.

At the dawn of the sixteenth century, the print trade was a small but well-established industry in England. In the decades following, it grew steadily into an important tool for the dissemination of information and news. The next significant advance in the industry came about, like so much else, as a result of Henry VIII's desire to divorce Catherine of Aragon in order to marry Anne Boleyn. Henry was a master of state propaganda, and he turned to the printing press to influence opinion throughout Europe. He needed to convince a reluctant Pope Clement VII to grant an annulment of his marriage; thus, he sought and ordered learned treatises to be published that explained and justified his actions. Pamphlet after pamphlet rolled off the presses stating Henry's case.

With the increasing importance of the press, the government moved to control and license print. This was accomplished by licensing printers and by using monopoly patents. By 1534, the early encouragement given to foreign printers disappeared, as Parliament passed legislation restricting their trade. Further restrictions on printing were implemented in 1538, when the government issued a proclamation to regulate the industry. The Crown thus exerted control over printing by granting certain privileges. For example, in 1538, Richard Grafton was awarded a patent that gave him sole right to print the Bible for a period of seven years.

Strict control of the press was a defining feature of Tudor England. Proclamation after proclamation was issued to restrict "seditious books" and to restrain anyone who interfered with or commented upon "affairs of state." For the Protestant Elizabethan government, faced with the "unnatural" rule of a woman in a patriarchal society, internal dissension from recusant Catholic nobles, and the threats posed by the papacy and Catholic Spain, control of the news was an urgent priority. This is not to say that all news was banned. Generally, it was safe to print news about murders, natural events, the appearance of witches, and criminals. Such news coverage took many forms, from single-sheet broadside ballads to lengthy pamphlets. Single-issue news items like *The Strange and Marueilous Newes Lately Come from the Great Kingdome of Chyna* (ca. 1577), which were as much travel narratives as actual news, also escaped the censor's wrath. But any attempt in England to discuss politics, government policies, or matters of state was quickly suppressed, and perpetrators often found their presses closed and were themselves thrown into prison. Most news, then, was spread via personal letters, at least until the 1620s when a revolution took place.

That revolution began on December 2, 1620, when the first newspaper arrived in England in the form of a coranto from an Amsterdam publisher, Pieter van den Keere (FIG.1). Amsterdam was the European center of the emerging news industry, and van den Keere had experience working in England. The first issue contained news from major European cities, as well as reports on the progress of the war. However, while publication was continuous, it was sporadic, and issues appeared, on average, only twice a month. Although there is no indication of how many copies were imported or sold, the coranto was evidently popular enough for English publishers to make its production a homegrown industry.

During the early decades of the seventeenth century, English news reporting was dominated by Nathaniel Butter and his business partner, Nicholas Bourne.

FIG. 1
The New Tydings out of Italie
Amsterdam: George Veseler, to be sold by Petrus Keerius dwelling in Calvert Street, 1620
C.55.1.2
Courtesy of the British Library

Newspapers first arrived in England in the form of corantos. The first coranto published in English was printed in Amsterdam and dated December 2, 1620. Its initial success led in 1621 to publication shifting to London. Early corantos followed a standard format of a single sheet, peppered with news from the major cities of Europe and the battlefields of the Thirty Years' War.

The new tydings out of Italie are not yet com.

Out of Weenen, the 6 November.

THe French Ambaſſadour hath cauſed the Earle of Dampier to be buried ſtately at Preſburg. In the meane vvhile hath Bethlem Gabor cited all the Hungeriſh States, to com together at Preſburg the 5. of this preſent, to diſcourſe aboute the Crovvning & other cauſes concerning the ſame Kingdom.

The Hungarians continue vvith roveing againſt theſe Lands. In like manner thoſe of Moravia, vvhich are fallen upon the Coſackes yeſter night by Hoſleyn, ſet them on fire, and ſlaine many dead, the reſt vvill revenge the ſame.

Heere is certaine nevves com, that the Crabats, as alſo the Lord Budean, are fallen unto Betlem Gabor.

The Emperour ſends the Earle of Altheim as Ambaſſadour to Crackovv in Polen, to appeare upon the ſame meeting-day.

Novv comes tidings, that Betlem Gabor is at Thurna, there doe gather to gether great ſtore of States.

The Emper. Maj. hath appoynted heere a meeting-day upon the 1. of Decemb. thereupon ſhould appeare the 4. Proclaimed States. The appoynted taxing ſhall bring up a great ſom of money.

Detail figure 1.

Butter already had an established career as a member of the Stationers' Company and had experience in publishing occasional newsbooks, such as *News from Spaine* (1613). These publications, despite the fact they contained only rare mentions of English troop movements on the Continent, aroused official ire. James I asked the Dutch government to ban the export of corantos in English and issued a proclamation prohibiting the discussion of matters of state. One of the first booksellers involved in the trade, Thomas Archer, was imprisoned for publishing news in the summer of 1621. Butter, however, had more success. In September 1621, he obtained a license to publish weekly corantos translated from the Dutch. He altered the format, changing it from a single sheet to a newsbook, which varied in length from eight to twenty-four pages, although the cost remained low, at a mere 2 *d.* each. Thereafter, the early newsbooks gradually evolved in both style and form. They did not have a set title, taking instead the headline news of the week as a way of defining each issue. But by mid-October 1622, they were numbered consecutively, and they later came to include the weekly dates which the news covered. It was stated prominently on the front page that they offered "a continuation of the weekly news."

Butter's news industry rapidly attracted unwelcome attention. He was mercilessly satirized in Ben Jonson's play *The Staple of News* (1626), in which he appeared as Cymbal, a purveyor of idle gossip and frivolity. More significantly for Butter, the government intervened once again in news publication. In 1627, faced with a crisis in foreign policy as war erupted between England and the two European superpowers, France and Spain, Butter was imprisoned for publishing news reports from the Continent. His incarceration did not last long, however, and both he and Bourne were soon back at work, although the news appeared with less regularity and was more circumspect. However, in 1632 the government acted once again, this time at the behest of the Spanish ambassador, Juan de Nicolaldo. On the Continent, the new Protestant champion, King Gustavus Adolphus of Sweden, was driving back Catholic forces in northern Europe. Fearful that the news would inflame public opinion in England toward a more interventionist role in the war, the Privy Council suppressed the publication of all newsbooks and commanded Butter and Bourne to cease printing.

However, it quickly became clear that while the government could pressure individuals and the Stationers' Company, it could not stop the news. Increasingly, the news appeared in the form of single-sheet ballads, a format that had not been suppressed when newsbooks were prohibited. After petitioning the King and negotiating with his agents, Butter and Bourne finally received a patent to start printing news again in December 1638. However, the renewal of their license came at a high cost. They were forced to pay £10 yearly toward the repair of St. Paul's Cathedral and to abide by the harsh restrictions placed upon news publications by a Star Chamber decree of 1637. The government edict appointed a censor for newsbooks and dramatically increased the penalties for publishing deemed to be seditious. Butter and Bourne struggled in this new environment. Government officials were slow to approve their copy, and the range of news

FIG. 2
James Cranford (1602/3–1657)
The Teares of Ireland
London: Printed by A.N. for John Rothwell, 1642
166- 401q, pp. 75, 79

Stories of wartime atrocities inspired as much outrage in the seventeenth century as they do today. As Britain drifted towards civil war following the Catholic rebellion in Ireland (1641), London's presses produced dozens of pamphlets with exaggerated tales of massacred Protestants. These images come from a compilation of such stories, produced by a Puritan minister in London, showing how brutality allegedly extended even to infant children, and also demonstrating how many people obtained their news from reading public notices.

they could safely provide was severely limited. In 1639, the regular publication of newsbooks ceased, and only a few issues appeared the following year.

The early decades of the seventeenth century reveal a burgeoning market for printed news and a demand for information about current affairs which seriously outstripped supply because the government was too nervous to allow the industry to flourish. During the late 1630s and early 1640s, however, a new and profound revolution in the news occurred, which can be attributed to three factors. First, the public desire for news became increasingly focused upon domestic affairs, as religious and political tensions mounted in England, Scotland, and Ireland. Second, the summoning of Parliament in 1640, after eleven years of so-called "personal rule" during which Charles I refused to call a Parliament, and the election of many political and religious reformers ensured that much more domestic news was generated. Third, these reforming impulses ensured the dismantling of the mechanisms for press censorship, as well as the trial and imprisonment of many bishops and clerics believed to have abused their licensing power by suppressing worthy books by Puritan authors, and promoting instead excessive royal powers, as well as displaying crypto-Catholic sympathies.

The result of these reforms was a dramatic explosion in topical tracts and pamphlets and a transformation of the news industry. In the opening weeks of the so-called Long Parliament, weekly manuscripts emerged, recounting the "diurnall" or daily events in Parliament and outlining the latest decisions taken in both the House of Lords and the House of Commons. In short order, these manuscripts were supplemented and eventually supplanted by printed weekly newspapers that concentrated on domestic news. Among these was the famous *Perfect Diurnall*, produced by Samuel Pecke, which soon became one of the most popular, respected, and long-running titles of the era. Although these early printed newspapers initially contained no more information than their manuscript predecessors, they could be produced at a fraction of the cost and thus be made available to a much wider audience. Newspapers were given stable titles, were consecutively numbered and paginated, and appeared regularly on set days of the week. As such, they offered the potential for transforming consumer habits and expectations in the acquisition of news.

Further impetus for the growth of this fledgling trade was provided by the drift toward armed conflict within the British Isles. Fighting began in Ireland with the outbreak of the Catholic rebellion in 1641, which revived fears of "popish" plots; these fears had scarcely diminished since the defeat of the Spanish Armada in 1588 and the associated plots against Elizabeth I's life. The Irish rebellion brought with it lurid stories of atrocities and massacres, and London's presses poured forth a torrent of short tracts and pamphlets filled with horrific news stories, with titles such as *Bloudy Newes from Ireland*. Some, like the tract entitled *The Teares of Ireland*, even added gruesome pictures (FIG. 2). The cumulative effect of such publications was to raise tensions and make civil war across Britain much more likely. As soon as this wider conflagration began, every skirmish was reported in newspapers and in pamphlets with titles such as *A True Relation of a Great Battel* and *True but Sad Newes from Shrewsbury*. In this time of upheaval and bloodshed, people scrabbled for information about the kingdom's descent into chaos and disorder, and the newspaper industry more than managed to cater to their needs.

As has so often been the case throughout history, war provided an incredibly powerful stimulus for change, and nowhere more so than in journalism and the news industry. To understand the nature of the changes that took place during the decades of civil war and revolution, it is possible to identify five key trends.

The first of these trends is marked not just by the dramatic growth in size of the domestic news industry, but also by the increasingly commercial nature of that industry. The number of available titles proliferated, to the point where consumers could get access to the latest information almost every day of the week. This sometimes bewildering variety reflected a response to a growing demand for information and the awareness that money could be made from producing short, topical pamphlets. This mixture of commercial pressure and popular demand ensured that journalists were in the forefront of the development of advertising, which became much more prevalent and much more sophisticated. Although these advertisements may seem quaint to modern readers, they display traits that persist into the modern world, from personal notices regarding lost and stolen property to overblown claims for new and exotic products. The growth of advertising, in turn, facilitated the explosion of commercial newspapers.

Many of the newspapers that were produced in the attempt to capitalize upon the popular thirst for information were unable to survive in an intensely competitive marketplace; several lasted only one or two issues. This is less significant than the fact that the industry was so open to newcomers and favorable to journalists from all walks of life. These included the former Thames bargeman John Taylor, the London ironmonger Henry Walker, and printers and publishers from the margins of the industry, including entrepreneurial women such as Jane Coe. The competitiveness of the news industry meant that consumers were regularly presented with the spectacle of journalistic rivalries spilling onto the pages of their newspapers, as editors reported on each other's errors, exaggerations, and outright lies and made allegations about their opponents' mercenary natures.

Another result of the commercialization of the news industry was that publishers and editors recognized that success lay in catering to niche markets. This did not necessarily mean that individual newspapers targeted audiences that were either exclusively populist or else uniformly elitist, and there is plentiful evidence that most titles were read by a cross-section of the population. But it is certainly evident that a paper like *The Kingdomes Weekly Intelligencer* was more factual and informative, while *Mercurius Elencticus* was gossipy and scandalous. Some publications, like *The Man in the Moon*, contained hardly any factual information, resorting instead to political commentary that could be highly offensive, even semipornographic.

The second trend in this competitive and commercial marketplace for news, amid the growth of specialized newspapers, was the industry's response to the nearly infinite variety of political and religious opinions that emerged during the Civil War. This meant not merely that Royalist newspapers such as *Mercurius Aulicus* lined up against Parliamentarian journals such as *Mercurius Britanicus*, but that all shades of opinion within these two sides were found in the news. Divisions within Royalist ranks, particularly during the late 1640s, were mirrored in the press, as journalists loyal to Charles I offered conflicting advice about the alliances and tactics that he should pursue and made very different interpretations of his likely fate. After 1646, this variety was matched and even exceeded among the king's opponents, as the victorious Parliamentarians split over options for the future and as new varieties of political radicalism emerged in the years before and after the king's execution. *The Scottish Dove*, among others, represented moderate Parliamentarian views, while *Perfect Occurrences* recorded the views of the army and its friends in Parliament. Tensions between such factions can be demonstrated neatly in the way in which a newspaper like *The Moderate Intelligencer* came under attack from a would-be usurper, inaptly named *The Moderate*, whose editor rejected his rival's willingness to countenance a peaceful settlement with Charles I and aired genuinely radical views from the Levellers and other fringe elements of the Parliamentarian cause. These radicals called for the trial of the king, religious toleration, and wholesale constitutional reform, including the abolition of the House of Lords and the democratization of the House of Commons, and newspapers provided one of the key ways in which their ideas spread across the country.

Perhaps the most dramatic means of highlighting the intensity of internal political rivalries—both Royalist and Parliamentarian—is to examine the phenomenon of the counterfeit newspaper. From the early 1640s, successful journalists, editors, and publishers had been threatened by usurpers producing works that closely mimicked their own, in attempts to capitalize upon their commercial success by fooling customers into buying fraudulent copies. By the end of the decade, however, the regular counterfeiting of newspapers such as *Mercurius Pragmaticus* represented attempts to silence journalists who pursued a troublesome political agenda. In this case, many powerful courtiers clearly objected to the refusal by Marchamont Nedham—one of the leading Royalist journalists, but someone with unorthodox views, who was mistrusted by many for his former allegiance to Parliament—to argue that the king should join forces with the Scots in order to restart the war and revive his fortunes.

A third trend that can be discerned during the Civil Wars is the growing professionalization of the press. This is not to say, of course, that standards in printing and design improved across the board, since many short-lived titles were shoddily produced, poorly informed, and badly written. These inferior products were made with cheap paper and worn type, and they generally offered little besides pilfered and recycled news items. But there was rapid improvement in the best newspapers of the age in both news coverage and quality of writing.

FIG 3.
Robert White (1645–1703)
"Petrus Heylyn. S.T.P."
Engraving, 1681
D9516
Courtesy of the National Portrait Gallery, London

Many of those involved in writing the first English newspapers were anything but professional journalists. Peter Heylyn was a Church of England clergyman and scholar, who became a chaplain to Charles I and a leading polemicist on behalf of his government's religious policies in the 1630s. He is perhaps best known as a participant in any number of learned controversies, as a church historian, and as the biographer of his patron, Archbishop William Laud.

The Moderate Intelligencer, *The Kingdomes Weekly Intelligencer*, and *The Perfect Diurnall* were very well respected and generally deemed reliable. Even those titles whose content was received skeptically, such as Nedham's *Britanicus* or Gilbert Mabbott's *Moderate*, often featured the work of talented writers who were successful newspaper correspondents.

What lay behind this last development was the emergence of a professional breed of newspapermen. Initially, many of the best newspapers were written by men with proven literary talent, among them clergymen with well-established credentials as polemical authors, such as Peter Heylyn (FIG.3). Such men practiced journalism on a part-time basis. But it became apparent that newspapers required a particular kind of rhetorical flair, and by the mid-1640s the industry was already dominated by writers such as John Taylor and Henry Walker, who may have had little formal academic training but displayed wit and a racy, often scandalous style. The greatest journalists of the age, from Nedham to Sir John Berkenhead, came from outside the political and religious elite and owed their fame and fortune (in the case of Berkenhead, his knighthood) to their journalistic skills. Indeed, whether producing the dry and factual prose of *The Perfect Diurnall* or the fiery polemic of *Mercurius Britanicus*, writers were professionals, in that they worked and lived by their pens full-time. As such, they were deemed to be less than principled, sometimes with some good reason. Many journalists, from Nedham to Henry Care, had little difficulty in changing political sides, sometimes more than once.

Like so many other attributes of the modern press, the popular image of the journalist as a cynical hack can be traced back to the very origins of the newspaper business in the seventeenth century. Indeed, this distrust of journalists was deliberately fostered by the kind of satirical and polemical attacks upon the industry that appeared as early as the 1620s from the pens of such literary giants as Ben Jonson and which were produced more or less consistently for the remainder of the century. In ballads, plays, satires, and polemics, journalists were accused of being moneygrubbing, untrustworthy, and downright mendacious. However, some journalists were genuinely respected by their contemporaries, and even the more colorful members of the profession garnered grudging respect and a sizeable audience for their work. Contemporaries enjoyed the opinionated and accusatory polemics of Marchamont Nedham as much as the reliable news service of Samuel Pecke.

A fourth trend, one more or less in constant tension with the commercial imperative already outlined, was the growing determination on the part of political leaders to interfere with the press. This was based upon an acute awareness of the power of the journalistic medium and involved attempts to both reimpose censorship and produce propaganda. From the early months of the Civil Wars, leading Royalists and Parliamentarians sought to establish official newspapers, beginning with the Royalist *Mercurius Aulicus*, which was produced at Oxford (the king's headquarters). This drew upon the resources of royal administrators, such as the secretary of state, Sir Edward Nicholas, and the talents of Charles I's favorite courtiers, such as Lord Digby, not to mention the printing presses co-opted from Oxford University. Parliamentarians responded with *Mercurius Britanicus*, widely regarded as Westminster's official mouthpiece. In the months that followed, the two newspapers engaged in furious attacks and counterattacks.

As the years progressed, these official newspapers became increasingly sophisticated and well resourced, particularly those produced by Parliamentarians and the kingless regimes of the 1650s. *Mercurius Politicus* (published 1650–60), for example, was founded by order of the Republican Council of State, on the basis of a proposal submitted by Marchamont Nedham. Recently imprisoned for journalism that supported Charles I and his son, the future Charles II, Nedham advocated a new title that would "undeceive the people," that would be written "in a jocular way, or else it will never be cried up, for those truths which the multitude regard not in a serious dress . . . make music to the common sense, and charm the fancies, which ever sways the sceptre in vulgar judgments much more than reason." Like other contemporary journalists, Nedham recognized the need to "tickle the ears of the giddy multitude."

Once established, *Mercurius Politicus* drew upon the skills of a government printer, Thomas Newcombe, another former Royalist, and of a journalist, Nedham, who received a salary of £100 a year from the government, as well as a share of the paper's substantial profits. Nedham worked closely with Cromwell's secretary of state, John Thurloe, to ensure a regular supply of intelligence and information. In addition to the official newspapers, politicians sponsored an array of semi-official titles written by allies such as John Dillingham, to whom information could be leaked surreptitiously and who could be relied on to maintain government-approved positions.

What is intriguing about the Civil War era is that political leaders on all sides recognized that they could no longer treat print culture in general, and journalism in particular, as they once had. Rather than merely imposing restrictions upon the publication of news, they realized the need to combine censorship with propaganda. And censorship was much more of a priority than historians have sometimes suggested. The collapse of censorship in 1641 can be regarded as the unintended consequence of attempts to reform the structures and personnel of the government of the early Stuart kings. More importantly, there were efforts to impose some form of press censorship, with orders and ordinances in 1642, 1643, 1647, 1649, and 1653, such as the requirement that pamphlets and newspapers be licensed prior to publication. Licensing was never really effective, however, and authorities were only occasionally able to influence the substance of the weekly journals before publication. Nevertheless, Parliamentarian officials did punish editorial indiscretions—Nedham and the publisher of *Mercurius Britanicus* were repeatedly in trouble over scandalous comments about the king and various politicians—and they probably capitalized on journalists' fear of imprisonment in order to nudge editors in different political directions. Such pressure ensured that *Mercurius Britanicus* changed its editorial tack fairly frequently during the early 1640s, as different factions within Parliament sought to secure Nedham's services as a spokesman for their views.

The frequency with which contemporaries complained about Parliament's power over the press after 1641 is a reminder that censorship was hardly ineffective. Attempts to reimpose censorship during the 1640s resulted in fascinating debates about the advantages and disadvantages of a free press. These debates persisted throughout the seventeenth century, producing some of the most important defenses of political liberty in the canon of political thought. These included not only John Milton's *Areopagitica*, subtitled "a speech . . . for the liberty of unlicenc'd printing," but also writings by radicals such as John Lilburne, one of the leaders of the Levellers, who was repeatedly imprisoned for his fiery tracts and pamphlets arguing for freedom of the press, religious toleration, and political reform.

The culmination of this process whereby political grandees tightened their grip upon the news press occurred in the summer of 1655, when Oliver Cromwell's government managed to close all but two newspapers. The two remaining titles were both written by Marchamont Nedham as a salaried, if sometimes unreliable, government official. Nedham's papers, *Mercurius Politicus* and *The Publick Intelligencer*, were essentially identical, differing only in the days of the week on which they were published. They were immensely popular both in Britain and on the Continent, even if they were considered rather dull, and they were universally acknowledged to be tools for government propaganda. In other words, Cromwell achieved what few people had even imagined before 1640 and what would not be feasible after his Protectorate: effective censorship combined with a strict government news monopoly. Historians can only wonder whether the fate of Charles I would have been different if he or his father, James I, had heeded the advice offered to them to adopt precisely such tactics.

The fifth and final trend that can be traced to the mid-seventeenth century is arguably the most important, but also the hardest to demonstrate—the profound transformation of national political culture and the political life of the average British citizen. What is certain is how popular newspapers were during the Civil Wars and how strongly readers responded to them—with both fascination and derision. The public grew addicted to journalism, although its producers and products were thought to be as much untrustworthy as useful. Newspapers were a political necessity and a guilty pleasure.

We know what readers thought because so many people commented upon news titles in their letters, recorded newspaper purchases in account books, and annotated and preserved their newspapers in their libraries. Newspapers were regularly read by the aristocracy—Parliamentarians such as the Earl of Salisbury and Royalists such as the Earl of Bath—and by shopkeepers, tradesmen, ploughmen, soldiers, and sailors, women as well as men. The Earl of Leicester bought multiple titles every week to compare rival accounts of particular events, but even a humble woodturner like Nehemiah Wallington recorded that his house was full of newspapers, which he likened to "so many thieves that had stole

FIG. 4
Attributed to John Michael Wright (ca.1617–1694)
Sir Roger L'Estrange
Oil on canvas, ca. 1680
NPG 3771
Courtesy of the National Portrait Gallery, London

After fighting for Charles I during the Civil Wars, and being imprisoned for his pains, Sir Roger L'Estrange became one of the most important pamphleteers and propagandists in the service of Charles II after 1660. In addition to his journalism, he is known to have published at least 130 books and pamphlets, which tended to display a particularly virulent and intolerant brand of royalism. Having served three Stuart monarchs, he opposed the Glorious Revolution of 1688–9, and was repeatedly arrested as a "Jacobite" enemy of William III's government.

away my money before I was aware of them." Throughout the country and across the social spectrum, readers were keenly aware of dependable newspapers and scandalous ones, although many continued to consume both kinds simultaneously; the public grew increasingly adept at discerning political manipulation of the industry and the connections between journalists and politicians.

But the widespread popularity of newspapers is only part of the story. More intriguing is how the news industry changed public participation in political life. Newspapers helped create a common political culture where different regions and localities shared a national focus and national issues; newspapers gave people from all walks of life unprecedented amounts of information about daily political events. They broke down the traditional levels of secrecy about the monarch, royal court, and Parliament, and they allowed readers to observe the workings of government and the performance of politicians by providing details of speeches made in Parliament and information about where and when parliamentary committees would meet and who would sit on those committees. While the degree of accountability that might have resulted is difficult to measure, contemporary commentators such as Sir Roger L'Estrange certainly bemoaned what we would describe as the democratizing effects of the press, saying that newspapers made "the multitude too familiar with the actions and counsels of their superiors" and gave them "not only an itch but a colourable right and license to be meddling with the government" (FIG. 4).

Where L'Estrange's fears proved most justified was in the development of election literature. From the mid-seventeenth century onward, it was common for cheap pamphlets and newspapers to be used in order to influence voters prior to elections; such advice became increasingly detailed about specific candidates. While candidates could publish their electioneering speeches and newspapers could report on the controversies surrounding particular polls, interested observers could supply details about candidates and their voting records in Parliament. Members of the public were able to campaign for (or against) candidates, which ensured that the electorate had much more information upon which to base their decisions and to analyze the behavior of their fellow voters.

The history of journalism after the Restoration in 1660 has received much less scholarly attention than the advances of preceding decades, but this was not an unimportant or uninteresting period for the industry. Because it is often assumed that Charles II's return represented a turning back of the political clock to pre–Civil War days, there are two reasons to argue that the most important fact relating to late seventeenth century news was the persistence of many of the earlier trends outlined above, rather than their reversal.

First, the period after 1660 witnessed the almost complete suppression of newspapers, where strict censorship was combined with a government news monopoly, reflecting a determination to pursue the tactics of Oliver Cromwell rather than those of Charles I. This was most evident from the power of Sir Roger L'Estrange who, as the official press overseer, was particularly zealous in

FIG. 5
Marcellus Laroon
The Cryes of the City of London
London: H. Overton, 1711
DA688 L2 Cage, plate 56

The news was not only available in bookstores or in coffeehouses. London resonated with the cries of street vendors selling all types of wares. Here a woman offers copies of the *London Gazette*, the official government newspaper that first appeared in 1665 and is still published today.

prosecuting government critics. It is also evident from the central position of the government-controlled *London Gazette*, which began publication in 1665 and was written by the best polemicists of the day, just as its predecessor *Mercurius Politicus* was (FIG. 5).

Second, there was a brief but dramatic resurgence of journalism after 1679, indicating another trend first witnessed in 1641, when the collapse of censorship, combined with heightened political tensions, produced a new wave of journalistic endeavor. One of the most striking features of political debate during the late 1670s and early 1680s was the fear of renewed civil war, and there were clear parallels with the press coverage of the early 1640s. The licensing system that had been introduced in 1662 temporarily ended when the required legislation was not renewed; new stories emerged of a "popish plot," with fears that the heirless Charles II would be succeeded by his Catholic brother, the Duke of York (later James II). Added to this volatile mixture was vigorous political agitation in and out of Parliament by men opposed to the government (Whigs), who had clearly learned how to exploit the newspapers and other print media.

Beyond such continuities with pre-Restoration journalism, the industry under Charles II witnessed the intensification of trends apparent since the earliest days of printed news. For example, crime reporting became thoroughly integrated with wider political and religious concerns. Journalists emphasized the repentance of imprisoned and executed criminals, and they exploited public fears of moral collapse and social degeneracy for political and religious ends. They also warned readers of the dangers of undermining established authority and of gaining too much political and religious liberty. Such tendencies were even more dramatically evident after 1660, when a new civil war appeared increasingly likely, or when particularly notorious crimes occurred, such as the mysterious murder of the magistrate Sir Edmund Berry Godfrey in 1678 or the assault upon poet laureate John Dryden in 1679. Tories exploited the attack on Dryden in Covent Garden in order to suggest that the social order was collapsing, while Whig politicians and journalists made the most of Godfrey's murder on Primrose Hill to suggest that Catholics had infiltrated the political elite and sought to overthrow Charles II's Protestant government.

As important as it is to recognize that trends from the Civil Wars persisted into the later seventeenth century, it is also vital to highlight some very significant advances that took place only after 1660, with new and intriguing directions for the dissemination of news. The first of these involves the changing ways in which news was presented, with a shift from small quarto pamphlets of eight or more pages toward a larger, single-sheet folio format with the news printed on both sides and arranged in columns, rather than in larger blocks of text. The second development was the increasing frequency with which individual titles appeared. This trend was first seen fleetingly during Charles I's 1649 trial, when journalists recognized that they were witnessing momentous events that the public would want to know about on more than a weekly basis. Nevertheless, this change in publication frequency did not survive the king's sentencing by the

FIG. 6
Edward Ward (1667–1731)
Vulgus Britannicus or, the British Hudibras
London: Printed for Sam Briscoe and sold by James Woodward and John Morphew, 1710
PR 3757 W8 V8 Cage Copy 1

Coffeehouses and news went hand-in-hand. Virtually all coffeehouses subscribed to a variety of newspapers and some proprietors even went so far as to set up their own news service. In this illustration we can see many traditional elements of the coffeehouse—newspapers scattered around the tables, the coffee-boy refilling cups and the matron serving coffee behind the bar. But even in the civilized atmosphere of the coffeehouse, violence could break out, especially at times of political tension as people argued over the news.

High Court of Justice. It was only after 1660 that newspapers appeared two, three, or even four times a week.

Perhaps the most important single development in post-Restoration news culture was how the public accessed the news, rather than the format in which the news appeared. Historians have become increasingly fascinated by the emergence of coffeehouses as a central feature of urban culture, in large part because the establishments where this newly fashionable drink was made available were focal points for the distribution of newspapers and the discussion of their contents (FIG. 6). That governments tried to outlaw coffeehouses after 1660, particularly as political tensions rose in the late 1670s, reflected the awareness that a coffeehouse was "the marketplace of news," where men and women from different social groups could mingle and gain access to information about current events, without even purchasing a newspaper. One 1683 complaint railed against coffeehouses as places "where false and seditious news is invented and spread." Coffeehouses were unwelcome because they fostered a well-informed, literate, and active citizenry, which could be mobilized by the leaders of the emerging political parties of the day.

Another significant advance was the emergence of a fledgling newspaper industry in the New World. *Publick Occurrences*, the first newspaper published in America, appeared in 1690, the work of Benjamin Harris, a recent arrival from England. Harris already had a long career in newspaper journalism. In 1679, he started the biweekly *Domestick Intelligence*, and he later produced *Protestant Intelligence* and the *Weekly Discoverer Strip'd Naked*. An ardent supporter of Protestantism who frequently found himself in conflict with the English government, Harris published anti-Catholic material during the Popish Plot scare, and he was continually under suspicion for sedition after James II came to the throne in 1685. Fearful of imprisonment, he fled to Boston, where he established himself as the proprietor of the London Coffee House.

Harris's venture into newspaper publication in America lasted only one issue. He had intended to publish *Publick Occurrences* "once a month (or if any Glut of occurrences happen, oftener)," but the colonial government put an immediate stop to his plans. A proclamation was issued that not only suppressed the newspaper but called in all remaining copies to be destroyed. The proclamation ensured that nothing would be printed in Massachusetts without official license. Harris's publication was censored not only because it was unlicensed but because its content was scandalous. Rather than simply reprinting items from the official *London Gazette*, Harris had included local news, a report of a suicide, and items on the practices of native Americans who had converted to Christianity, a Boston fire, and "fevers and agues" in the countryside. More importantly, at a time of war and high political tension, Harris's suggestion that Louis XIV of France had had an affair with his daughter-in-law was seen as unnecessarily provocative.

The next newspaper to appear in America, the *Boston News-Letter*, was far more successful, and one with some degree of official backing. In 1704, John Campbell, the Boston postmaster, received the approval of the Massachusetts authorities to circulate local government decrees, as well as economic and maritime reports and a selection of foreign news. Campbell had previously operated a handwritten newsletter service, and the switch to print commercialized his activities. The *News-Letter* was closely modeled on the *London Gazette*, both in its format and as a source for foreign news. The first issue of April 24, 1704, when 250 copies were printed, contained mainly events from abroad. It appeared every Monday, timed to coincide with the postal service. On Sundays, riders arrived with the mail from New York, Philadelphia, and the northeastern seaboard; on Tuesdays, the return mail left Boston, enabling Campbell to incorporate up-to-date information received over the weekend and to disseminate his newspaper via the Tuesday post. Campbell continued the *Boston News-Letter* until 1722, by which time competitors such as the *Boston Gazette* and the *New England Courant* had emerged. Under different proprietors, the *Boston News-Letter* survived until 1776.

Meanwhile, the delivery of news back in England forged ahead. In 1695, the government decided not to renew the Licensing Act. The Stationers' Company was widely perceived to have abused its monopoly on publishing, and this, combined with greater parliamentary control over the monarchy due to the Glorious Revolution of 1688–89, meant that many saw official control of the press as unnecessary. The lapse of the Act led to an explosion of new titles. Benjamin Harris, back from his New England exile, started *Intelligence Domestick and Foreign*, while *The Flying Post*, *The Post-Boy*, and *The Post Man* commenced publication in 1695. These papers were published three times a week on Tuesday, Thursday, and Saturday, coinciding with the days on which the mail left London for the provinces. However, a few of the new titles shied away from this schedule, publishing on Monday, Wednesday, and Friday, most likely seeking a London audience rather than cultivating readers in the country with out-of-date news. Another advantage of this schedule was that the news arrived off the boats from France, Flanders, and Holland on Tuesdays and Fridays, so the Monday, Wednesday, and Friday papers could relay foreign news first.

Apart from the thrice-weekly paper, another significant advance in the 1690s was the appearance of an evening newspaper, *Dawks's News-Letter*, which debuted on June 23, 1696. In order to further distance his publication from those of his rivals, Ichabod Dawks's paper was printed in an unusual typeface, known as *civilité*, which gave it the appearance of a hand-written newsletter. Again, unlike most newspapers at this time, Dawks's was not available on the streets but required a quarterly subscription. The paper was further personalized by having blank spaces, which allowed the insertion of handwritten messages for individual subscribers. The venture was clearly a success, and the newsletter was produced until 1716.

Industry competition was heightened by the arrival of more newspapers, many of them short lived. Dawks, not content with relying solely on his evening newsletter, started a standard thrice-weekly morning paper in 1697, *The Protestant Mercury*. *The Foreign Post* appearing in 1697, lasted for just under a year, and the ubiquitous Benjamin Harris founded *The London Post* in 1699. But the next significant advance in the industry was the arrival of the daily newspaper. On March 11, 1702, Samuel Buckley issued *The Daily Courant*, printed in a single-sheet format like the thrice-weekly competitors. However, in the early days Buckley struggled to find sufficient news, and the reverse of the paper was often left blank. As with the first newspapers in 1620, however, the progress of warfare across Europe soon helped to fill *The Daily Courant*'s pages and make it commercially viable. In the coffeehouses, the salons of the wealthy, and the countryside, the progress of the Duke of Marlborough's armies against the French was the talk of the day, and Buckley tapped into this market. He readily acknowledged that he mainly printed news translated from Continental papers and *The Daily Courant* closely followed the military campaigning season. Buckley's paper had no competitors until 1719, when the *Daily Post* began publication; by 1728, there were as many as four dailies, published Monday through Saturday.

Running in parallel to the growth of daily newspapers after 1695 was the rise of the periodical magazine. These weekly or biweekly publications offered not only news reports, but also social and political commentary. One of the earliest and most successful was Daniel Defoe's *Review*. Although Defoe is best known today as the author of *Robinson Crusoe* and *Moll Flanders*, his primary career was as a journalist and political pamphleteer. *The Review* was published three times a week to great acclaim, and Defoe's commentaries foreshadowed the success of later periodicals, such as *The Tatler* (started in 1709 by *London Gazette* editor Richard Steele) and *The Spectator*.

Like the *Gazette*, *The Tatler* was a single sheet with two columns printed on both sides, but each edition of this thrice-weekly journal featured a lengthy essay on some aspect of society—theater, politics, or the reformation of manners. The venture was enormously successful, and Steele was soon joined by Richard Addison, although the two men wrote under the pseudonym "Isaac Bickerstaff, Esq." *The Tatler* turned into a literary prank, where the journal was populated by the Bickerstaff's imaginary kin, including his half-sister, Jenny Distaff, and Humphrey Wagstaff, the pen name of Jonathan Swift. Increasingly, however, *The Tatler* became more politicized, and Steele, a committed Whig, was attacked by Tory newspapers and the establishment. He eventually resigned as editor of the *Gazette*, while *The Tatler* ceased production on January 2, 1711, with Steele signing off with a flourish by using his own name.

The runaway success of *The Tatler*—selling 3,000 copies per issue—demonstrated unequivocally that there was a market for the essay periodical, and Addison and Steele joined forces again to create *The Spectator*. In contrast to *The Tatler*, *The Spectator* was nonpartisan, although its style of creating enduring literary characters, such as the Whig merchant Sir Andrew Freeport and the Tory country squire Sir Roger de Coverley, was similar. Published Monday through Saturday, it was an instant success and regularly sold 4,000 copies a day. However, after 555 issues Steele and Addison discontinued *The Spectator* to pursue other publishing opportunities. Nevertheless, its impact was immense in its pioneering literary criticism and social commentary.

By 1710, fifteen years after the lapse of the Licensing Act, all of the key elements of the modern printed news industry were largely in place. Journalism had come a long way in little more than a century, from the early reports of crimes and strange apparitions to the imported corantos and the first faltering steps toward serialized newspapers taken by Butter and Bourne. The tumultuous events of the seventeenth century provided the impetus for rapid change in many walks of life, and news was no exception, as publishers, editors, and writers experimented with the elements of news journalism that we now take for granted. They invented a plethora of strange titles for their papers before settling on many of the names that remain familiar to modern news enthusiasts, and they deployed editorials, headlines, and even illustrations. The introduction of advertisements not only sheds light upon the culture of a bygone age but also indicates how rapidly the news industry expanded and became commercialized. Writers, printers, and publishers flocked into the profession as if it were a paper gold rush, confident that the reading public had an insatiable appetite for news of the latest events both at home and abroad. That politicians and governments were determined to impose censorship and licensing or to manipulate the news to produce propaganda reflects their awareness of the power of the print medium and journalism's potential to communicate with the public. It also reflects the understanding that political support required persuasion rather than unthinking obedience. By the end of the Renaissance, daily newspapers competed for readers along party political lines, advertisements filled the pages, editorials opined, theater reviews discussed the merits of individual plays, and letters to the editor critiqued previous stories. The coffeehouses patronized by the literate and educated were filled with newspapers and periodicals, hawkers populated street corners selling titles hot off the presses, and even provincial newspapers had begun to appear. Although the press could hardly yet be described as free, government control was much more difficult to achieve. News was the news of the day, and readers in both England and America arguably already had access to all the news that was fit to print.

CATALOG OF THE EXHIBITION

IN SIXTEENTH AND SEVENTEENTH CENTURY ENGLAND, when the printing of domestic news was banned by the government and the newspaper had not yet been invented, letters were the most common form for the transmission of news. People also copied news reports into their personal diaries. One of the most popular ways to obtain information was to purchase separates. These were manuscript copies of speeches and reports of events of high political drama. Avidly collected and read, they were often circulated among family and friends.

My most Honorable good La: uppon occasion of my continuall followinge of his Matie in his Jerneys I have ben longer silent then I should have ben: The newes heere is all in parlament busines the matter of religion to compell every man to the communion hath much troubled them but now they are agreed that all shall come to the communion within the space of 2 yeares or els they shall be in the nature of recusants for the matter of purveance the Kinge is very desirous for the ease of the subiect to have a composition and to pay a yearely some of mony and to be freed from the purveior But as yet the Lower house will not hear of any composition for that they feare they can have no assurance from the Kinge and then they should both give their mony and be troubled with the Kinges takers so It is thought the parlament is like to continue yet a good while for they must part with on subsidy more and 2 fifteenes or else this is nothinge that they have don: The provinciall of the Jesuites Garnet who is in the Tower will prove a notorious traytor and to have had his hand in all these treasons and a principall man that caused them to take armes when the powder plott fayled The Earle of Northumberland will goe cleere in this matter his Lady is permitted to come to him and ther is expectance of his liberty shortly But with the rest of the Lords it will goe hard There be many

1 James Montagu (1568?–1618)
Autograph letter signed to
Elizabeth Hardwick Talbot,
Countess of Shrewsbury
Whitehall: March 7, 1606
X.d.428 (60)

BEFORE THE ADVENT OF THE NEWSPAPER, most people received news in the form of a personalized letter. The oft-married and socially ambitious Bess of Hardwick liked to be kept informed of the goings-on in London. From news that Queen Anne was pregnant to the capture of the Jesuit priest Father Garnet—England's most-wanted man—and the work of Parliament, she was well-versed in the latest stories from London.

(9) 17

Number 2.

THE LONDON POST

Communicating the High Counsels of both Parliaments in *England* and *Scotland*, and all other Remarkable passages, both Civill and Martiall in his Weekly Travells through the three Kingdoms.

Printed and entred according to order.

From Thursday January the 14. *to Thursday January* 21.

HAving of late been silent, and almost speechlesse by reason of a Fever, my present condition (if instances of weake account may carry weight, compared with such great examples) doth much repre-

B

sent

2 *The London Post,*
Number 2, 1646
E.371 (17)
Courtesy of the British Library

3 “Ladyes ladyes howle yee and cry”
Manuscript miscellany, ca. 1630
V.a.345, p. 36

EARLY MODERN ENGLAND WAS EAGER TO HEAR SALACIOUS GOSSIP about political figures. King James’ chief minister, Robert Cecil, Earl of Salisbury, was the target of much rumor and innuendo after his death in 1612. This anonymous verse libel, a typical format for mocking the powerful, reports that Cecil died from the “pox,” referring to whispers that he was having affairs with Lady Walsingham and the Countess of Suffolk, the “ladyes” referenced in the first line of the second paragraph.

Strange Reportes.

Mr Wilkes of Horton in Northamptonshire
had (as he saith) of one Barly Corne set alone
by it selfe in his garden 224 Eares.
whereof the greatest part had 20, & some
30 graines in each Eare.

Sargeant Harvy reported yt in Dunstable
a Market Towne, there is neither hay
nor butter made within the Parish.

Mr More Schoolemaister of Thurloe, saith, that
this verse Mes, fles, res et rex, mus, mons,
mons, mons, simul et fons, Is to be varied
twenty thousand times.

In the west about Lemster there was a Morris
of some men & a maid marrion whose ages
together made 12 hundred yeares.

In Kent, A Knight his Lady & 2 Children
all theire ages together, made but 31 yeares.

Mris Honiwood of Kent had 13 score & odd that
came out of her loynes, & did aske her blessinge.

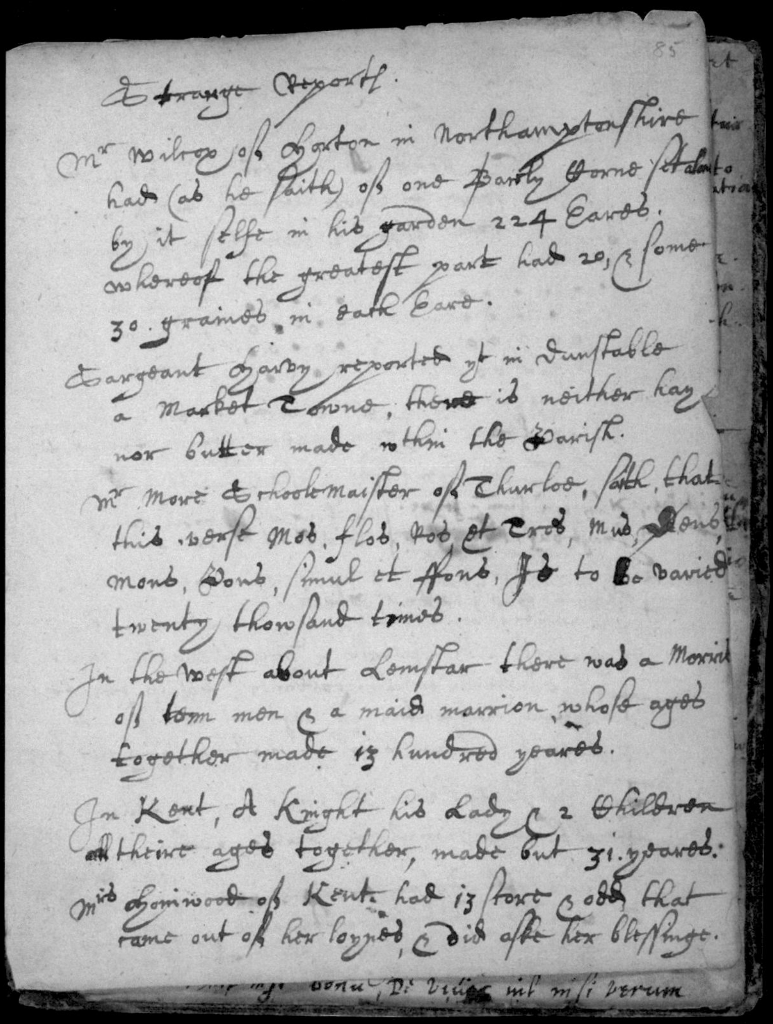

4 "Strange Reportes"
Manuscript miscellany,
1650–1670
E.a.6, fol. 85

THE TITLE *STRANGE REPORTES* SUMS UP THE GOSSIPY NEWS collected by the anonymous compiler of this private journal. He collected weird snippets of news including many scarcely believable. For example, it does seem unlikely that Mrs. Honiswood of Kent gave birth to over 260 children. Perhaps more feasible, though still astonishing, is the example of the husband, wife and two children whose combined ages equaled thirty-one years.

34

5A Newsletter from the Secretary of State's Office, received by Richard Newdigate, October 21, 1678
L.c.695

SIR EDMUND BERRY GODFREY, the judge investigating the "popish plot" of 1678, had gone missing; many speculated that a major Catholic conspiracy was at hand. The news set all of England abuzz. Sir Richard Newdigate (1644–1710), a Warwickshire gentleman, received the latest reports of the plot and other matters from a regular subscription newsletter service run out of the office of the secretary of state. The letters were sent three times a week, so the newsletter writer promised updates on Godfrey—"a little time may better informe us."

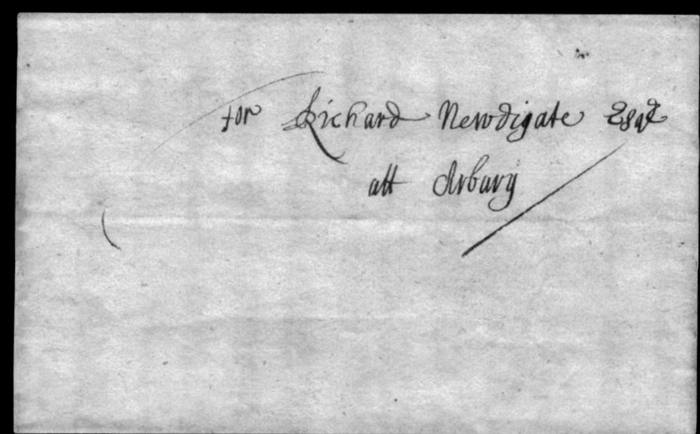

for Richard Newdigate Esqr
att Arbury

5B Newsletter from the Secretary of State's Office, received by Richard Newdigate, October 21, 1678
L.c.696

WHEN SIR RICHARD NEWDIGATE RECEIVED HIS NEWSLETTERS from London, they arrived folded into a small packet with a wax seal affixed. In 1635, Charles I had authorized the government postal service to carry private letters and a fixed rate was established dependent upon the distance traveled. However, many letters went missing en route and important news was often conveyed verbally rather than by letter.

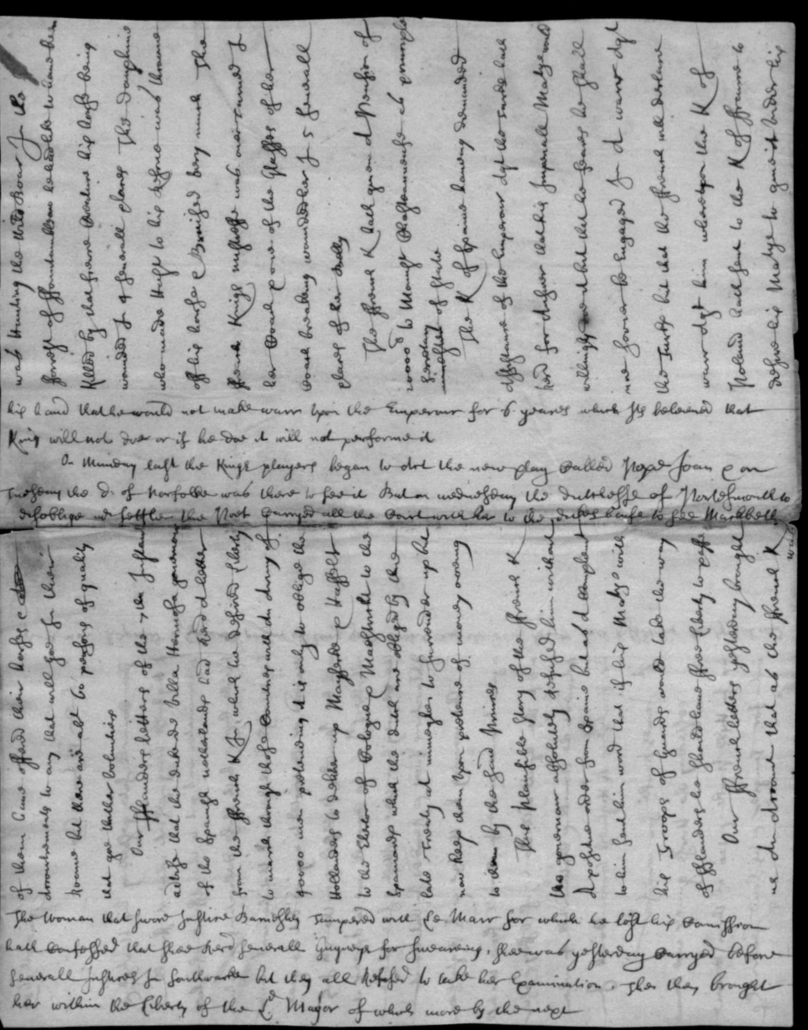

5C Newsletter from the Secretary of State's Office, received by Richard Newdigate, June 5, 1680
L.c.943

DURING THE POLITICALLY TENSE MONTHS OF 1680, as Whigs sought to exclude the Catholic Duke of York from the royal succession and to prove the legitimacy of the Duke of Monmouth, theater assumed almost unprecedented political importance. The newsletter dated June 5, 1680 mentions the staging of a notorious anti-Catholic play by the Whig agitator, Elkanah Settle, as well as a pointed response to the turmoil from Charles II's much vilified Catholic mistress: she took members of the court to see a private performance of Shakespeare's *Macbeth*, probably the adaptation by Sir William Davenant.

Transcription of passage from letter: *"On Munday last the Kings players began to Act the new play Called Pope Joan & on Tuesday the d: of Norfolke was there to see it but on Wednesday the dutchesse of Portesmouth to disoblige mr settle the Poet Carryed all the Court with her to the dukes house to see Mackbeth."*

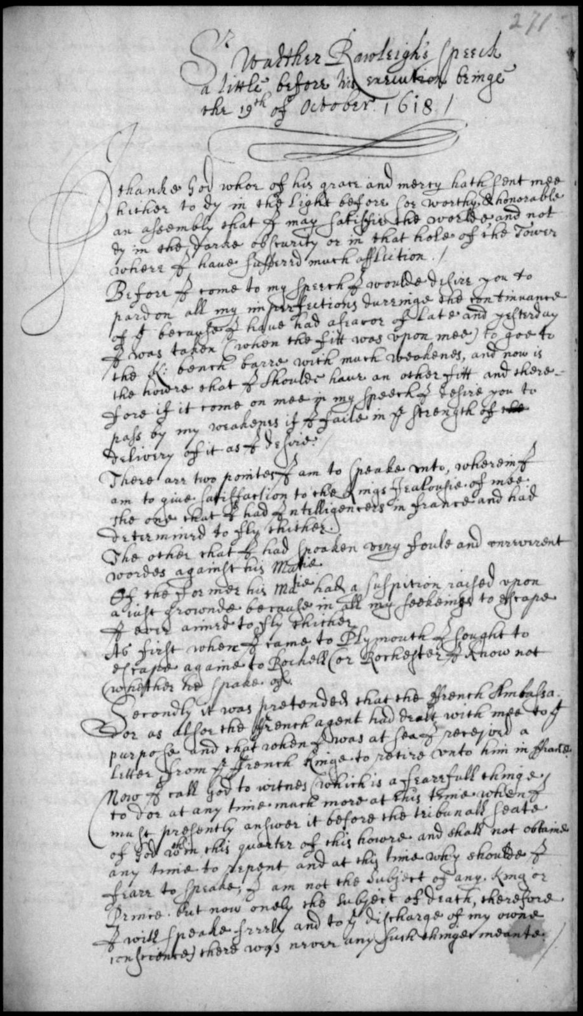

271

Sr Walther Rawleigh's speech a little before his execution beinge the 19th of October 1618

I thanke God who of his grace and mercy hath sent mee hither to dy in the light before soe worthy & honorable an assembly that I may satisfie the world, and not dy in the darke obscurity or in that hole of the Tower where I haue suffered much affliction.

Before I come to my speech I would desire you to pardon all my imperfections duringe the continuance of it beinge (as I haue had a feavor of late and yesterday I was taken (when the fitt was vpon mee) to goe to the K. bench barre with much weakenes, and now is the howre that I should haue an other fitt and therefore if it come on mee in my speeche I desire you to pass by my weakenes if I faile in ye strength of the deliuery of it as I desire.

There are two pointes I am to speake vnto, whereinn I am to giue satisfaction to the Kings Jealousie of mee. the one that I had intelligences in Fraunce and had determined to fly thither.

The other that I had spoken very fowle and irreuerent wordes against his Matie.

Of the former his Matie had a suspition raised vpon a iust grownde because in all my seekinge to escape I was aimed to fly thither

As first when I came to Plymouth I sought to escape againe to Rochell (or Rochester I know not whether he spake of.

Secondly it was pretended that the French Ambassador or as Monsieur the French agent had dealt with mee to yt purpose and that when I was at sea I receiued a letter from ye French Kinge to retire vnto him in France.

Now I call God to witnes (which is a fearfull thinge, to doe at any time much more at this time when I must presently answer it before the tribunall seate of God within this quarter of this howre and shall not obtaine any time to repent and at this time why should I feare to speake, I am not the subject of any Kinge or Prince but now onely the subject of death, therefore I will speake freely and to ye discharge of my owne conscience) there was neuer any such thinge intended

6 "Sir Walther Rawleigh's speech a little before his execution being the 19th of October 1618"
Manuscript collection of political and parliamentary documents, ca. 1550–1650
V.b.303, p. 271

SIR WALTER RALEGH'S EVENTFUL LIFE came to an end in 1618. The poet, explorer, scientist, and one-time favorite of Queen Elizabeth had been convicted in 1603 on flimsy evidence of treason and imprisoned in the Tower. As was customary, those on the scaffold were permitted a final speech. Ralegh spoke eloquently for forty-five minutes from notes he had made the night before. Then the executioner severed his head in two blows. Ralegh was a popular figure and reports of his speech quickly circulated in manuscript and were copied into personal journals.

MAJOR EVENTS AND NATURAL DISASTERS provided an opportunity to publish lengthy news pamphlets. Dramatic political events from the courts of Europe, reports of strange weather, attacks on the Pope, and news of far-away and exotic lands were all available for purchase by the reading public. The government also spread the news in printed propaganda campaigns, taking full advantage of its ability to reach the populace from the pulpit and the town square.

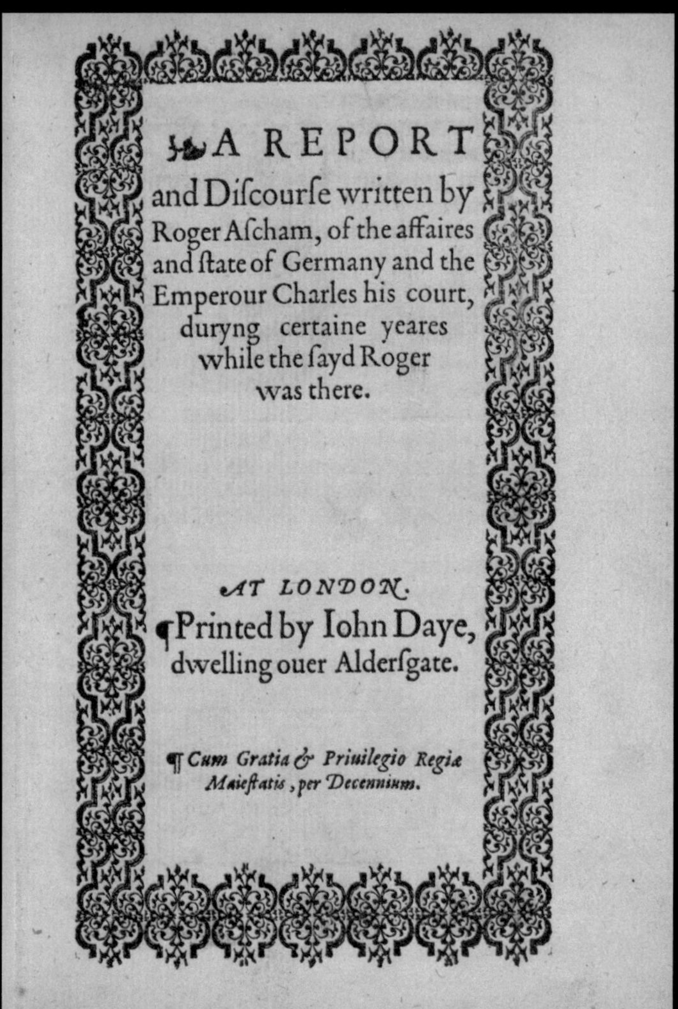

A REPORT and Diſcourſe written by Roger Aſcham, of the affaires and ſtate of Germany and the Emperour Charles his court, duryng certaine yeares while the ſayd Roger was there.

AT LONDON.
¶Printed by Iohn Daye, dwelling ouer Alderſgate.

¶ *Cum Gratia & Priuilegio Regiæ Maieſtatis, per Decennium.*

7 Roger Ascham (1514/15–1568)
A report and discourse written by Roger Ascham, of the affaires and state of Germany and the Emperour Charles his court, duryng certaine yeares while the sayd Roger was there
London: Printed by John Daye dwelling over Aldersgate, [1570?]
STC 830 Copy 1, title page

ROGER ASCHAM WAS THE TUTOR TO PRINCESS ELIZABETH and author of *The Scholemaster*, a popular book on education. In 1550, Ascham traveled to Germany as the secretary to Sir Richard Morison, the English ambassador to the Court of Charles V, the Holy Roman Emperor. In order to satisfy the demand in England for news from Germany, Ascham began to compile a daily report on affairs of the court. Although written as a series of manuscript newsletters, Ascham's reports were of sufficient interest to be published after his death, perhaps to capitalize on his popularity as an educator. Published twenty years after the events described, this report shows that for many Elizabethans, news did not have to be current.

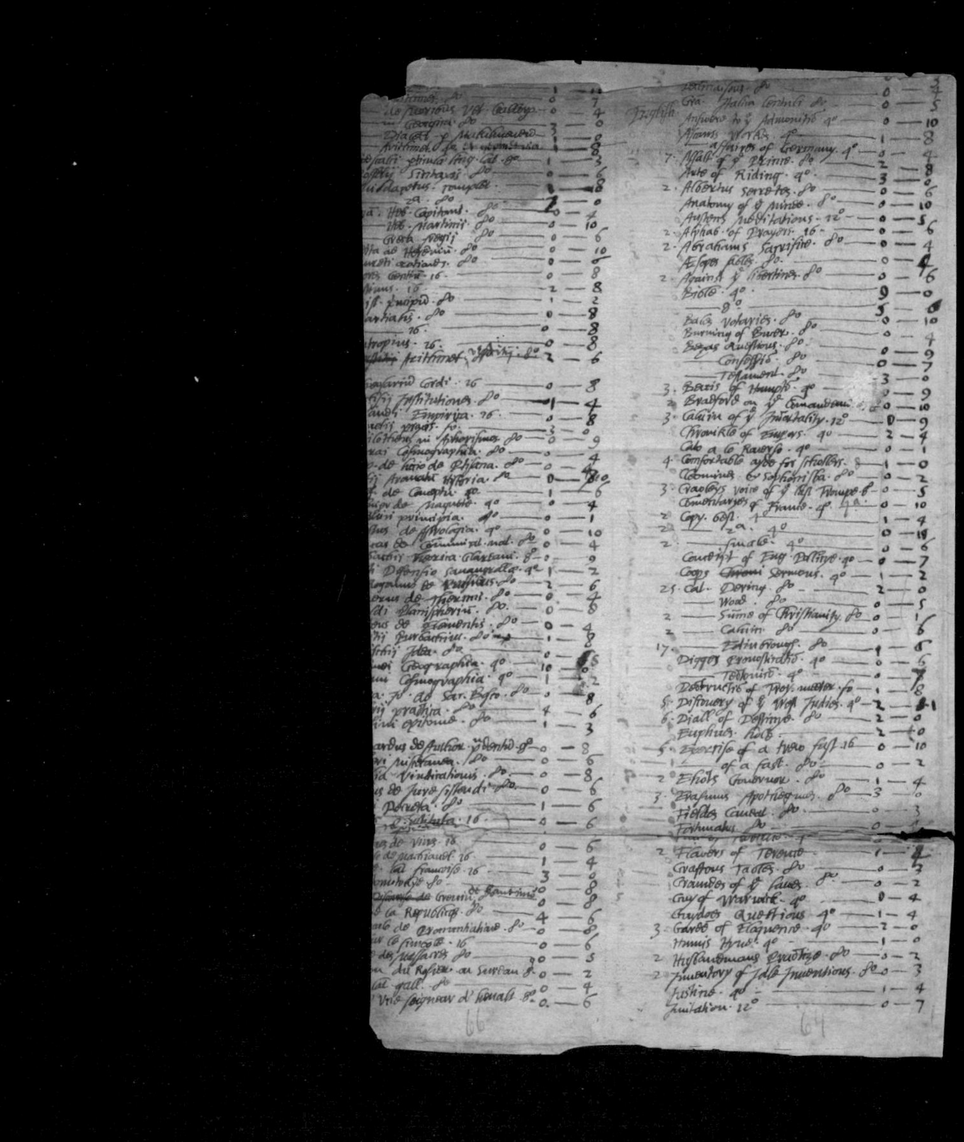

8 Thomas Chard
Manuscript booklist,
1583–1584
X.d.168 (3)

THOMAS CHARD WAS A LONDON BOOKSELLER who dabbled in newsbooks as well as great works of literature. On his list of books to be sent to two Cambridge booksellers, Chard records as four pence the trade price of Roger Ascham's work on Germany (column 2, item 5).

Good Newes to Chriſtendome.

Sent to a Venetian in Ligorne, from a Merchant in ALEXANDRIA.

Diſcouering a wonderfull and ſtrange Apparition, viſibly ſeene for many day[es] together in Arabia, ouer the place, where the ſuppoſed Tombe of MAHOMET (th[e] Turkiſh Prophet) is incloſed: By which the learned Arabians prognoſticate the Reducing & Calling of the great Turke to Chriſtianitie. With many other notable Accidents: But the moſt remarkable is the miraculous rayning of Bloud about ROME.

Done out of the Italian.

LONDON,
Printed for NATHANIEL BUTTER. 1620.

9 Ludovico Cortano
Good newes to Christendome
London: Printed [by G. Purslowe] for Nathaniel Butter, 1620
STC 5796, title page

WEIRD AND WONDERFUL APPARITIONS always made for popular news. They also offered an opportunity for illustrators to catch the eye of the buying public with dramatic woodcuts of the event. This title page conveys both a vision seen over the prophet Mohammed's tomb in "Arabia" and a depiction of the skies raining blood in Rome. The pamphlet is a good example of how news was transmitted in England before the newspaper. Originally written as a letter, it was then translated from Italian into English, before being printed.

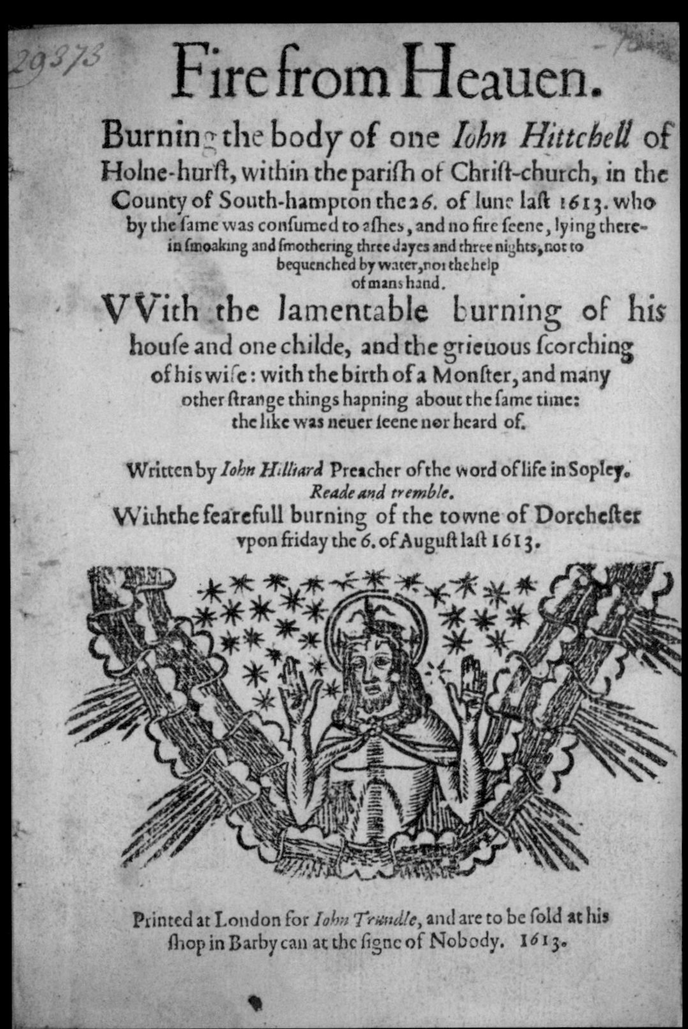

Fire from Heauen.

Burning the body of one *Iohn Hittchell* of Holne-hurſt, within the pariſh of Chriſt-church, in the County of South-hampton the 26. of Iune laſt 1613. who by the ſame was conſumed to aſhes, and no fire ſeene, lying therein ſmoaking and ſmothering three dayes and three nights, not to be quenched by water, nor the help of mans hand.

VVith the lamentable burning of his houſe and one childe, and the grieuous ſcorching of his wife: with the birth of a Monſter, and many other ſtrange things hapning about the ſame time: the like was neuer ſeene nor heard of.

Written by *Iohn Hilliard* Preacher of the word of life in Sopley.
Reade and tremble.
With the fearefull burning of the towne of Dorcheſter vpon friday the 6. of Auguſt laſt 1613.

Printed at London for *Iohn Trundle*, and are to be ſold at his ſhop in Barbycan at the ſigne of Nobody. 1613.

10 John Hilliard (fl. 1613)
Fire From Heaven
London: By [E. Allde] for John Trundle and are to be sold at his shop in Barby can [sic] at the signe of Nobody, [1613]
STC 13507, title page

ON AUGUST 6, 1613, A GROCER IN DORCHESTER was melting tallow to make candles when his shop caught on fire. Fanned by a strong wind, within no time half the town had burned to the ground. For many inhabitants and onlookers, this catastrophe represented God's vengeance on the town for the moral corruption of its citizens. *Fire from Heaven* relates not only the story of the Dorchester fire but also includes other "miraculous" stories of divine fire visited on the ungodly. News was not the author's sole intent; moral persuasion and fear were motivators as well—"read and tremble," the subtitle advised.

The ſtrange and marueilous Newes lately come from the great kingdome of Chyna, which adioyneth to the East Indya.
Tranſlated out of the Caſtlyn tongue, by T.N.
(∴)

Imprinted at London, nigh vnto the three Cranes in the Vintree, by Thomas Gardyner, and Thomas Dawſon.

11 *The strange and marueilous newes lately come from the great kingdome of Chyna, which adioyneth to the East Indya. Translated out of the Castlyn tongue, by T.N.* London: Nigh vnto the three Cranes in the Vintree, by Thomas Gardyner, and Thomas Dawson, [1577?] STC 5141, title page

OFTEN NEWS WHICH CIRCULATED IN CONTINENTAL EUROPE was translated into English and re-published in an effort to satisfy the increasing appetite for exotic news. This report from China marvels at shaven-headed Buddhist priests, the fine quality of Chinese horses, and the small stature of people. It also laments the lack of grapes to make wine. It was originally written in Castilian, a regional dialect of Spanish, and translated by T.N.—probably Thomas Nicholas, a travel writer.

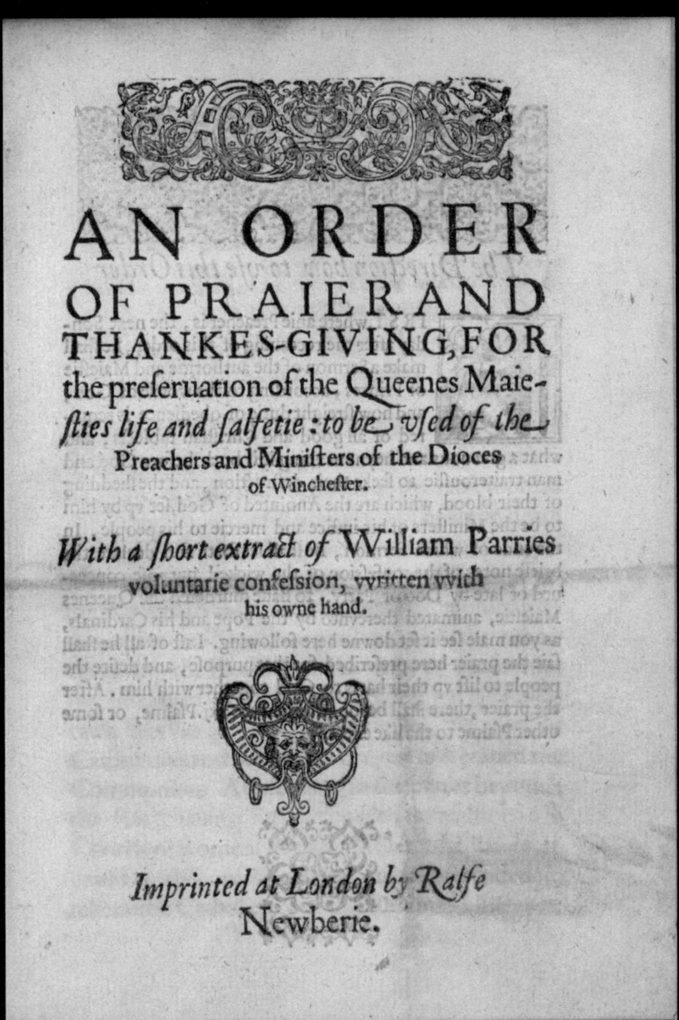

AN ORDER
OF PRAIER AND
THANKES-GIVING, FOR
the preſeruation of the Queenes Maieſties life and ſalfetie: to be vſed of the
Preachers and Miniſters of the Dioces
of Wincheſter.

With a ſhort extract of William Parries
voluntarie confeſsion, vvritten vvith
his owne hand.

Imprinted at London by Ralfe
Newberie.

12 *An order of praier and thankes-giuing, for the preseruation of the Queenes Maiesties life and salfetie…* London: By [Henry Denham for] Ralfe Newberie, [1585] STC 16516, title page

PRAYERS OFFERED AN EFFECTIVE AVENUE for the dissemination of news by the Elizabethan government. Designed to be read from church pulpits, orders of prayer and thanksgiving gave detailed accounts of the latest royal happenings—in this instance, William Parry's confession that he had plotted the assassination of Queen Elizabeth. Whether Parry was guilty or not remains a puzzle. He appears to have been a spy for the Elizabethan regime before converting to Catholicism. Parry claimed that he had simply acted as an agent, and his actions were designed to draw into the open those who wished to see Elizabeth dead. The government, however, did not give credence to his tale, and he was executed on March 2, 1585 in the Palace of Westminster's Old Palace Yard.

A true and perfect declaration of the Treaſons practiſed and attempted by Francis Throckemorton, late of London, againſt the Queenes Maieſtie and the Realme.

Hereas there haue bene verie lewde and ſlaunderous bruites and reportes giuen out, of the due and orderly proceedings held with *Francis Throckemorton* lately arraigned and condemned of high treaſon at the Guildhall in London the xxi. day of May laſt, whereby ſuch as are euill affected toward her Maieſtie, and the preſent gouernement, haue indeuoured falſely and iniuriouſly to charge her Maieſtie and her faithfull miniſters with crueltie and iniuſtice vſed againſt the ſaid *Throckemorton* by extorting from him by torture, ſuch confeſſions as he hath made againſt himſelfe, and by inforcing the ſame to make them lawful euidence to conuict him of the treaſons therein ſpecified: Albeit her Maieſties ſubiects in general, calling to minde ẏ milde and temperate courſe ſhe hath helde all the time of her moſt happie Reigne, might rather impute her clemencie and lenitie vſed towards all ſortes of offenders to a kinde of fault, then taxe her ẘ the contrarie: yet ſuch as allowe of practiſes and treaſons againſt her Maieſtie, do alwayes interprete both of the one and of the other, according to the particular affections that doe poſſeſſe them, that is, to the worſt. And foraſmuch as the caſe of *Throckemorton* at this time hath bene ſubiect to their ſiniſter conſtructions, and conſidering that lies and falſe bruites caſt abroad are moſt commonly beleeued, vntil they be controlled by

A.i. the

13 *A discouerie of the treasons practised and attempted against the Queenes Maiestie and the realme*
[London: C. Barker], 1584
STC 24050 Copy 2, sig. A1

ELIZABETH'S GOVERNMENT MADE EFFECTIVE USE of the printing press to get the news out, especially when it concerned the safety of the Queen. As described in this tract, Francis Throckmorton conspired with Elizabeth's cousin, Mary, Queen of Scots, to overthrow Elizabeth. He had contacted Mary's kinsman, the Duke of Guise, who was ready to land an invasion force in the south of England and forcibly remove Elizabeth from the throne. Throckmorton was betrayed by an agent in the pay of the Elizabethan secret service, and captured and tortured. He was executed for treason on July 10, 1584.

14 *Newes from Rome, Spaine, Palermo, Geneuæ and France* London: Printed [by J. Wolfe?] for Thomas Nelson, and are to be sold by William Wright, [1590] STC 21293, sig. A3v

PROTESTANT ENGLAND DELIGHTED IN READING SCANDALS about the Pope and the Catholic Church. The author of this newsbook has reproduced a woodcut which was circulated in Rome attacking corrupt Catholics and the papacy. The empty speech bubble allowed the buyer to fill in his own unflattering caption. The original probably contained a biblical verse "redde rationem villitionis tuae"—often translated as "make me an account of your administration" (Luke 16.2). In this case, the gentleman challenges the Pope at the barrel of a gun. One section of the pamphlet reports that a Jewish army was allegedly sent to besiege Turkey. It was once thought that this was the pamphlet from which Shakespeare found the name Shylock, the moneylender in *The Merchant of Venice.*

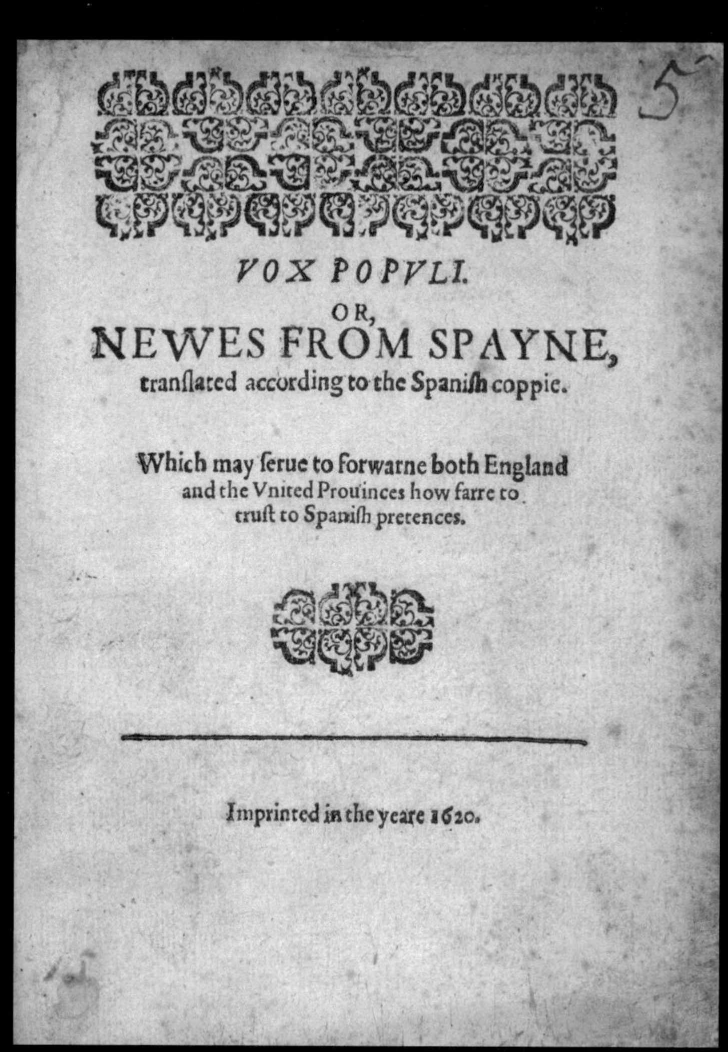
VOX POPVLI.
OR,
NEWES FROM SPAYNE,
translated according to the Spanish coppie.
Which may serue to forwarne both England and the Vnited Prouinces how farre to trust to Spanish pretences.
Imprinted in the yeare 1620.

15 Thomas Scott (1580? –1626)
Vox populi. Or, Nevves from Spayne
[London]: Imprinted in the yeare 1620
STC 22103.3 Copy 1, title page

THOMAS SCOTT, A RADICAL PROTESTANT, anonymously published *Vox Populi* in 1620 before fleeing to the Netherlands. It was a highly critical attack on the foreign policy of James I and his negotiations with Catholic Spain to marry his son, Charles, to a Spanish Princess. The pamphlet, designed to look like a news report from the Spanish ambassador to his superiors in Madrid, and widely believed to be accurate, quickly became a cause célèbre as the government hunted for its author and attempted to stop its publication. Hastily and poorly printed editions flowed off the presses before government pressure halted the production. Quickly though they handed the text to scriveners and manuscript copies continued to circulate. Some, like Thomas Legge (Cat. No. 16) copied *Vox Populi* into their own journals. Printed news had become manuscript news.

16 "Vox populi or Newes from Spaine translated accordinge to the Spanish copie which may serue to forewarne both England and the Vnited prouences how farr to trust the Spanish pretences"
Bound with scribal copy of Thomas Legge (1535–1607), *Richardus tertius*
Manuscript, ca. 1620
V.a.310, fol. 54

50

THE NEWSPAPER ARRIVES

GEntle Readers, this Intelligencer the Curranto having been
long ſilenced, and now permitted by Authority to ſpeake a-
gain, preſents you here at firſ
vith ſuch things as paſſed ſome months ſince, no
ecauſe we conceive that they are abſolutely Novels unto you, but firſt becauſe there is fraud i
eneralities, we thought fit to acquaint you with
ach particular ; and ſecondly, that by theſe Ante-
edents you may the better underſtand the Conſe-
uents, which wee ſhall now publiſh weekely a

THE OUTBREAK OF THE PAN-EUROPEAN THIRTY YEARS WAR in 1618 created an insatiable demand in England for news from the Continent. Two enterprising English publishers, Nathaniel Butter and Nicholas Bourne, soon dominated the news market. By 1642, with the breakdown of state control over the printing presses due to the British Civil Wars (1642–1651), newspapers like *A Perfect Diurnall* began to print domestic as well as foreign news. This signified the advent of the weekly newspaper.

N° 47 213

EXTRAORDINAIRE

DV XXIe AVRIL M. DC. XXXIX.

CONTENANT

La ſortie du Roy d'Angleterre hors de Londres contre les Eſcoſſois du Convenant ſigné en Février 1638. Avec les noms des principaux ſeigneurs de l'vn & l'autre parti.

Et la défaite & priſe de trois compagnies de cavalerie du Comte Kurtz Vice-Chancellier de l'Empire.

LE Comte Kurtz ayant, comme vous avez ſceu, long-temps eſſayé à Hambourg & ailleurs, de débaucher les eſprits des Alemans & de leurs Alliez, & les gangner pour le parti, qui prend & auquel pour la ſeule diſtinction nous donnons le nom d'Imperial: voyant toutes ſes mines ſi biẽ éventées qu'elles n'avoient eu aucun effet, ſe réſolut vers la fin du mois paſsé de ſ'en retourner à Vienne, y rendre conte des motifs qui avoient empeſché l'effet de ſa légation. Mais ſur le chemin il receut nouvel ordre du Roy de Hongrie d'aller trouver de ſa part le Cardinal Infant. Dequoi le General Major King Süedois eſtant averti par ſes eſpions, & qu'il devoit aller à Meppen, apres avoir ſejourné huit jours à Bremen, où il avoit eſté viſité par le Prince de Portugal, & qu'il eſtoit eſcorté de trois cornettes de cavalerie conduites par le Baron de Luterſum, & de quelques autres troupes Imperiales: Ce General Major délaſcha à ſes trouſſes vne partie des troupes Süedoiſes qu'il commande ſur le Weſer dans la Weſtphalie: laquelle ayant rencontré les Imperiaux dans le village de Goldenſtede pres de Meppen, les y ſurprit & enveloppa de ſorte que ces trois cõpagnies ſe rendirent à eux avec ce Baron, & tous ſes Officiers: cependant que le reſte de l'eſcorte ſe ſauvoit par vn autre coſté avec ce Vice-Chancelier, à Meppen: juſques où les Süedois le pourſuivirent, & l'y tiennent comme aſſiégé. Aucuns ont eſcrit que tous les titres & papiers de ſa Chancellerie ont eſté pris par eux: qui ont tout brûlé, pillé & degaſté en ces quartiers-là, & particuliérement autour de la ville de Milshouſen.

HHh

17A Théophraste Renaudot (1586–1653)
Nouvelles Ordinaires
Paris: Bureau d'Adresse, 1631–
248336 No. 47

THE FRENCH GOVERNMENT WAS QUICK TO REALIZE the value of news as propaganda and the importance of controlling the presses. With the support of Cardinal Richelieu, the publisher Théophraste Renaudot held a monopoly over news publication in Paris from 1631 onwards. *Nouvelles,* along with its sister publication the *Gazette,* was published weekly each Saturday. Unlike his English counterparts, Renaudot published domestic news, especially the "heroic" deeds of King Louis XIII.

N° 94 417

LE TRAITE' FAIT ENTRE LE ROY de la grand' Bretagne & les Eſcoſſois du Convenant, ſes ſujets.

Es Eſcoſſois du Convenant eſtoient dans leur camp pres de Wederburne : lors que les principaux d'entr'eux deſirans voir quelque fin à ces troubles, envoyérent le Comte de Dumfermlin Seton fils du défunt Chancelier d'Eſcoſſe du meſme nom, par devers le Roy de la grand' Bretagne, avec cette requeſte, qu'il luy préſenta le 16e du mois de Iuin dernier.

SIRE, Puis que tous les moyens precédens par nous employez n'ont eu aucun effet pour nous faire recouvrer les bonnes graces de Voſtre Majeſté, & la paix de ce Royaume voſtre païs natal : Nous nous preſentons de rechef à ſes pieds, la ſuppliant tres-humblement qu'il lui plaiſe envoyer quelques-vns du grand nombre de ceux de voſtre Royaume d'Angleterre, qui ſont bien affectionnez à la religion & à la paix commune, pour entendre de quelques-vns des noſtres de la meſme diſpoſition nos humbles ſupplications, & de nous faire connoiſtre le gratieux traitement qu'il plaiſt à V. M. nous faire: A fin que, comme ſous vn meſme Roy ainſi par la grande ſageſſe & prudence de V. M. nous puiſſions vivre en paix & felicité, ſous le long & gratieux regne de V. M. pour lequel nous ne ceſſerons jamais de prier Dieu, comme il appartient aux tres-fidelles ſujets de V. M. Signé, Arguylle, Rotheſſe, Hume, Laudien, Caſſelles, Montroſe, Laudun, Forbus & autres.

En ſuïte dequoi les Comtes d'Arondel, d'Eſſex, Briſtou & Hollant, le Chevalier Henry de Veine & le Secretaire Cooxe, de la part du Roy de la grand' Bretagne, ſe ſont rendus dans la tente dudit Comte d'Arondel : où les Comtes de Rotheſſe, Leſlé, le Milord Laudun Cambell, le Chevalier Douglas Schirref de la province de Tiffendale, & le Miniſtre Alexandre Hendreſon, de la part des Eſcoſſois, ſe ſont auſſi rendus pour traiter.

Apres quelques abouchemens de ces Députez, les Eſcóſſois preſentérent aux Commiſſaires dudit Roy, les articles ſuivans.

Humbles pétitions des Sujets de Sa Majeſté en Eſcoſſe.

I, Qu'il plaiſe à Sa Majeſté nous donner aſſeurance que les articles de l'Aſſemblée de Glaſcow ſeront ratifiez du Parlement qui ſe doit tenir le 3e d'Aouſt *1639*, puis que la paix de l'Egliſe & du Royaume n'en peuvent ſouffrir plus longue dilation.

II, Que Sa Majeſté, ſelon la tendre affection qu'elle porte à la conſervation de noſtre religion & loix, ait agréable de declarer

NNNNn

17B Théophraste Renaudot (1586–1653)
Nouvelles Ordinaires
Paris: Bureau d'Adresse, 1631–
248336 No. 94

345

N° 181

NOVVELLES Ordinaires du dernier Decembre 1639.

De Stokolm, capitale de Suede, le 25 Novembre 1639.

LA contagion comme elle eſt fort rare en ce païs ; ainſi y eſt-elle tellement opiniaſtrée, que nonobſtant la froideur du climat & de la ſaiſon, elle rend encor cette ville moins frequentée.

De Dantzic, le 26 Novembre 1639.

Apres pluſieurs conteſtations des Députez, ſouſtenans avec trop de vigueur chacun l'intereſt de ſon maiſtre & de l'Eſtat qui l'avoit envoyé, la Diette de Warſaw eſt finie le 16ᵉ de ce mois ſans aucune réſolution : les Eſtats ſ'eſtans ſeparez particulierement mal ſatisfaits du Roy de Pologne. On n'y a point du tout parlé de noſtre nouvel impoſt.

De Vienne, le premier Decembre 1639.

Le 28ᵉ du paſſé, le Roy de Hongrie inveſtit l'Archiduc Leopold Guillaume ſon frere, des Eveſchez de Straſbourg, Halberſtat & Paſſaw : cet Archiduc ayant pour cette fin envoyé ici ſes Députez. Le General Galas a eu audiance dudit Roy, & croid-on à preſent qu'il ſera employé au traité qu'on parle tousjours de faire avec les Süedois en particulier : mais avec fort peu d'apparence d'y pouvoir reuſſir, pour le peu de ſeureté que trouve hors d'vne paix generale, cette nation que la longue habitude qu'elle a euë avec nous a pleinement inſtruite de nos affaires. Le principal ſujet pourquoi on lui a oſté ſon Generalat, eſt la jalouſie qui eſtoit entre lui & le Comte de Hazfeld. Bien que les Turcs ne nous faſſent pas encor ouvertement la guerre ; ils font neantmoins de grands préparatifs par terre & par mer, qui donnent de grandes terreurs à tous les Eſtats de la maiſon d'Auſtriche. Les Eſtats de ce païs n'ont eſté ici aſſemblez que pour contribuer des hommes & des munitions pour la forteresſe de Raab en Hongrie, & pour la ville de Budweis en Boheme, places particulierement menacées : cette-là du Turc, & cet-

XXXXXXxxx

17C Théophraste Renaudot (1586–1653)
Nouvelles Ordinaires
Paris: Bureau d'Adresse, 1631–
248336 No. 181

Honorable Sr

Finsbury this 20th of October 1632

Yor Servant to be commanded
Rich: Mason

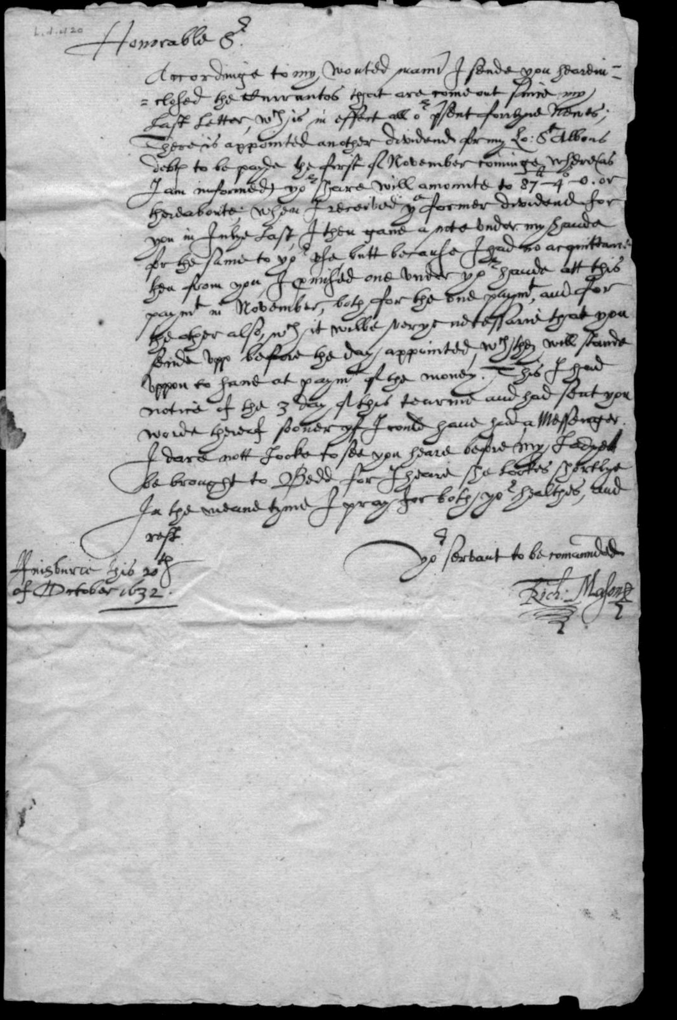

18 Richard Mason
Autograph letter signed to
Roger Townshend
Finsbury: October 20, 1632
L.d.420

THE ADVENT OF THE CORANTO fundamentally changed the way many newsletter writers operated. While pages of news were once laboriously copied by hand, this short note sent from London to a Norfolk country gentleman accompanied a packet of printed news. Mason's first sentence reads in part: "I sende you heare inclosed the Currantos that are come out since my last letter, w[hi]ch is in effect all o[u]r p[re]sent forreyne newes."

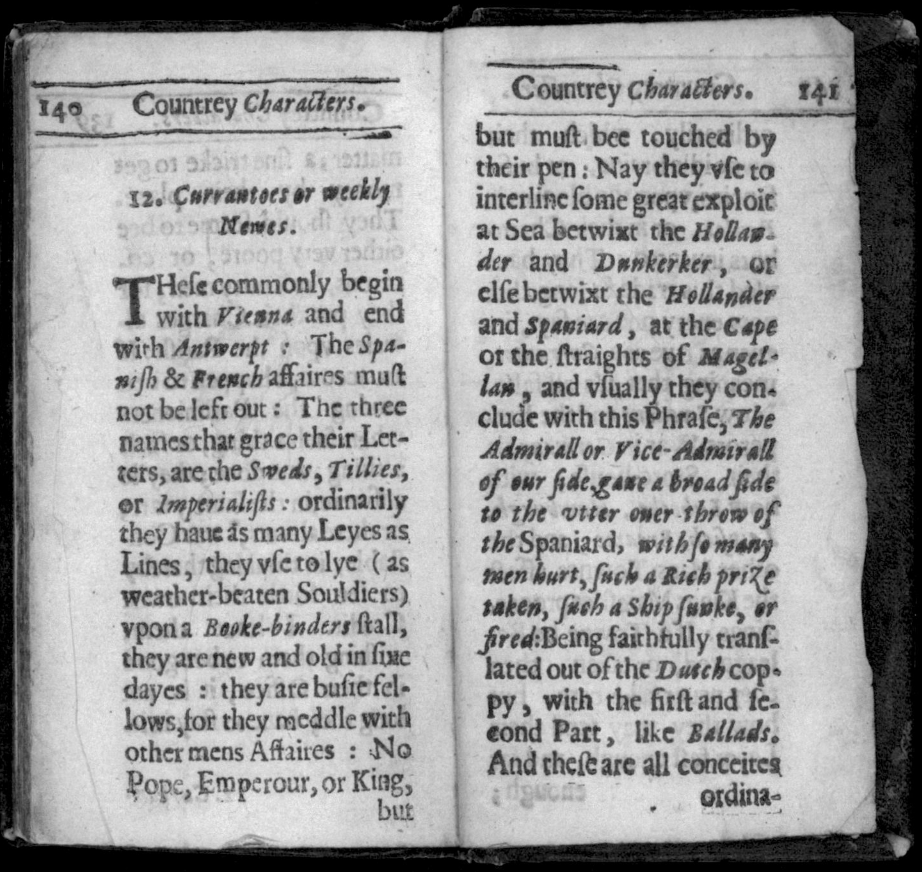

140 Countrey *Characters.*

12. *Currantoes or weekly Newes.*

THeſe commonly begin with *Vienna* and end with *Antwerpt* : The *Spaniſh* & *French* affaires muſt not be left out : The three names that grace their Letters, are the *Sweds*, *Tillies*, or *Imperialiſts* : ordinarily they haue as many Leyes as Lines, they vſe to lye (as weather-beaten Souldiers) vpon a *Booke-binders* ſtall, they are new and old in fiue dayes : they are buſie fellows, for they meddle with other mens Affaires : No Pope, Emperour, or King, but

Countrey *Characters.* 141

but muſt bee touched by their pen : Nay they vſe to interline ſome great exploit at Sea betwixt the *Hollander* and *Dunkerker*, or elſe betwixt the *Hollander* and *Spaniard*, at the *Cape* or the ſtraights of *Magellan*, and vſually they conclude with this Phraſe, *The Admirall or Vice-Admirall of our ſide gaue a broad ſide to the vtter ouer-throw of the* Spaniard, *with ſo many men hurt, ſuch a Rich prize taken, ſuch a Ship ſunke, or fired:* Being faithfully tranſlated out of the *Dutch* coppy, with the firſt and ſecond Part, like *Ballads.* And theſe are all conceites ordina-

19 Donald Lupton (d. 1676)
London and the Countrey Carbonadoed and Quartred into Severall Characters
London: Printed by Nicholas Okes, 1632
STC 16944 Copy 1, pp. 140–141

DONALD LUPTON WAS A CLERGYMAN who occasionally turned his hand to social commentary. In this witty portrait of characters, he takes gentle aim at corantos, commentating on how their format had become standardized. He writes that they all start with news from Vienna and end with the affairs at Antwerp, and must include reports from Spain and France. His most telling comment shows the importance of up-to-date reports: "they are new and old in five days."

The Currantiers to the Readers.

Gentle Readers, this Intelligencer the Curranto *having been long ſilenced, and now permitted by Authority to ſpeake again, preſents you here at firſt with ſuch things as paſſed ſome months ſince, not becauſe we conceive that they are abſolutely Novels unto you, but firſt becauſe there is fraud in generalities, we thought fit to acquaint you with each particular; and ſecondly, that by theſe Antecedents you may the better underſtand the Conſequents, which wee ſhall now publiſh weekely as heretofore.*

A 3

20 *An Abstract of Some Speciall Forreigne Occurences*
London: Printed [by T. Harper?] for Nathaniel Butter and Nicholas Bourne, by permission, 1638
STC 82, A3r

IN 1632, THE GOVERNMENT OF CHARLES I banned the publication of corantos. As the king commented in his letter to the Stationers' Company, the news in corantos was "unfit for popular view and discourse." However, fearful of losing a propaganda opportunity, in 1638 the Crown licensed the publishers Nathaniel Butter and Nicholas Bourne to produce newsbooks of foreign affairs, subject to government scrutiny before publication. In this epistle to coranto readers, Butter and Bourne inform their reading public that they can look forward to a resumption of frequent news reports. It was clear that the government could not stop the news, only attempt to control it.

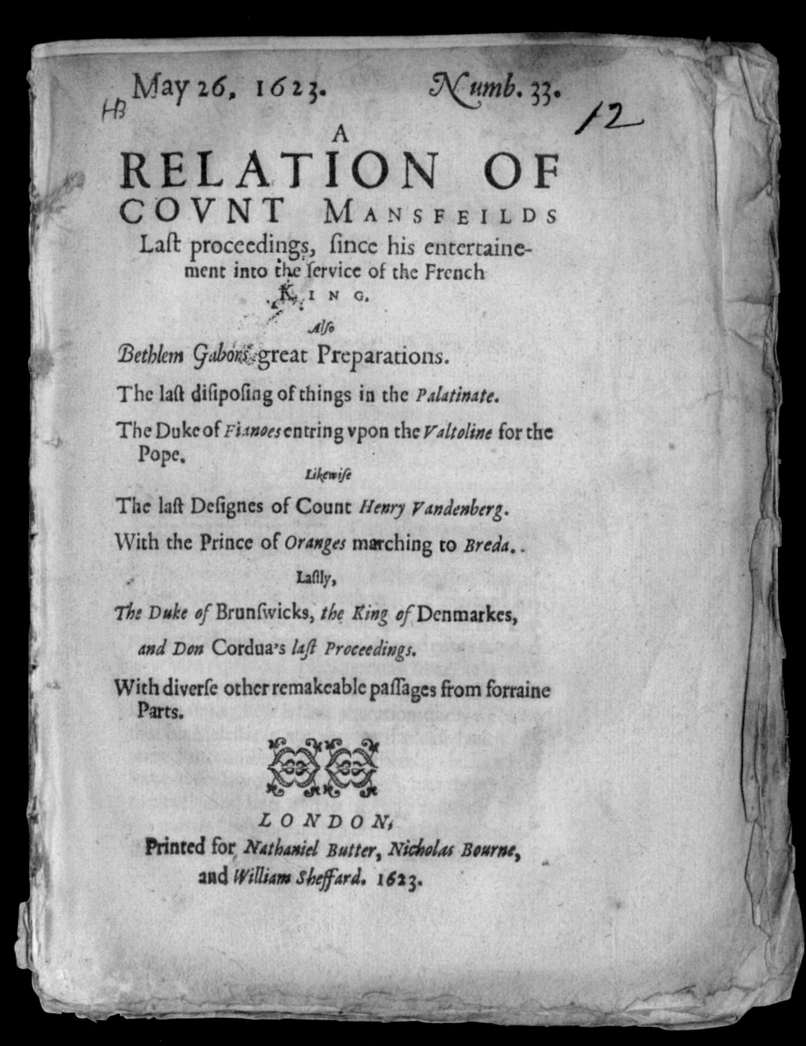

May 26. 1623. Numb. 33.

A

RELATION OF

COVNT MANSFEILDS

Laſt proceedings, ſince his entertaine-
ment into the ſervice of the French
KING.

Alſo

Bethlem Gabors great Preparations.

The laſt diſpoſing of things in the *Palatinate*.

The Duke of *Fianoes* entring vpon the *Valtoline* for the Pope.

Likewiſe

The laſt Deſignes of Count *Henry Vandenberg*.

With the Prince of *Oranges* marching to *Breda*.

Laſtly,

The Duke of Brunſwicks, *the King of* Denmarkes, *and Don* Cordua's *laſt Proceedings.*

With diverſe other remakeable paſſages from forraine Parts.

LONDON,

Printed for *Nathaniel Butter*, *Nicholas Bourne*, and *William Sheffard*. 1623.

21 *A Relation of Count Mansfeilds Last Proceedings*
London: Printed [by John Dawson] for Nathaniel Butter, Nicholas Bourne, and William Sheffard, 1623
STC 25198.8, title page

CORANTOS QUICKLY BECAME POPULAR and publishers introduced the idea of serialization—in this case dating and numbering each issue. However, they had yet to employ the idea of a standard title. Early corantos took as their title what the publishers thought was the most important news of the week. In Issue 33, news of the English expeditionary force to Germany led by Count Mansfeild provided the headline, and thus the title.

A true Report of all the ſpeciall *Paſſages of note lately happened in the Ile of Ree*, betwixt the Lord Duke of *Buckingham* his Grace, *Generall for the King of England, and Monſieur Thorax*, Gouernour of the Fort in the ſaid Ile, as alſo *betwixt the Duke and the* French *King, likewiſe the preſent ſtate of the* Rochellers, and of the Kings Armie lying before it

Nouemb. 1. *Numb.* 40.

The Continuation of our vveekly *Newes from the* 24. *of* October *to* the 2. of *Nouember.*

Containing amongſt the reſt theſe ſpeciall particulars following.

Vnto which is added Newes from *Germany, France, and diuers parts of Chriſtendome.*

The warlike proceedings of the Imperialiſts, and *Daniſh.*

The Treatie of Peace betwixt *Poland* and *Sweden.*

The Emperours Iourney towards Prage.

Beſides diuers other matters of moment.

Printed by Authoritie.

LONDON

Printed for *Nathaniell Butter*, 1627.

22 *A True Report of all the Speciall Passages*
London: Printed [by W. Stansby] for Nathaniel Butter, 1627
STC 25201a.2, title page

ALTHOUGH NATHANIEL BUTTER WAS IMPRISONED in August 1627 as a result of the government's increasingly hostile attitude towards news publication, he continued to publish corantos. The title page, though still not completely standardized, now reflected the exact dates of the news included in the issue—October 24–November 2—and included the phrase, "the continuation of our weekly news."

Numb. 10. 3

A
Perfect Diurnall
OF THE
PASSAGES
IN
PARLIAMENT:

From the fourteenth of March, to the twenty firſt. 1641.

Printed for *William Cook.*

Monday the fourteenth of March.

There were divers Letters read in the Houſe of Commons, which came from the Lords Juſtices of *Ireland*, Sir *Symon Harecourt*, and others, ſetting forth the preſent ſtate and condition of *Ireland*; And the ſeverall Victories they have lately obtained againſt the Rebells.

That the 27. of February laſt, they relieved *Tredagh* with proviſions, for ſeven weeks longer.

That the Proclamation which came from the King, requiring the Rebells immediately to lay down their Arms, or that otherwiſe they ſhould bee proſecuted with fire and ſword, as Traitors to the Crowne, takes no effect with them; But they have lately taken a new Oath of Confederacy againſt the King and his liege people.

That the Lords Juſtices are reſolved very ſuddenly to ſend a ſtrong Army into the *Pale*, to burn, ſpoile, and deſtroy the Rebells there, and to beat them off from before *Drogheda*, for that the Rebellion had its firſt root from the *Pale*.

That the returns from *England*, to aſſiſt the Proteſtants, are very ſlow, and not ſo full as a cauſe of ſo high nature requires; and that it is much feared, the want of moneys and clothes will breed great diſtractions in the Army, if not prevented by a ſudden and ample ſupply.

H And

23A *A Perfect Diurnall of the Passages in Parliament*
London: William Cook, 1642
P1486.6 Nos. 10, 11, title page

UNLIKE PREVIOUS NEWS PRINTERS who primarily translated foreign news, Samuel Pecke—considered the first English journalist— found his own sources of information and published domestic news gleaned from the proceedings in Parliament. *A Perfect Diurnall* was published weekly from 1642 through 1655 and quickly spawned imitators. By the end of 1642, seven other newsbooks had copied his title and over sixty different domestic newsbooks had appeared. Unlike many of his contemporaries, Pecke was not an educated man.

9

Numb. 11.

A Perfect Diurnall OF THE PASSAGES IN PARLIAMENT:

From the twenty first of March, 1641. to the twenty eighth, 1642.

Printed for *William Cook.*

Monday the 21. of March.

THere was a Bill read in the House of Commons, for the taking away of all Innovations in any Churches or Chappel, that hath been set up within this twenty yeeres: As the Altar, Rayles before the Communion Table, Pictures, Images or Crucifixes; and that all Chancells be laid even, and the steps before the Communion Table or Altar taken away.

In this Bill, there is a Clause for the strict keeping and observing of the Lords day, and that week-day-Lectures be set up in all places.

The Commons received information, that Master *Binion* Citizen of London, formerly committed to the Tower about the crosse Petition of the City for the ordering of the *Militia*, was upon his Petition to the Lords discharged from his imprisonment. But the Commons understanding him

I

23B *A Perfect Diurnall of the Passages in Parliament*
London: William Cook, 1642
P1486.6 Nos. 10, 11, title page

Numb. 135.

THE Moderate Intelligencer:

Impartially communicating Martial Affaires to the KINGDOME of ENGLAND.

From Thurſday October. 14. *to Thurſday October* 21. 1647.

October 14.

HE Commons proceeded in the Propoſitions, and perfected them the day before voted, and added that the Common Prayer book ſhall not be uſed in private. A Letter from his Majeſty to Sir *Tho. Fairfax*, deſiring that his children may be permitted to

THE BRITISH CIVIL WARS PROVIDED AN IMPORTANT IMPETUS for innovation and improvement in the newspaper industry. Newspapers became much better established, and a new generation of professional writers, publishers and printers emerged from within social groups that had not previously been involved in literary endeavors. Such men and women were willing and able to report on the progress of the war, and the issues involved with a combination of information and wit, although neither their loyalty nor their reliability could be taken for granted.

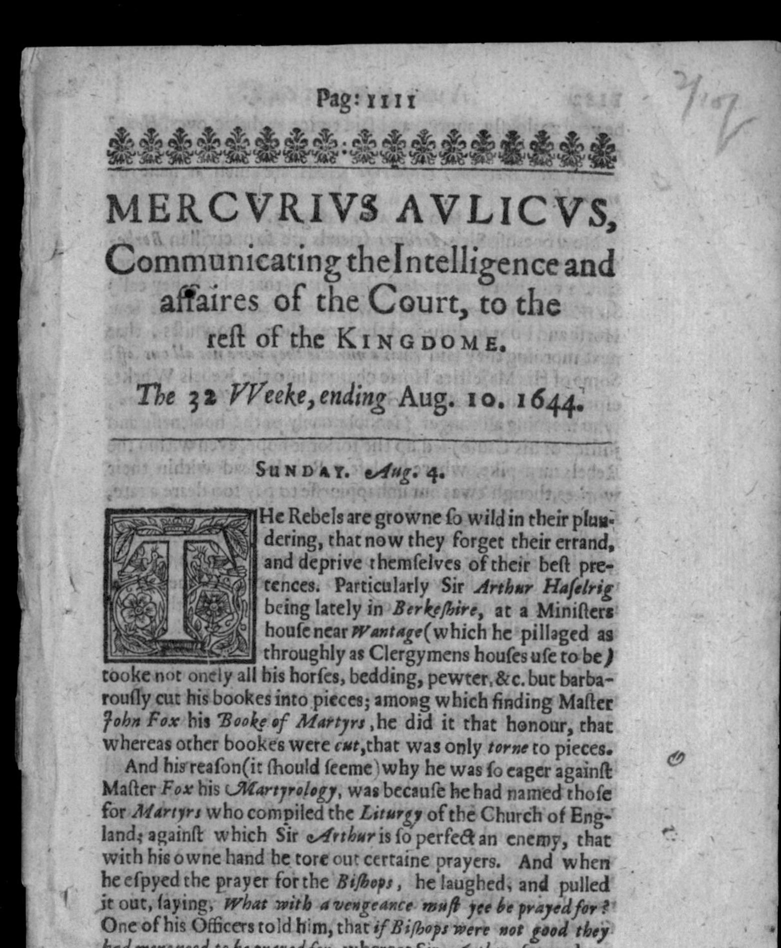

Pag: 1111

MERCVRIVS AVLICVS,

Communicating the Intelligence and affaires of the Court, to the reſt of the KINGDOME.

The 32 VVeeke, ending Aug. 10. 1644.

SUNDAY. *Aug.* 4.

THe Rebels are growne ſo wild in their plundering, that now they forget their errand, and deprive themſelves of their beſt pretences. Particularly Sir *Arthur Haſelrig* being lately in *Berkeſhire*, at a Miniſters houſe near *Wantage* (which he pillaged as throughly as Clergymens houſes uſe to be) tooke not onely all his horſes, bedding, pewter, &c. but barbarouſly cut his bookes into pieces; among which finding Maſter *John Fox* his *Booke of Martyrs*, he did it that honour, that whereas other bookes were *cut*, that was only *torne* to pieces.

And his reaſon (it ſhould ſeeme) why he was ſo eager againſt Maſter *Fox* his *Martyrology*, was becauſe he had named thoſe for *Martyrs* who compiled the *Liturgy* of the Church of England; againſt which Sir *Arthur* is ſo perfect an enemy, that with his owne hand he tore out certaine prayers. And when he eſpyed the prayer for the *Biſhops*, he laughed, and pulled it out, ſaying, *What with a vengeance muſt yee be prayed for?* One of his Officers told him, that *if Biſhops were not good they had more need to be prayed for*, whereat Sir *Arthur* ſeemed to

hhh be

24 *Mercurius Aulicus*, 32 (August 4–10, 1644)
Oxford: Printed by Henry Hall for William Webb?, 1644
M1752.5 No. 84, title page

RUNNING FROM JANUARY 1643 UNTIL SEPTEMBER 1645, *Mercurius Aulicus* was the first truly substantial newspaper printed during the Civil Wars, operating with court backing out of the royalist headquarters at Oxford and reprinted illicitly in London. It was initially written by the cleric, Peter Heylyn. However, beginning in the summer of 1644, it was penned by Sir John Berkenhead, although he was widely assumed to have received assistance from other leading courtiers. *Aulicus* offered military reports and political intelligence, and biting attacks upon parliamentarians. Despite this, it was often read by supporters of both sides.

(1103)

Numb. 129.

Mercurius Britanicus,

Communicating the affaires of great

BRITAINE:

For the better Information of the People.

From Monday May 4. to Monday, May 11. 1646.

I Hope ye all know ere this where the *King* is: Truly, his going to the *Scots* hath not *overtaken me unexpectedly*, nor *filled me with amazement*: for now my *dream* proves true; I alwayes thought he would go any whither rather then come to his *Parliament*, though truly it had been more honourable a great deal to come, than be ſent hither, for every body thinks the *Scots* will diſpoſe of him according to the determination of the *Parliament*, rather then *weaken the union and confidence between the Nations*: whatſoever people talk, I cannot believe otherwiſe, for the *Engliſh* Nation are bold, gallant, undaunted *ſpirits*, and do not expect the contrary, they cannot endure to ſee their *Parliament* ſlighted, they cry, Why not come in to us as well as to the *Scots*? What's the meaning of it, ſayes one? Why ſhould he truſt them more then us, ſayes another? I am ſure they have been worſt abuſed by him of any, branded for *Rebels* by him long before us, and now at laſt as *Invaders*, and all the worſt *mockeries* and *ſcandals* beſtowed on them ſtill at *Court*, yet the *King* preſumes moſt upon them: I will not ſay this is a *myſterie*, but it *fils me with amazement* when I ſee how *Malignants* are joyed at his going thither, how they *ſhew their teeth* together in *Corner-diſcourſe*, how they *ſtrut, clap their Wings*, and *crow* here upon our *dunghill*, as if all were on their ſide, as if they had their hearts deſire: this makes me

The King with the Scots.

Engliſhmen not to be neglected.

Iiiii *dream*

25 *Mercurius Britanicus*, 129 (May 4–11, 1646) [London: Printed by G. Bishop and R. White], 1646 262- 441q, title page

MERCURIUS BRITANICUS **WAS LAUNCHED IN THE SUMMER OF 1643** with the explicit aim of responding to *Aulicus*, and the two newsbooks traded blows, and accusations of inaccuracy, every week. An extremely influential newspaper, which was widely assumed to have had political backing, it launched the journalistic career of Marchamont Nedham, under whose guidance it became witty, acerbic, and scurrilous. His willingness to experiment with editorializing about both king and Parliament ensured a less than smooth relationship with the authorities, who shut the paper down and imprisoned its editor the week after this issue appeared.

MERCVRIVS Num. 4.
PRAGMATICUS.
Communicating Intelligence from all parts, touching all Affaires, Designes, Humours, and Conditions, throughout the Kingdome.
Especially from *Westminster*, and the *Head-Quarters*.

From Tuesday, *Octob.* 5. to Tuesday, *Octob.* 12. 1647.

Our wise Reformers, *brave and gay,*
Have ta'ne a godly *course,*
To fight, *to* feast, *to* fast *and* pray,
And milk *each honest* purse.

The Crownes Revenue *goes to wrack,*
While they sing Hymnes *and* Psalmes,
And rather then themselves will lack,
The King *must live on* Almes.

We are, the learned Synod *sayes,*
The Church of England's *Nurse,*
Who make them blesse *the* Sabbath-dayes,
And all the week *to* curse.

The Plough *stands still, and* Trade *is small,*
For, Goods, Lands, Townes, *and* Cities,
Nay, I dare say, the Devill *and all*
Payes Tribute *to* Committees.

——Nemo me Impunè lacessit.

I Know ye all look for *Newes*, but what can I do, when the *Houses* bring so few *grists to the mill*? Sure, they want the other *Purge*; for, they are very *costive* toward any *conclusion*: they are *hard bound*, and *hide-bound*, nay, *bound hand and foot*, so that they only wait the good houre, to be cast into *outer darknesse*, seeing the *worm that never dies* begins to quicken within already.

D And

26 *Mercurius Pragmaticus*, 4 (October 5–12, 1647)
London, 1647
M1768.49, title page

HAVING MADE HIS PEACE WITH THE KING, Marchamont Nedham resurfaced in September 1647 as editor of the royalist *Mercurius Pragmaticus*, thus ensuring his reputation as an unprincipled turncoat. In reality, Nedham remained a maverick on key issues, and his ideas did not meet with universal approval among fellow royalists. Despite his new political leanings, he remained a biting wit with regards to the characters and foibles of parliamentarian grandees, referenced in the verses with which he opened each week's issue.

MERCURIUS Num.2

PRAGMATICUS.

Communicating Intelligence from all Parts, touching all Conditions, Affayres, Deſignes, and humours, throughout the whole Kingdome.

Eſpecially from *Weſtminſter*, and the *Head-Quarters*.

From Tueſday 21. *Sept.* to Tueſday 28. *Sept.* 1647.

O goodly Kirke that we have got
By Lowdons *Information;*
What thankes we owe unto the Scot
For our bleſt Reformation.

The Crowne and Scepter's out of date,
The Miter low doth lie,
While we are governd by a State,
And hugge Democracy.

We have no King, we all are Kings,
And each doth doe his pleaſure,
And therefore tis we all ſtrange things,
And ſin beyond all meaſure.

When we have toyld our ſelves in vaine
For to be Rulers all,
We muſt intreat our Soveraigne
For to be Principall.

MAY we yet venture to ſpeake Truth (thinke you) and not feare the checkes of the Chayre man of the Cloſe Committee, and to be examined upon ſtrict Interrogatories, by thoſe bloody Inquiſi-

B tors

Gift of The Gladys Brooks Acquisitions Endowment Fund.

27 *Mercurius Pragmaticus*, 2 (September 21–28, 1647) [counterfeit]
London, 1647
252- 399q, title page

THE RUNAWAY SUCCESS OF NEWSBOOKS DURING THE 1640S ensured that there was money to be made from journalism, both for editors and publishers. As such, leading titles repeatedly found themselves counterfeited, as entrepreneurs sought to trick readers into buying illicit titles. The production of this inferior quality imitator, whose publication coincided with the second week of the authentic newsbook, was almost certainly motivated purely by profit.

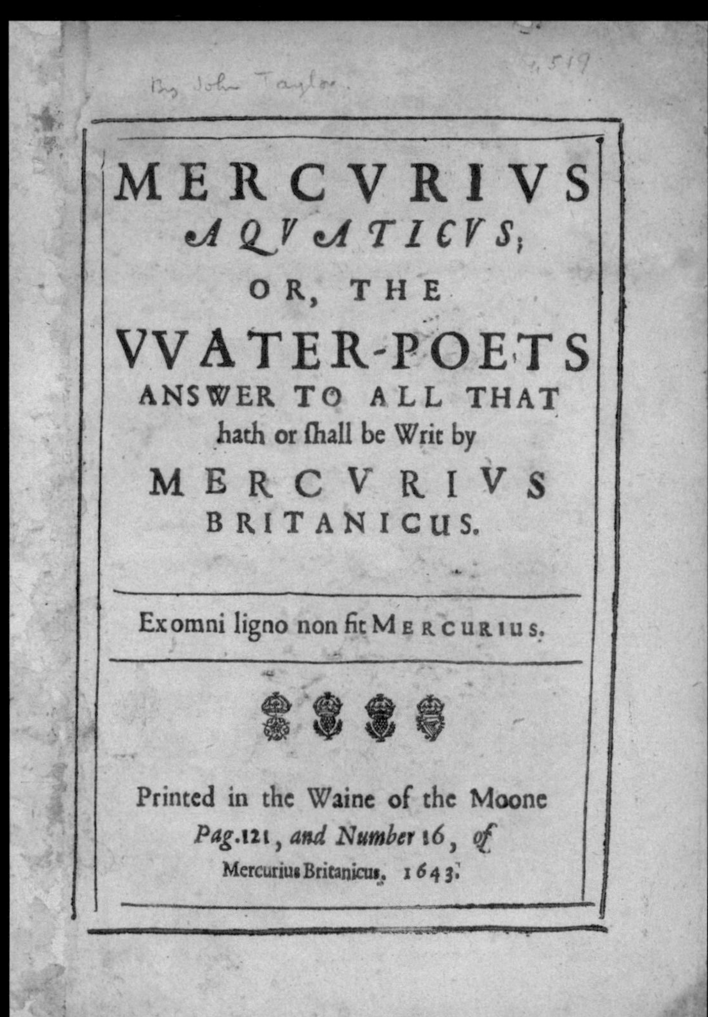

By John Taylor.

MERCVRIVS
AQVATICVS;
OR, THE
VVATER-POETS
ANSWER TO ALL THAT
hath or ſhall be Writ by
MERCVRIVS
BRITANICUS.

Ex omni ligno non fit MERCURIUS.

Printed in the Waine of the Moone
*Pag.*121, *and Number* 16, *of*
Mercurius Britanicus, 1643.

28 *Mercurius Aquaticus, or, the Water Poet's Answer to all that hath or shall be writ by Mercurius Britannicus* [Oxford]: Printed [by Leonard Lichfield] in the Waine of the Moone pag. 121, and Number 16, of Mercurius Britanicus, 1643 T481, title page

THE POPULARITY OF *MERCURIUS BRITANICUS* can be gauged by the strenuous efforts made by royalists to undermine Nedham's influence, including the suggestion that he was employed by Parliament. This news pamphlet, which employed a newsbook-style title, adopted the unusual strategy of reprinting an entire issue of *Britanicus* before subjecting it to a detailed critique. It was written by one of the most colorful literary characters of the age, the Water Poet John Taylor, who began life as a Thames bargeman and ended up running an alehouse. In between, he pioneered "professional" authorship, making money from his witty royalist poetry in cheap and sometimes scurrilous pamphlets.

(1285)

Numb. 132.

THE Moderate Intelligencer:

Impartially communicating Martial Affaires to the Kingdome of ENGLAND.

From Thurſday Septemb. 23. to Thurſday Septemb. 30. 1647.

Septemb. 23.

THE Commons this day went on to reſolve what was farther neceſſary for the ſettlement of the Kingdom, and having the day before agreed to the Militia, as formerly; they this day Voted the downfall of Epiſcopacy root and branch likewiſe that their Lands be ſold; a good Vote for them that have purchaſed: alſo that all that his Majeſty hath done by the great Seal during the late differences be null; that all Declarations by him publiſhed againſt the Parliament be recalled; that no Lords be made but by conſent of Parliament; that all done by the Parliaments great Seal be confirmed, with that of payment of the publique debts of the Kingdom, and upon the matter all the materiall ones, except that of ſetling the Presbyterian governmant and the taking the Covenant upon a penalty was not inſiſted upon, but forborn: They are two things upon which many eyes are and all parties look for ſatisfaction in them, ſome one way, and ſome another, and indeed it will be the great work to content all in theſe, the Conſcience ſatisfying is the great work.

An Ordinance paſt for continuing the Committee of the Army: Mr. *Glyn* being outed, Mr. *Fienes* was put in; the Ordinance continues the Treaſurers, and gives them power to diſpoſe of monies according to inſtructions therein. Ordered how the 20000 li. out of the Exciſe for Ireland be paid to the Committee of the Army, which the Exciſe is to take notice of, and do: The Committee for the

Rrrrrr Army,

29A *The Moderate Intelligencer*, 132 (September 23–30, 1647), London: Printed for Robert White, 1647
M2324.6 No. 132, title page

JOHN DILLINGHAM WAS A LONDON TAILOR who provided a bespoke intelligence service to wealthy individuals through manuscript newsletters before emerging as a prominent journalist during the 1640s. He developed a style that was less racy and more informative than some of his rivals, and was respected for his reliability. Nevertheless, his various titles served the interests of a particular group of moderate parliamentarian politicians to whom he was close. Like them, he was eventually eclipsed by more radical figures with more extreme ideas.

(1321)

Numb. 135.

THE Moderate Intelligencer: Impartially communicating Martial Affaires to the KINGDOME of ENGLAND.

From Thurſday October. 14. *to Thurſday October* 21. 1647.

October 14.

THE Commons proceeded in the Propoſitions, and perfected them the day before voted, and added that the Common Prayer book ſhall not be uſed in private. A Letter from his Majeſty to Sir *Tho. Fairfax*, deſiring that his children may be permitted to come once in ten dayes to him to *Hampton-Court*, and ſtay a night or two, their returne to Saint *James's*, not permitting this winter, the comming and going of a day as was uſuall; and this he is deſired to move the Parliament for.

The 15.

THE Commons conſidered of the Ordnance for poundage and tunnage. This day alſo the buſineſſe of Lieutenant Colonel *John Lilburne* was reported, and after a long debate, it was referred to a Committee of the long Robe, to conſult and declare in point of Law, what they conceive is juſt.

Letters from Munſter came this day, which ſpeak, that the Lord

Vuuuuu *Inchequin*

29B *The Moderate Intelligencer*, 135 (October 14–21, 1647), London: Printed for Robert White, 1647 M2324.6 No. 135, title page

(1345)

Numb. 137.

THE Moderate Intelligencer:

Impartially communicating Martial Affaires to the KINGDOME of ENGLAND.

From Thurſday October. 28. *to Thurſday November* 4. 1647.

October 28.

THE Contractors who have divers obſtructions in their ſales of Biſhops lands, had their deſires conſidered, and Committed it; being not yet reſolved, nor is like to be, that they ſhall ſell Lands for ten years purchaſe and no more, nor 21 yeers Leaſe, and three lives, for two yeers and no more.

Impeachments againſt ſeverall Lords were agreed, alſo againſt Sir *John Maynard*; Colonell *[illegible]* being an active man in the late buſineſſe, was Ordered to the Tower: Captain *[illegible]*, made Captain of the Primroſe; a great Detection offered, and to be found in Captain *Vernons* Chamber, proved nothing. A great aſſembly this day at Putney Church, where was debated matters of high concernment, *viz.* Whether the Army were obliged to make good their late Declarations and whether they might not be waved, ſome affirming they were not lawfull to be made, others, that they would be prejudiciall to ſome to whom they were made, and ſo to be kept, but when all profeſt to aym at nothing but the publique good, there was reſolution taken to meet the next day, and proceed, and firſt to put up ſupplications to God for a good iſſue.

The 29.

The Commons ſpent the whole day as a grand Committee about Tunnage and Poundage, and went through that long Bill; the Counſell ſate this day at *Putney*, whoſe

Yyyyyy

29C *The Moderate Intelligencer*, 137 (October 28–November 4, 1647)
London: Printed for Robert White, 1647
M2324.6 No. 137, title page

Mercurius Somnioſus

COMMVNICATING

His Packet of Intelligence from the ſeverall WATCHES of divers parts of the Kingdome:

CERTIFYING

How the three Major Generalls, with the loſſe of the Noble Sir WILLIAM FAIRFAX and others, rayſed the Siege at *Montgomery* Caſtle.

Taken priſoners.	*Slaine.*
The two Generalls of Foot and Horſe.	5 Colonells and Majors.
12 Coulours Majors and Captaines.	Divers Captains and Officers.
23 Lievetenants.	300 Common Souldiers.
33 Enſignes.	500 Wounded.
57 Sergeants.	200 Armes taken, and
11 Drums.	12 Barrells of powder.
1480 Common ſouldiers.	All their Bag and Baggage.

Beſides other Newes from the King Prince *Rupert*, the Lord *Hopton*: and Collections of Strange Dreames, ſuch as are not uſually Committed to the Preſſe.

LONDON,
Printed by JANE COE. 1644.

30 *Mercurius Somniosus*
London: Printed by Jane Coe, 1644
181- 414q, title page

NOT STRICTLY A NEWSPAPER because it appeared on only one occasion, this publication demonstrates how quickly titles such as "Mercurius" came to be regarded as suitable for any form of news pamphlet. This example came from a press operated by Jane Coe, one of London's few female printers. Coe capitalized upon strong contacts within the parliamentarian army to provide information for her many pamphlets and newspapers, as well as to forge links with a number of religious radicals.

(1)

MERCURIUS Num.5.

ANTI-PRAGMATICVS.

Communicating Intelligence from all parts, Touching all Affaires, Deſignes, Humours, and Conditions, throughout the Kingdome.

Eſpecially from *Weſtminſter*, and the *Head-Quarters.*

From Thurſd. *Novem.* 11. to Thurſd. *Novem.* 18. 1647

That Dagon *falls before the Ark,*
No rites to Moloch *given,*
Make Hamon *bleat,* Anubis *bark*
Diſtracts the hoſts of heaven.

Lets know that Kings *and* Peoples *ſin*
Do work a Nations *bane:*
So Roderigos *fault brought in*
The Moores *to conquer* Spaine.

We crie, an error of the Prince
Abimelech *combin'd,*
Forc'd by a ſupreme providence,
Sichem *and* Mello *joyn'd.*

Britain *was ſlav'd to* Saxons *power,*
France *for her ſins they ſcourg'd:*
If neighbouring lands do us devoure,
Our crimes their ſpleen have urg'd.

SEat me now on ſome high turret, whoſe heighth menaceth the clouds, that my Stentorian voice may be heard from Gades even to the Eaſt, while I bewaile the deplorable condition of our diſtracted land: what ſpirit of enmity

E praćtiſeth

31 *Mercurius Anti-Pragmaticus*, 5 (November 11–18, 1647) [London]: Printed for William Ley, 1647 M1752.45, title page

SOME OF THE MOST INFLUENTIAL AND CONTROVERSIAL NEWSPAPERS during the Civil Wars were considered so troubling that they inspired determined attempts to respond to their arguments and evidence. This particular journal, which ran for nine issues from October 1647 until February 1648, offered an explicit response to Nedham's royalist newspaper, *Mercurius Pragmaticus* (Cat. No. 26). Its unknown parliamentarian editor mimicked the appearance of his rival, and subjected Nedham to some of his own barbed and invective medicine.

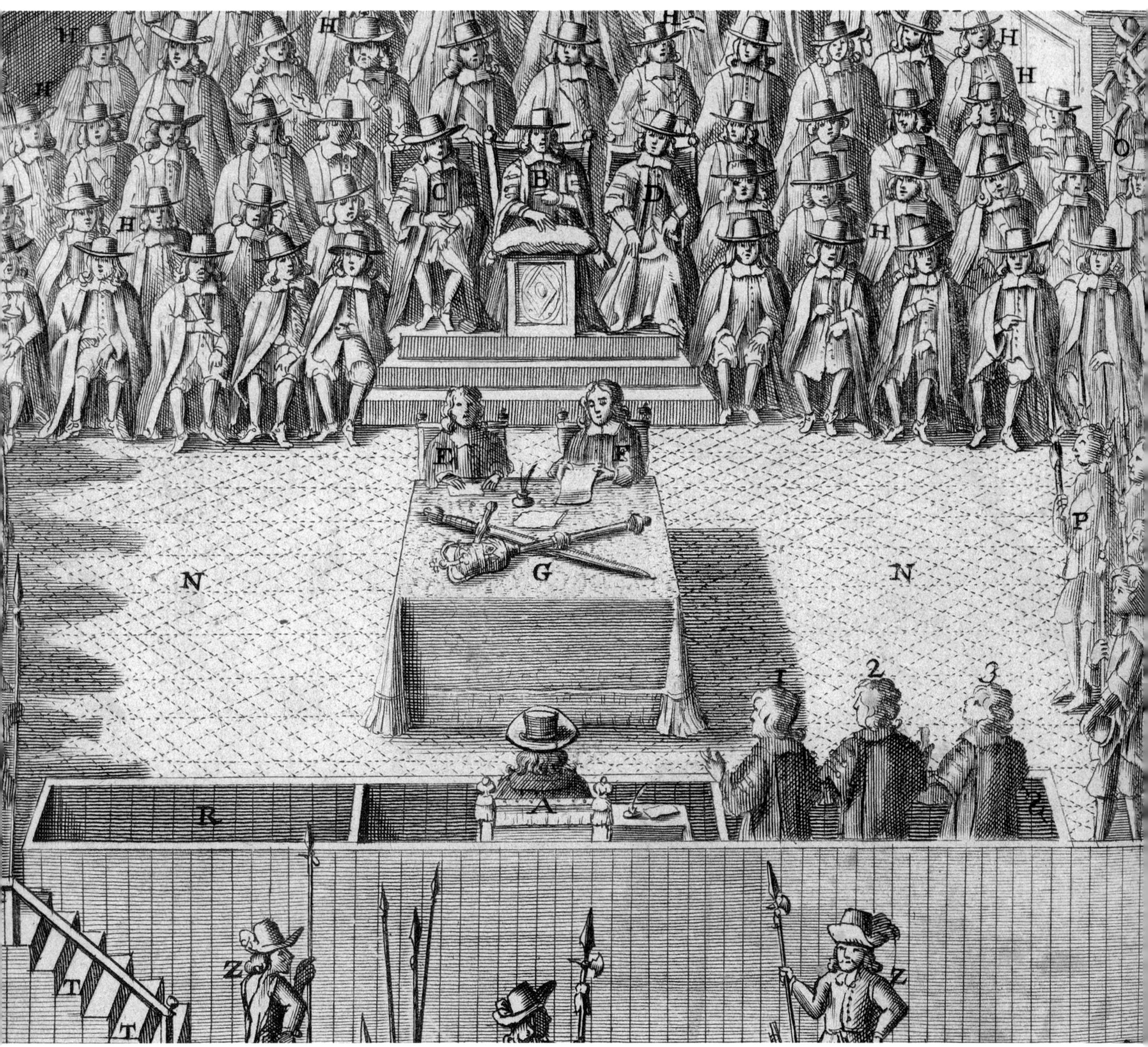

THE END OF THE BRITISH CIVIL WARS brought radicalism and political volatility, which presented new challenges for the fledgling newspaper industry. Journalists needed to navigate uncharted political territory, and their papers very quickly adopted novel ideas and innovative methods for conveying the news. The greatest challenge, involved a republican regime which, like those of earlier and later generations, sought to tame the industry, and exploit its potential for political purposes.

32 John Nalson (1637–1686)
A True Copy of the Journal of the High Court of Justice, for the Tryal of K. Charles I
London: Printed by H.C. for Thomas Dring, 1684
144- 155f, 2A1r

THE TRIAL OF CHARLES I IN JANUARY 1649 was one of the defining events of the seventeenth century—a high profile news event. This depiction of the scene was published as part of historical reflection upon the Civil Wars later in the century by an ardent supporter of the Stuart cause. It demonstrates how many people crowded into Westminster Hall. Amongst those present during the trial were a number of journalists, who reported on the proceedings in their newspapers.

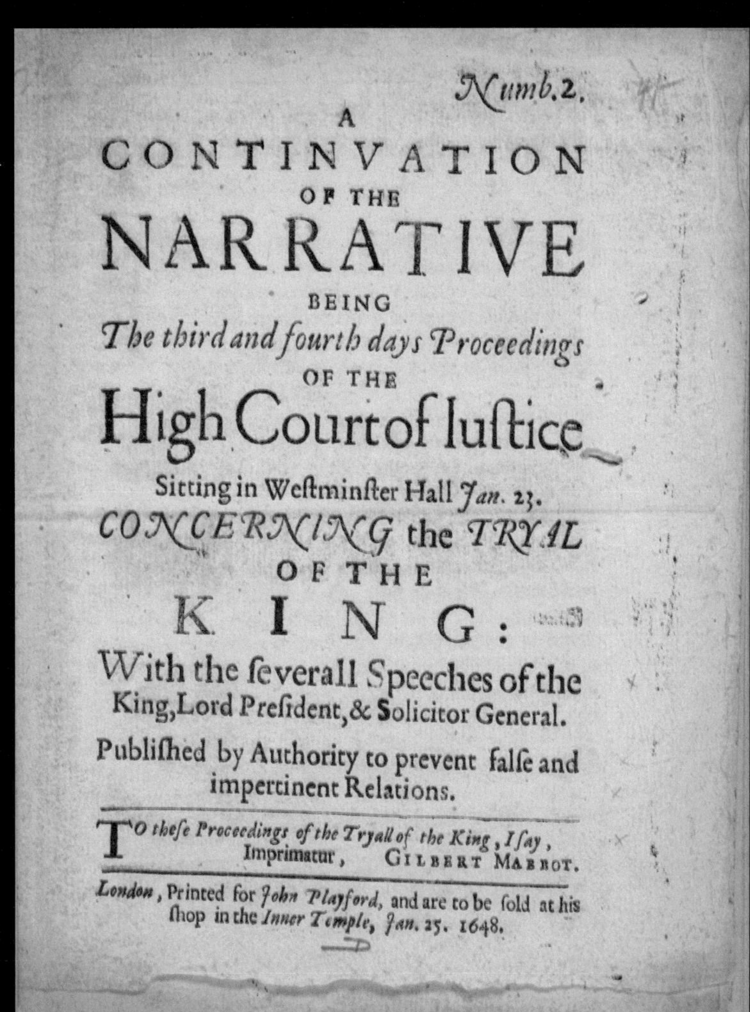

Numb. 2.

A
CONTINVATION
OF THE
NARRATIVE
BEING
The third and fourth days Proceedings
OF THE
High Court of Iuſtice
Sitting in Weſtminſter Hall *Jan.* 23.
CONCERNING the *TRYAL*
OF THE
KING:
With the ſeverall Speeches of the
King, Lord Preſident, & Solicitor General.
Publiſhed by Authority to prevent falſe and
impertinent Relations.

To theſe Proceedings of the Tryall of the King, I ſay,
Imprimatur, GILBERT MABBOT.

London, Printed for *John Playford*, and are to be ſold at his
ſhop in the *Inner Temple*, *Jan.* 25. 1648.

33 Gilbert Mabbott (1622–c.1670)
A Continuation of the Narrative… Concerning the Tryal of the King, 2
London: Printed for John Playford, 1648[9]
W9A, title page

THE TRIAL OF THE KING HIGHLIGHTED the difficulty which weekly newspapers had in keeping up with rapidly changing events. A number of journalists responded by producing special issues after each day's proceedings in the court had ended. These publications, including this example by Gilbert Mabbott, provided customers with their most regular printed news yet. Such reports also offered evocative verbatim accounts of the heated courtroom exchanges between the king and his prosecutors, as recorded by the army secretary, William Clarke.

(81)

Numb. 11.

The IModerate Rogue

Impartially communicating Martial Affaires to the KINGDOME of ENGLAND.

From Tuesday Septemb 19. to Tuesday Septemb 26. 1648.

WHere the peoples judgements are rectified, the Traytors purposes are prevented; but when affections blinde the judgement, judgements by Treason bring speedy ruin. It is the greatest of all Princely policy, to keep their subjects in simplicity; the Papists must hear Mass and say their Prayers in a Language they understand not, and desire of God they know not what, of their Laws made more ignorant, and consequently more fit for vassalage and slavery The English too much affected with the Mode of *France*, gives encouragement to their Prince to espouse himself with a Daughter of the Church of *Rome*, which occasions the Popish Faction and Councel to creep into the Court of the *English* Nation: The chiefest Peers, and the only Favorites, must be of the *Romish* interest, which for fifteen years together vassalize and enslave the people, by Monopolies, Ship-money, Coat and Conduct-money, and what not; making them believe that Kings are Gods anointed, and Vicegerents though Tirants; and that it is Damnation to oppose them in whatsoever they do, though it be to the ruine of the Nation; for the better effecting whereof, the people must be kept in greater ignorance by a Book of Common-Prayer the Bishops must silence Preaching Ministers, and others of the Popish and Royal Faction must be preferred to great Benifices, to Preach down Puritans, and introduce Popery, by erecting of Altars, and bowing down with all reverence towards them, with Copes and Surplices, making the people believe that God was worshipped Complementally and Formally, more then Spiritually and Cordially; their Laws continued in French, that they may not understand their Liberty, or the bounded power of their P. by them: The Bodies and Souls of the people thus enslaved *a la mode de France*, a Parl. is called, upon

34A *The Moderate*, 11 (September 19–26, 1648) London: Printed for Robert White, 1648 M2324.5

THE 1640S WITNESSED THE EMERGENCE of increasingly radical political ideas which were well represented in newspapers like *The Moderate*, written by Gilbert Mabbott. Mabbott had strong ties to the parliamentarian army, and perhaps even to groups on the radical republican fringe, such as the Levellers. Like many of the best newspapers, *The Moderate* was widely derided but avidly read. The owner of this particular copy has renamed it *The IModerate Rogue.* The pages remain in the unopened state in which newspapers were sold (Cap. No. 34B).

(81) Numb. 11.

The Moderate

Impartially communicating Martial Affaires to the Kingdome of ENGLAND.

From Tuesday Septemb. 19. to Tuesday Septemb. 26. 1648.

34B *The Moderate*, 11
(September 19–26, 1648)
London: Printed for Robert White, 1648
M2324.5

This afternoone, the new Court sate in the Painted Chamber, where met Sir *David Watkins*, Lieut.Gen.*Hammond*. Col.*Whaly*, M.*Silvanus Taylor*, Commissioners for Articles, upon the Act lately published, M.*Edward Friend* (being appointed Usher by the Serjeant at Armes,) had Orders given him to desire all the Commissioners to meet there on Tuesday at three a clocke, till which time the Court adjourned. *Thursday June* 21.

THe House of Commons Ordered that Sir *William Dicks* businesse should be Reported the first thing on Munday morning next, Col. *Allits* accounts also to be reported on Munday, and severall other businesse referred to days.

The great businesse of this day was about a long Act brought in, for regulating the Excise. and all things pertaining thereto.

The Reports from the Councell of State concerning what is fit to be done before the Parliament adjournes, is ready to bee made, so that there is likely to bee an adjournment suddainly.

From *Ireland* is news come, That Maj.Gen *Stradling* (called Sir *Henry Stradling*) the Lord *Inchequeens* chiefe officer and manager of his designes, is dead; that P. *Rupert* hath sent to *Plunket* to hasten his ships, which are not near ready. That *Rupert* is not in a condition to goe out with his Navy. That he hath sent a letter to the Generalls at Sea to desire Capt. *Allen* to be exchanged for Capt *Thomas*, that as Cap. *Allen* is used, and proceeded against here, so he will use Cap. *Thomas*. There are no letters come yet that the Parliaments ships are come againe before Kingsale, but yet it is probable enough that they are there by this:

Prince *Charles* hath sent a letter to his mother, late Queen of *England*, in answer to one that he received about the Irish Agent, which concernes the differences between *Owen Roe*, and the Marquesse of *Ormond*.

The chiefe Heads this week are these,

Letters from the Admirals at Sea, to the Parliament. The Stormes at Sea. And particulars of what ships were taken by Prince Charleses *ships. And Prince* Ruperts *peremptory Letter to the Admirals. Sir* Henry Stradling *dead. A Fight in* Shropshire, *and how divers of the Country rise, and fell upon the Souldiers, disarmed them, and stript them to their shirts. A fight at* Enfield Chase, *between the Country people and the Souldiers. Prince* Charleses *Letter to his Mother, late Queen of* England. *The Message sent by the Scots Commissioners from Prince* Charles *their King, to the Parliament of* Scotland. *The Votes of the House of Commons, and proceedings of the* Councell *of State, for the Parliament to adjourn, And an Order concerning new Propositions, An Order of the House of Commons concerning Major Gen.* Brown, *and the rest of the members imprisoned, And the copy of a Declaration which passed the House of Commons on Wednesday last. Fourteen hundred and eighty pounds taken at Gravesend. And L.G.* Crumwels *speech concerning his going to* Irel.

I Desire all people to take notice that I denie to give any authority to a Pamphlet called, *The Kingdomes Weekly Scout*, because the Common-wealth hath been so extreamly abused by it, by *Rob. Wood* of *Grubstreet*, who contrives false inventions at an Alehouse to adde to it what he fancies as news, after M. *Border* the Author hath write it, and the Licenser perused it, and thus he hath abused the Judge Advocate, and my selfe and the Common-wealth, and the Author who did it formerly doth now disclaim it, refusing any more to write it for him: and if he be so impudent as still to publish it, I desire all those whom it concernes to suppresse it that the people may not be cheated by it. 21 June. 1649. *Imprimatur Theo. Jennings.* Finis.

35 *Perfect Occurrences*, 129 (June 15–22, 1649) London: Printed by R.I. for Robert Ibbitson, 1649 150- 373q, p. 1081

ONE EDITOR FAVORED BY THE REPUBLICAN GOVERNMENT was Henry Walker, a former ironmonger turned news writer. During the 1640s he emerged as one of the most colorful and controversial of the new breed of professional journalists, often in association with the publisher Robert Ibbitson. Here he announces the withdrawal of an official license to a rival newspaper, whose publisher, Robert Wood, was accused, like many involved in journalism at the time, of contriving false inventions at an alehouse, after the text had been prepared by the editor, Daniel Border.

(485) *Numb.35.*

A

BRIEF RELATION

OF

Some Affairs and Tranſactions,

CIVIL and MILITARY,

BOTH

Forraign and Domeſtique.

Licenſed by Gualter Froſt *Eſq*; *Secretary to the Councel of State, according to the direction of the late Act.*

From Tueſday *April* 16. to Tueſday *April* 23. 1650.

Breda, 12 *April*, 1650.

SIR, I believe I ſhall write you no more from hence, nor much at preſent, things being come to a concluſion; for though they will not ſpeak it publiquely, yet it is believed by thoſe who obſerve all actions cloſely, that they are indeed agreed: for here hath been the Prince of *Orange* theſe three or four days, and been extreme earneſt with both parties to agree them, and hath indeed brought both to a Subſcription. What the Articles are, I yet cannot give you, for they will not acknowledge the thing it ſelf; but you may be confident of it, it is onely that they may be aforehand with you. But all the Scotiſh difficulties are not over, for 'tis evident they know not what to do with their King when they have him: They are not willing to have him into *Scotland*, the charge of it will be inſupportable to them, but they are willing to make uſe of his Authority. The Prince of *Orange* is all to have him go, becauſe ſo long as he ſtay in theſe parts, he is like to keep him, which will be a great burthen to his indebted Eſtate, which hath ſuffered ſo deeply already by his Royal Allyance, therefore be confident he will give him all the aſſiſtance he can to be rid of him; and there is no doubt 'tis moſt for his Intereſt to go pre-

Rrr ſently

36 Walter (Gualter) Frost (1598–1652)
A Briefe Relation of Some Affairs, 35 (April 16–23, 1650)
[London]: Printed by M[atthew] Simmons, in Aldersgate Street, 1650
B4624.5, title page

GOVERNMENT INTEREST IN THE NEWSPAPER INDUSTRY was evident from the work of men like Marchamont Nedham and, in this case, Walter Frost, who had been involved in intelligence gathering for Parliament during the Civil Wars, as well as in writing pamphlets against the proto-democratic Levellers. During the republic, he was employed as secretary to the Council of State, and his newspaper was produced by Parliament's official printers. These favors helped to ensure that he was widely recognized as an official "newshound."

CENSORSHIP AND THE FREE PRESS

IT is this day Ordered by the Commons Houſe of Parliament, That the Committee for examinations, or any four of them, have power to appoint ſuch perſons as they thinke fit, to ſearch in any houſe or place where there is juſt cauſe of ſuſpicion, that Preſſes are kept and employed in the printing of Scandalous and lying Pamphlets, and that they do demolliſh and take away ſuch Preſſes and their materials, & the Printers Nuts and Spindles which they find ſo employed, and bring the Maſter-Printers, and

OPINIONS HAVE ALWAYS DIFFERED about the degree to which the media should be controlled by political and religious authorities, and the sixteenth and seventeenth centuries witnessed persistent tension between the forces of order and liberation. Brutal punishment of wayward authors produced stirring calls for press freedom. Few contemporaries adopted entirely straightforward views on this issue, however, and many changed their views depending on their proximity to power. As a result, successive regimes continued to restrict the dissemination of news and opinion.

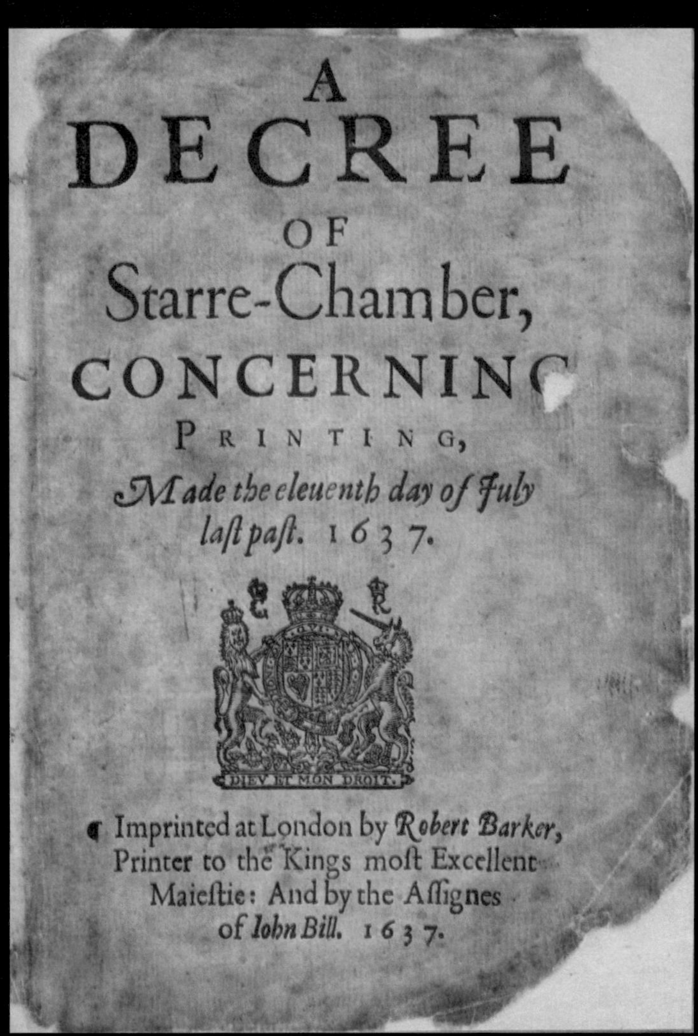

A

DECREE

OF

Starre-Chamber,

CONCERNING

PRINTING,

Made the eleuenth day of July last past. 1637.

DIEV ET MON DROIT.

¶ Imprinted at London by *Robert Barker*, Printer to the Kings most Excellent Maiestie: And by the Assignes of *Iohn Bill*. 1637.

37 *A Decree of Starre-Chamber, Concerning Printing*
London: By Robert Barker, printer to the Kings most Excellent Maiestie: and by the assignes of Iohn Bill, 1637
STC 7757 Copy 2, title page

AS RELIGIOUS DIVISIONS DEEPENED IN THE 1630S, Elizabethan legislation was deemed insufficiently rigorous to deal with Puritan tracts debating the affairs of church and state. This decree targeted "seditious, schismatical or offensive" pamphlets, and "secret printing in corners," and underpinned the notoriety of the court of Star Chamber, which sentenced a number of authors and activists to heavy fines, lengthy imprisonments, and savage punishments.

(6)

Die Jovis 9° Martii, 1642,

IT is this day Ordered by the Commons Houſe of Parliament, That the Committee for examinations, or any four of them, have power to appoint ſuch perſons as they thinke fit, to ſearch in any houſe or place where there is juſt cauſe of ſuſpicion, that Preſſes are kept and employed in the printing of Scandalous and lying Pamphlets, and that they do demolliſh and take away ſuch Preſſes and their materials, & the Printers Nuts and Spindles which they find ſo employed, and bring the Maſter-Printers, and VVork-

(7)

VVork-men Printers before the ſayd *Committee*; And that the *Committee* or any four of them, have power to commit to priſon any of the ſayd Printers, or any other perſons that do contrive, or publikely or privately vend, ſell, or publiſh any Pamphlet, ſcandalous to his Majeſty or the proceedings of both or either Houſes of Parliament, or that ſhall refuſe to ſuffer any Houſes or Shops to be ſearched, where ſuch Preſſes or Pamphlets as aforeſayd are kept: And that the perſons imployed by the ſayd *Committee*, ſhall have power to ſeize ſuch ſcandalous and lying Pamphlets as they find upon ſearch, to be in any Shop or VVarehouſe, ſold, or diſperſed by any perſon whomſoever, and to bring the perſons that ſo kept, publiſhed, or ſold the ſame, before the *Committee*; And that ſuch

38 *An Order of the Commons in Parliament Prohibiting the Printing or Publishing of any Lying Pamphlet*
[London]: Printed for Edw. Husbands and are to be sold at his shop in the Middle-Temple 1642[3]
142- 666q, pp. 6–7

THE REFORMS IMPLEMENTED DURING 1640 AND 1641 by critics of the government of Charles I included the abolition of the Star Chamber and the removal of individual press licensers. By 1643, however, Parliament was determined to try and re-impose order in the face of an explosion in pamphleteering and journalism. This order sanctioned searches for illicit presses and the seizure of any pamphlets which were deemed scandalous either to the king or to the proceedings of Parliament.

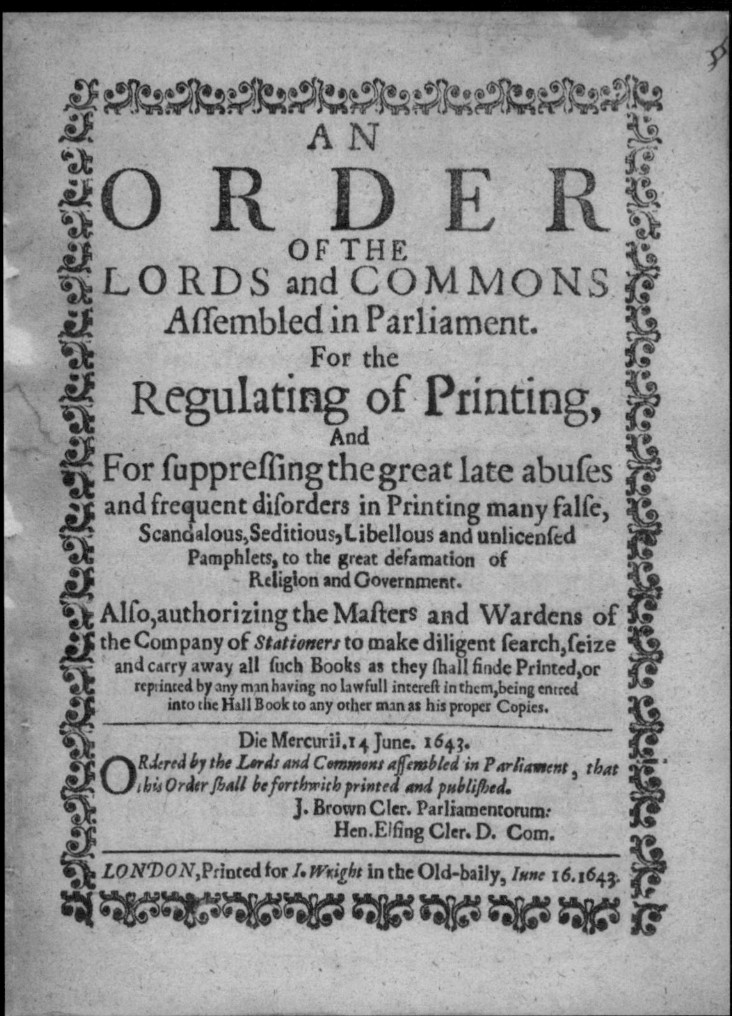

AN
ORDER
OF THE
LORDS and COMMONS
Aſſembled in Parliament.
For the
Regulating of Printing,
And
For ſuppreſſing the great late abuſes and frequent diſorders in Printing many falſe, Scandalous, Seditious, Libellous and unlicenſed Pamphlets, to the great defamation of Religion and Government.
Alſo, authorizing the Maſters and Wardens of the Company of *Stationers* to make diligent ſearch, ſeize and carry away all ſuch Books as they ſhall finde Printed, or reprinted by any man having no lawfull intereſt in them, being entred into the Hall Book to any other man as his proper Copies.

Die Mercurii, 14 June. 1643.

O*Rdered by the Lords and Commons aſſembled in Parliament, that this Order ſhall be forthwith printed and publiſhed.*

J. Brown Cler. Parliamentorum.
Hen. Elſing Cler. D. Com.

LONDON, Printed for *I. Wright* in the Old-baily, *Iune* 16. 1643.

39 *An Order of the Lords and Commons… For the Regulation of Printing*
London: Printed for I. Wright in the Old-baily, 1643
134- 929q, title page

A FULL-SCALE ATTEMPT TO RE-IMPOSE CENSORSHIP began in June 1643, with the establishment of a roster of clerics and lawyers to license new publications. This enabled the punishment of wayward journalists, not least those who attacked prominent members of Parliament and peers, as well as the king. Subsequent years witnessed the struggles between competing political factions over the power to license newspapers, more rigorous attempts to silence radical and royalist titles, and eventually the creation of a government news monopoly in 1655.

AREOPAGITICA;

A

SPEECH

OF

Mr. JOHN MILTON

For the Liberty of VNLICENC'D PRINTING,

To the PARLAMENT of ENGLAND.

Τοὐλεύθερον δ' ἐκεῖνο, εἴ τις θέλει πόλει
Χρηστόν τι βούλευμ' εἰς μέσον φέρειν, ἔχων.
Καὶ ταῦθ' ὁ χρῄζων, λαμπρὸς ἔσθ', ὁ μὴ θέλων,
Σιγᾷ, τί τούτων ἐστὶν ἰσαίτερον πόλει;
Euripid. Hicetid.

This is true Liberty when free born men
Having to advise the public may speak free,
Which he who can, and will, deserv's high praise,
Who neither can nor will, may hold his peace;
What can be juster in a State then this?
Euripid. Hicetid.

LONDON,
Printed in the Yeare, 1644.

40 John Milton (1608–1674)
Areopagitica; a Speech of Mr John Milton for the Liberty of Unlicenc'd Printing
London, 1644
M2092, title page

FOR AT LEAST SOME CONTEMPORARIES, the attempts by Parliament to re-impose censorship in 1643 came as a bitter disappointment. Foremost among those who bemoaned attacks upon "the people's birthright" was the poet John Milton who himself had faced punishment for his notorious pamphlets defending the practice of divorce. Milton argued that the authorities might as well "kill a man as kill a good book," that faith thrived "by exercise," and that truth would emerge from freedom. He made exceptions, however, for Catholicism and newspapers, and himself became a newspaper licenser in 1651.

Gaze not vpon this shaddow that is vaine.
But rather raise thy thoughts a higher straine.
To GOD (I meane) who set this young-man free.
And in like straits can eke deliuer thee.
Yea though the lords have him in bonds againe
the LORD of lords will his just cause maintaine.

A
REMONSTRANCE
OF
Many Thousand Citizens, and other Free-born
PEOPLE OF ENGLAND,
To their owne House of
COMMONS.
Occasioned through the Illegall and Barbarous Imprisonment of that Famous and Worthy Sufferer for his Countries Freedoms, Lievtenant Col.
JOHN LILBURNE.

Wherein their just Demands in behalfe of themselves and the whole Kingdome, concerning their Publike Safety, Peace and Freedome, is Express'd; calling those their Commissioners in Parliament to an Account, how they (since the beginning of their Session, to this present) have discharged their Duties to the Universallity of the People, their Soveraigne LORD, from whom their Power and Strength is derived, and by whom (ad bene placitum,) it is continued.

Printed in the Year, 1646.

41A Richard Overton
(fl. 1640–1663)
A Remonstrance of Many Thousand Citizens and other Free-Born People of England
[London], 1646
R993

THE MOST VEHEMENT CRITICS OF PRESS CENSORSHIP during the 1640s were political radicals, like the future Leveller, Richard Overton, who defended his recently imprisoned friend and ally, John Lilburne. Lilburne was as unpopular with the parliamentary authorities as he had been with Charles I as a result of his many intemperate pamphlets attacking parliamentary tyranny and individual politicians. On this occasion, the printer has superimposed prison bars upon an earlier engraving of Lilburne.

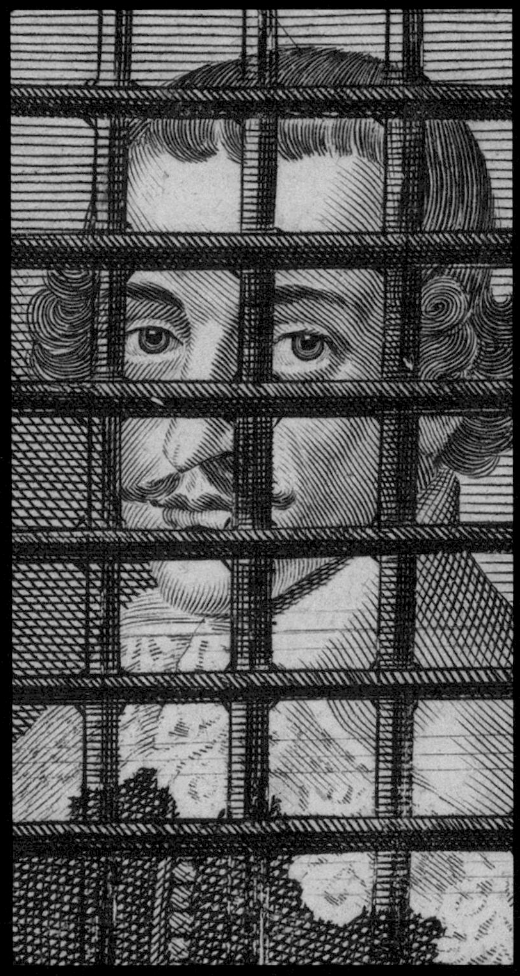

41B Richard Overton
(fl. 1640–1663)
A Remonstrance of Many Thousand Citizens and other Free-Born People of England
[London], 1646
R993

REASONS
Humbly offered for the
LIBERTY
OF
Unlicens'd Printing.

To which is Subjoin'd,
The Juſt and True CHARACTER
OF
Edmund Bohun,
The Licenſer of the Preſs.

In a Letter from a Gentleman in the Country, to a Member of Parliament.

London, Printed in the Year MDCXCIII.

42 Charles Blount (1654–1693)
Reasons Humbly Offered for the Liberty of Unlicens'd Printing
London, 1693
B3313 Bd.w. M3014, title page

ASIDE FROM BRIEF LAPSES IN LEGISLATION, press licensing remained in force until 1695, despite the controversy which continued to surround individual licensers, and the severity with which offenders were punished. One such victim was the freethinker and polemicist, Charles Blount, whose religious and political tracts were publicly burned on more than one occasion. Blount sought to keep Milton's ideas alive during the Restoration, and may thus have been responsible for this adaptation of *Areopagitica* (Cat. No. 38), published under the authorship of "J.M."

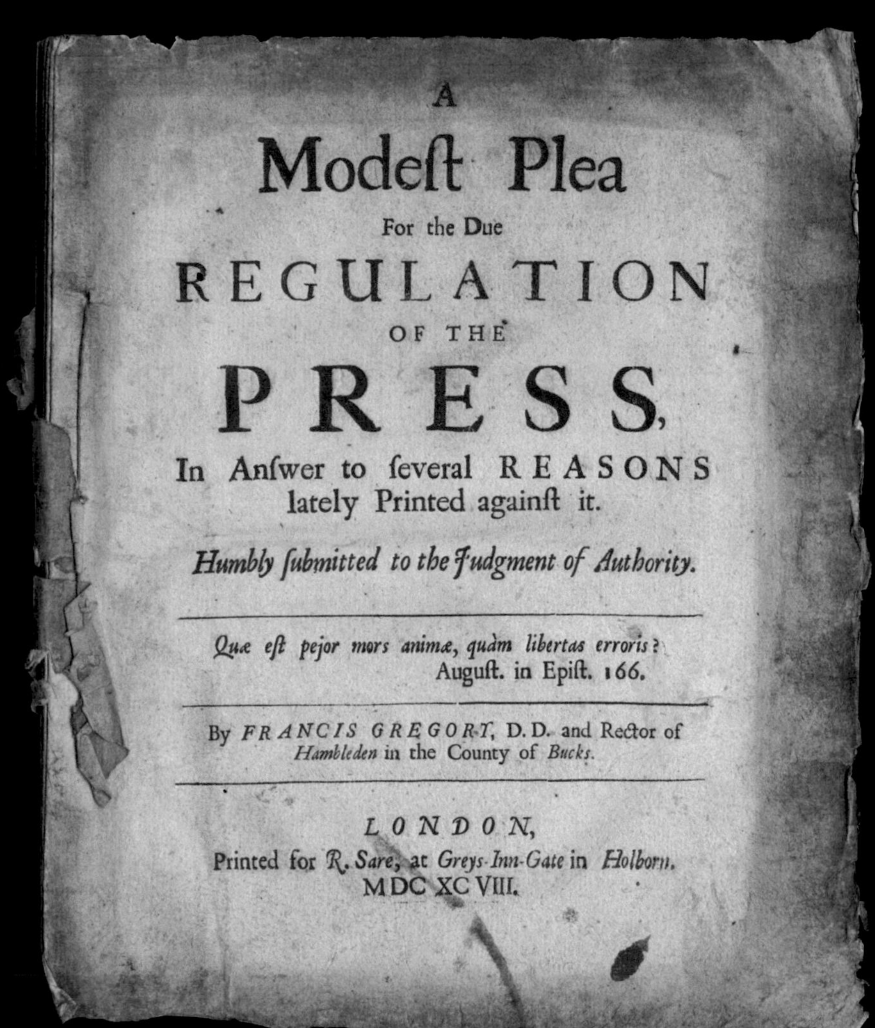
A
Modeſt Plea
For the Due
REGULATION
OF THE
PRESS,
In Anſwer to ſeveral REASONS
lately Printed againſt it.
Humbly ſubmitted to the Judgment of Authority.

Quæ eſt pejor mors animæ, quàm libertas erroris?
Auguſt. in Epiſt. 166.

By *FRANCIS GREGORY*, D.D. and Rector of
Hambleden in the County of *Bucks*.

LONDON,
Printed for R. *Sare*, at *Greys-Inn-Gate* in *Holborn*.
MDC XC VIII.

43 Francis Gregory (1623–1707)
A Modest Plea for the Due Regulation of the Press
London: Printed for R. Sare, at the Greys-Inn-Gate in Holborn, 1698
260- 739q, title page

THE END OF LICENSING IN 1695 did not result in press freedom, because other methods, such as the imposition of libel laws, were soon found to punish views that were considered scandalous or seditious. The ongoing debate about the issue is evident from this tract, written by an Anglican clergyman, which offered a point-by-point response to a recent pamphlet by the Whig philosopher and tolerationist, John Toland. In the same year Toland republished Milton's works, including *Areopagitica.*

Elizabeth R

Wheras divers bookes made or translated by
other side of the Sea without lawfull licence, conteyning
estate of her Mate: and styrring and nourishing
malicious persons amongst sundry her Mats subjects
from their duetie and allegeaunce due to her Ma: a
wicked example hath ben made in the state of

ONE OF THE WAYS IN WHICH THE GOVERNMENT CONTROLLED and censored the press was through proclamations. These royal edicts were often issued at times of political crisis. Fears over the spread of Catholic propaganda in Elizabeth's reign and the Exclusion crisis in the late seventeenth century drove the government to issue proclamations suppressing the news. Elizabeth's signature authorized the manuscript proclamation, while the printed version was distributed in towns around England.

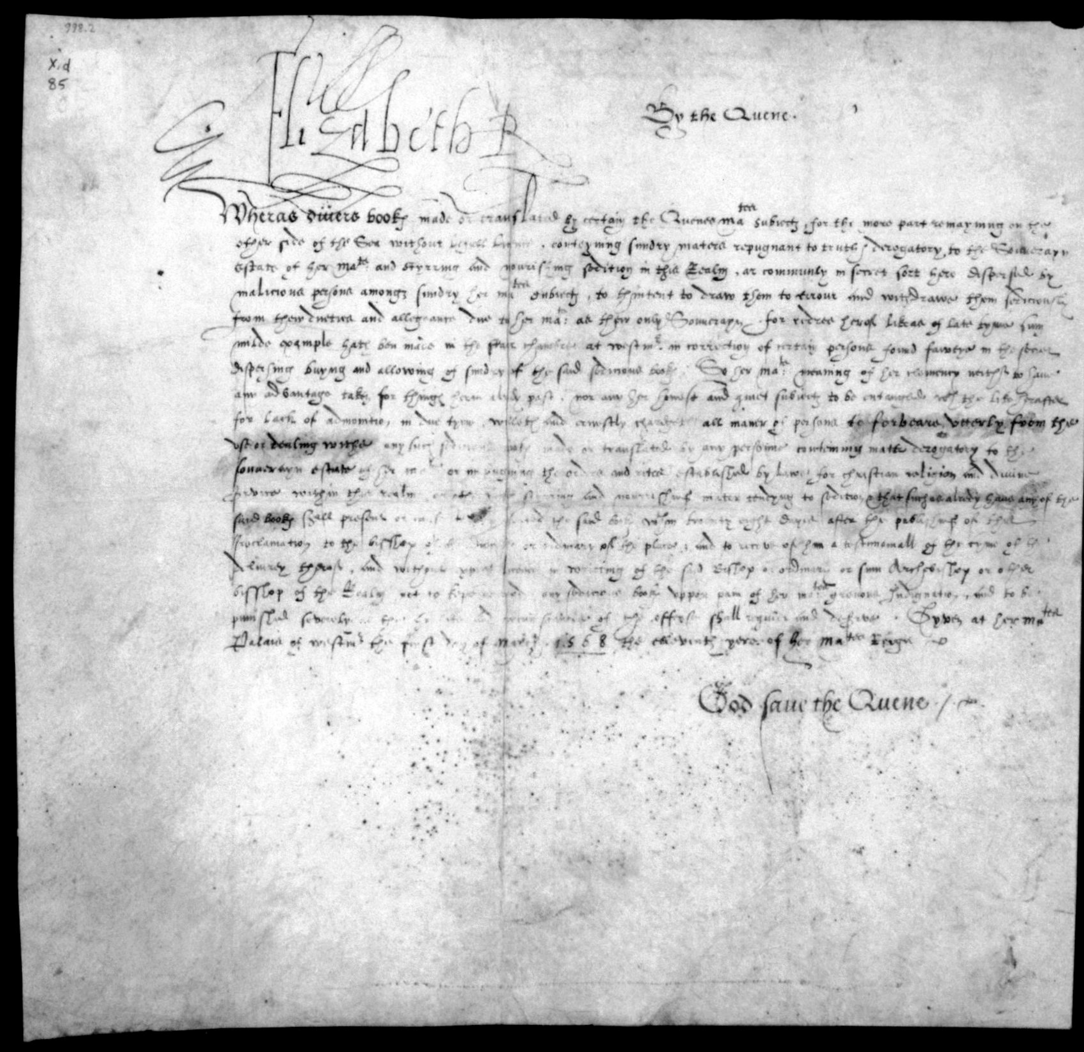

44 England and Wales. Sovereigns (1558–1603: Elizabeth I)
"By the Quene. Wheras diuers book[es] made or translated by certain the Quenes Ma[ies]ties subiect[es]..."
Manuscript proclamation signed by Elizabeth I
March 1, 1568/69
X.d.85

114

By the Queene.

A Proclamation for bringing into the Realme of vnlawfull and ſeditious bookes.

Wheras diuers bookes made or tranſlated by certayne the Queenes Maieſties ſubiectes, for the more part remayning on the other ſyde of the ſea, without lawfull licence, contayning ſundry matters repugnaunt to trueth, derogatorie to the ſoueraigne eſtate of her Maieſtie, and ſtirring and nouriſhing ſedition in this Realme, are commonly in ſecrete ſort here diſpearſed by malicious perſons among ſundry her Maieſties ſubiectes, to thintent to drawe them to errour, and withdrawe them ſediciouſly from their ducties and allegiance due to her Maieſtie, as their onlye ſoueraigne. For redreſſe hereof, lyke as of late tyme ſome mylde example hath ben made in the ſtarre chaumber at Weſtminſter, in correction of certayne perſons founde faultie in the ſecrete diſpearſing, buying, and allowing of ſundry of the ſayde ſeditious bookes: So her Maieſtie meaning of her clemencie neither to haue any aduauntage taken for thinges herein alredy paſt, nor any her honeſt and quiet ſubiectes to be entangled with the lyke hereafter for lacke of admonition in due tyme: wylleth and earneſtlye chargeth all maner of perſons, to forbeare vtterly from the vſe or dealing with any ſuch ſeditious bookes, made or tranſlated by any perſon, contayning matter derogatorie to the ſoueraigne eſtate of her Maieſtie, or impugning the orders and rites eſtabliſhed by lawe for Chriſtian religion and deuine ſeruice within this Realme, or otherwyſe ſtyrring and nouriſhing matter tending to ſedition: and that ſuch as alredy haue any of the ſayde bookes, ſhall preſent, or cauſe to be preſented the ſayde bookes, within twentie and eyght dayes after the publiſhing of this proclamation, to the byſhop of the dioceſſe, or ordinarie of the place, and to receaue of hym a teſtimoniall of the tyme of the deliuerie thereof: and without expreſſe licence in wryting of the ſayde byſhop or ordinarie, or ſome archbyſhop, or other byſhop of the Realme, not to kepe or reade any ſeditious bookes, vpon payne of her Maieſties greeuous indignation, and to be puniſhed ſeuerely, as the qualitie and circumſtaunces of the offence ſhall require and deſerue.

Gyuen at her Maieſties pallaice of Weſtminſter, the firſt day of March, 1568. the eleuenth yere of her Maieſties raigne.

God ſaue the Queene.

Imprinted at London in Powles Churcheyarde by Richarde Iugge and Iohn Cawood, Printers to the Queenes Maieſtie.

Cum priuilegio Regiæ Maieſtatis.

45 England and Wales. Sovereigns (1558–1603: Elizabeth I)
A Proclamation for Bringing into the Realm Unlawful and Seditious Bookes
London: In Powles Churcheyarde by Richarde Iugge and Iohn Cawood, printers to the Queenes Maiestie, [1569]
STC 8014 Bd.w. STC 7758.3

By the King.

A PROCLAMATION

To Reſtrain the Spreading of Falſe News, and Licentious talking of Matters OF

State and Government.

CHARLES R.

Whereas of late many perſons ill affected to the Government have aſſumed to themſelves a Liberty in their ordinary Diſcourſes to cenſure and defame the Proceedings of State, whereby they endeavour to create and nouriſh in the minds of His Majeſties good Subjects an evil opinion of things they underſtand not; And further to promote their Seditious ends, they do daily invent falſe News, and ſpread the ſame abroad amongſt the People, to the great ſcandal of His Majeſties Government: Whereof His Majeſty taking notice, and in particular of that very falſe Report of an intention to diſſolve this preſent Parliament, which hath not been under deliberation, His Majeſty ſeeing no cauſe to change His reſolutions taken touching their meeting: His Majeſty therefore looks upon the Spreaders of that Report as perſons Seditiouſly inclined and ill affected to His Service; And conſidering that by the Laws of this Realm great and heavy penalties are to be inflicted upon all ſuch as ſhall be found to be Spreaders of falſe News, or promoters of any Malicious Calumnies againſt the State by their ordinary and common Diſcourſes to ſtir up diſlike in the People of His Majeſties Perſon and the eſtabliſhed Government, whereof His Majeſty is ſenſible the perſons offending are not ignorant. Nevertheleſs, that all men may be left without excuſe who ſhall not hereafter contain themſelves within that modeſt and dutiful regard which they ought, His Majeſty hath thought fit, by the advice of His Council, to publiſh this His Royal Proclamation, And doth hereby forewarn and ſtraightly Command all His Loving Subjects of what ſtate or condition ſoever they be, from the Higheſt to the Loweſt, that they preſume not henceforth by any Writing or Speaking to utter or publiſh any falſe News or Reports, or to intermeddle with the Affairs of State and Government, or with the perſons of any of His Majeſties Counſellors or Miniſters, in their common and ordinary Diſcourſes, as they will anſwer the contrary at their utmoſt perils. And whereas all bold and irreverent ſpeeches touching matters of this high nature are puniſhable not onely in the Speakers but the Hearers alſo, unleſs they do ſpeedily Reveal the ſame unto ſome of His Majeſties Privy Council, or ſome other His Majeſties Judges or Juſtices of the Peace; His Majeſty doth hereby further Declare, that he will proceed with all ſeverity not onely againſt ſuch perſons as ſhall uſe any bold and unlawful ſpeeches of this nature, but alſo againſt thoſe perſons who ſhall be preſent where ſuch ſpeeches are uſed, without Revealing the ſame in due time, His Majeſty being reſolved to Suppreſs this Unlawfull and Undutifull kind of Diſcourſe, by a moſt ſtrict and exemplary Puniſhment of all ſuch Offenders as ſhall hereafter be Diſcovered.

Given at Our Court at *Whitehall*, the Second day of *May*, 1674. in the Six and twentieth year of Our Reign.

God ſave the King.

LONDON,
Printed by the Aſſigns of *John Bill* and *Chriſtopher Barker*, Printers to the Kings moſt Excellent Majeſty. 1674.

46 England and Wales. Sovereigns (1660–1685: Charles II)
A Proclamation to Restrain the Spreading of False News, and Licentious talking in Matters of State and Government
London: Printed by the Assigns of John Bill and Christopher Barker 1674
239- 609b

By the King.

A PROCLAMATION

For Suppreſſing the Printing and Publiſhing Unlicenſed News-Books, and Pamphlets of News.

CHARLES R.

Whereas it is of great Importance to the State, That all News Printed and Publiſhed to the People, as well concerning Foreign, as Domeſtick Affairs, ſhould be agreeable to Truth, or at leaſt Warranted by good Intelligence, that the minds of His Majeſties Subjects may not be diſturbed, or amuſed by Lies or vain Reports, which are many times raiſed on purpoſe to Scandalize the Government, or for other indirect Ends; And whereas of late many Evil-diſpoſed Perſons have made it a common Practice to Print and Publiſh Pamphlets of News, without Licenſe or Authority, and therein have vended to His Majeſties People, all the idle and malicious Reports that they could Collect or Invent, contrary to Law; The continuance whereof would in a ſhort time endanger the Peace of the Kingdom, the ſame manifeſtly tending thereto, as has been declared by all His Majeſties Judges unanimouſly: His Majeſty therefore conſidering the great Miſchief that may enſue upon ſuch Licencious and Illegal Practices, if not timely prevented, hath thought fit by this His Royal Proclamation (with the Advice of His Privy Council) ſtrictly to Prohibit and Forbid all Perſons whatſoever to Print or Publiſh any News-Books, or Pamphlets of News not Licenſed by His Majeſties Authority. And to the intent all Offenders may know their Danger, and deſiſt from any further Proceedings of this kind, His Majeſty is Graciouſly pleaſed hereby to Declare, That they ſhall be proceeded againſt according to the utmoſt Severity of the Law: And for that purpoſe, His Majeſty doth hereby Will and Command all His Judges, Juſtices of Peace, and all other His Officers and Miniſters of Juſtice whatſoever, That they take effectual Care, that all ſuch as ſhall Offend in the Premiſſes, be proceeded againſt, and puniſhed according to their Demerits.

Given at Our Court at *Whitehall* this 12th day of *May*, in the Two and thirtieth year of Our Reign.

God ſave the King.

London, Printed by *John Bill*, *Thomas Newcomb*, and *Henry Hills*, Printers to the Kings moſt Excellent Majeſty. 1680.

47 England and Wales. Sovereigns (1660–1685: Charles II)
A Proclamation for Suppressing the Printing and Publishing of Unlicensed News-books and Pamphlets of News
London: Printed by John Bill, Thomas Newcomb and Henry Hills, 1680
238- 661b

IT DID NOT TAKE LONG for the news industry to come under attack, and criticism became even more scathing after the explosion of partisan newspapers in the 1640s. Many saw newspapers as vehicles for biased propaganda and outright lies. In *The Staple of News*, Ben Jonson had ridiculed the foolishness of people wasting their money on salacious and inaccurate news. By 1660, newspapers were under sustained criticism and all pretense of objectivity was lost in a wave of bitter invective.

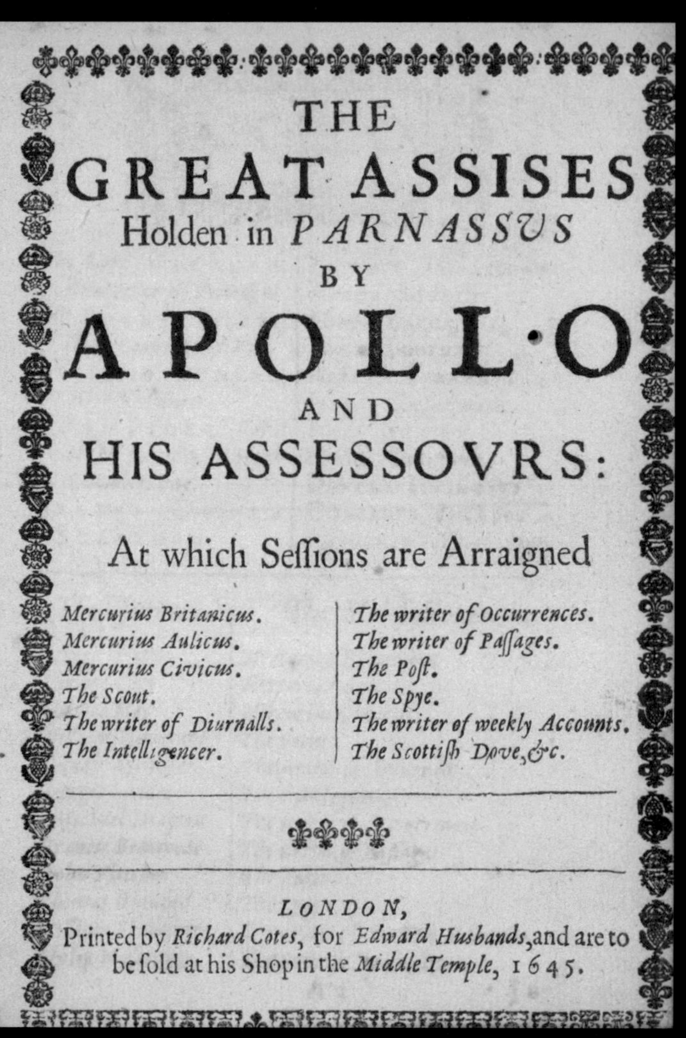

THE
GREAT ASSISES
Holden in *PARNASSVS*
BY
APOLLO
AND
HIS ASSESSOVRS:

At which Sessions are Arraigned

Mercurius Britanicus.	*The writer of Occurrences.*
Mercurius Aulicus.	*The writer of Passages.*
Mercurius Civicus.	*The Post.*
The Scout.	*The Spye.*
The writer of Diurnalls.	*The writer of weekly Accounts.*
The Intelligencer.	*The Scottish Dove,&c.*

LONDON,
Printed by *Richard Cotes*, for *Edward Husbands*, and are to be sold at his Shop in the *Middle Temple*, 1645.

48 George Wither (1588–1667)
The Great Assises holden in Parnassus by Apollo
London: Printed by Richard Cotes, for Edward Husbands, and are to be sold at his shop in the Middle Temple, 1645
W3160, title page

"NO NEWS, BUT ROMANCE" is how the author of this critique of London newsbooks referred to the information found in the *London Post.* In this prose satire, newsbooks are put on trial and a verdict on each one is given as they are brought to the dock to answer the charges. Neither royalist nor parliamentarian pamphlets escaped censure in this scathing attack on the exaggerations and falsehoods propagated in the news.

A
ROPE
FOR
POL.
OR,
A HUE and CRY after
MARCHEMONT NEDHAM.
The late Scurrulous News-writer.

Being a Collection of his horrid Blasphemies and Revilings against the King's Majesty, his Person, his Cause, and his Friends; published in his weekly *Politicus.*

2 Sam. 19. 21.
Shall not Shimei *be put to death for this, because he cursed the Lords annointed.*

1 Kings 2. 44, 45.
The King said moreover to Shimei, *Thou knowest all the wickednesse thy heart is privy to, that thou didst to* David *my Father, therefore the Lord shall return thy wickednesse upon thine own head.*
And King Solomon *shall be blessed, and the throne of* David *shall be established before the Lord for ever.*

LONDON, Printed in the Year, 1660.

49 Marchamont Nedham (1620–1678)
A Rope for Pol
London, 1660
184- 052q, title page

MARCHAMONT NEDHAM HAD BEEN ONE OF THE CHIEF PROPAGANDISTS for the Republican regime in the 1650s. A friend of John Milton, Nedham edited one of the most influential and widely read newspapers, *Mercurius Politcus.* By 1660, following the restoration of the monarchy, he was under attack for his republican views. This pamphlet, compiled by Roger L'Estrange, who later became the government press regulator, compares Nedham to the devil and calls for him to be "marked" so all could see his faults.

(3)

PIGGES
CORANTOE.

He generall newes is, no body knowes what to make of this World, and that all think there is a better, but its ten to one they doe not hit on't, that future ages are more ſubject to alteration then the preſent, that the Rumors of warres makes all beleeve Doomeſday is at hand, and hath cauſed more tales in every mans mouth then truth.

Forraigne Newes.

That thoſe *Politicians* that ſteere the courſe of all the States beyond the Seas imitates ***Hocus Pocus*** his Majeſties Jugler, that can play faſt, and looſe when he liſt, for they know the Engliſh affairs at that diſtance, better then honeſt pigge a great deale nearer.

From France 1. *March*, Stilo Novo.

That the Chriſtian King is in a ſtrange Quandary, and reſolves with Fortie thouſand men (remembring that Jerſey and Garnſey were once his) to dance French broiles after the Defender of the Faiths Muſick, So makes good, old Tarltons ſong.

The King of France with forty thouſand men,
Went up a Hill, and ſo came downe agen.

A 2 From

50 *Pigges Coranto or Newes from the North*
London: Printed for L. C. and M. W, 1642
236- 540q, A2

IN 1642, AS CIVIL WAR ERUPTED IN ENGLAND, newsbooks proliferated, and satires on news and newspapers started to appear in larger numbers. "The general news is, nobody knows what to make of the World," the author of *Pigge's Coranto* laments. Included on the first page is the news about the king of France in the form of a nursery rhyme. This rhyme was later made famous during the American Revolutionary War, recast as "The Grand Old Duke of York, he had ten thousand men."

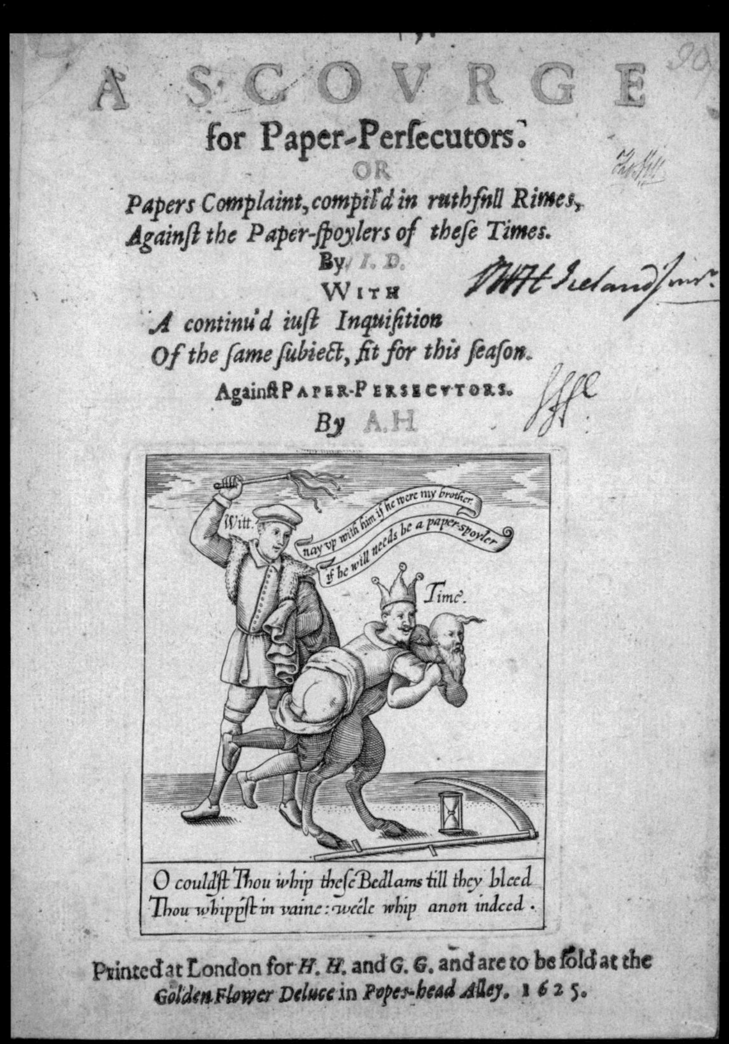

A SCOVRGE
for Paper-Perſecutors.
OR
Papers Complaint, compil'd in ruthfull Rimes,
Againſt the Paper-ſpoylers of theſe Times.
By I. D.
WITH
A continu'd iuſt Inquiſition
Of the ſame ſubiect, fit for this ſeaſon.
Againſt Paper-Persecvtors.
By A.H

O couldſt Thou whip theſe Bedlams till they bleed
Thou whippſt in vaine: weele whip anon indeed.

Printed at London for H. H. and G. G. and are to be ſold at the Golden Flower Deluce in Popes-head Alley. 1625.

51 John Davies (1565?–1618)
A Scourge for Paper-Persecutors
London: For H. H[olland] and G. G[ibbs] and are to be sold at the Golden Flower Deluce in Popes-head Alley, 1625
STC 6340 Copy 1, title page

THIS SATIRE COMPLAINS ABOUT THE ABUNDANCE OF WRITERS now publishing their works and "murdering paper," as the author, John Davies, eloquently put it. In the illustration, the author is referred to as "wit" and is seen whipping and shaming those who dared to publish their unworthy pamphlets. Newsletter writers were particularly scorned: "behold the walls buttered with weekly news composed in Pauls." The precinct of St. Paul's Cathedral was the home of the London book trade and the author derides the practice of smearing the church with advertisements for the latest news. The joke also satirizes Nathaniel Butter, the publisher of the corantos (Cat. No. 20).

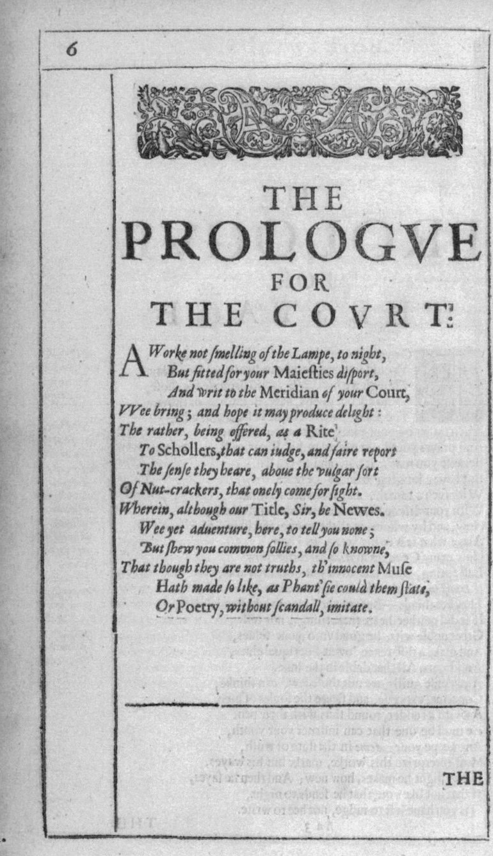

6

THE PROLOGVE FOR THE COVRT.

A Worke not smelling of the Lampe, to night,
But fitted for your Maiesties *disport,*
And writ to the Meridian *of your* Court,
VVee bring; and hope it may produce delight:
The rather, being offered, as a Rite
To Schollers,*that can iudge, and faire report*
The sense they heare, aboue the vulgar sort
Of Nut-crackers, that onely come for sight.
Wherein, although our Title, *Sir, be* Newes.
Wee yet aduenture, here, to tell you none;
But shew you common follies, and so knowne,
That though they are not truths, th'innocent Muse
Hath made so like, as Phant'sie could them state,
Or Poetry, *without scandall, imitate.*

THE

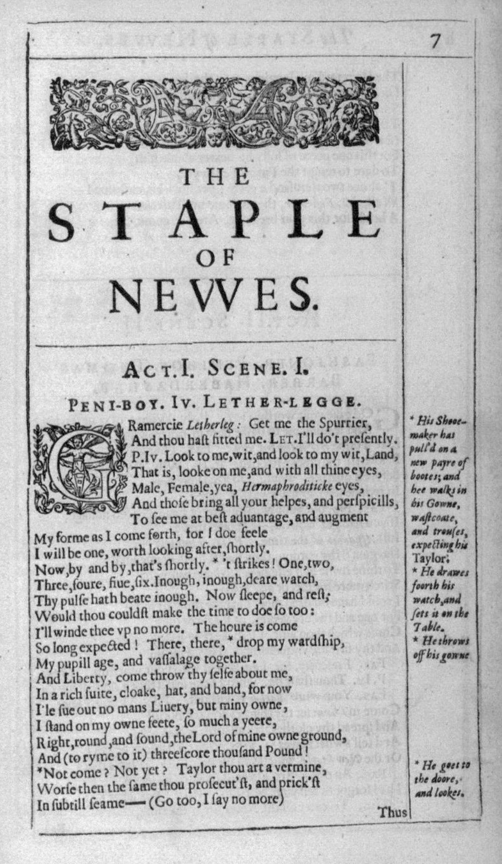

7

THE STAPLE OF NEWES.

ACT.I. SCENE.I.

PENI-BOY. IV. LETHER-LEGGE.

GRamercie *Letherleg:* Get me the Spurrier,
And thou hast fitted me. LET.I'll do't presently.
P.IV. Look to me,wit,and look to my wit, Land,
That is, looke on me,and with all thine eyes,
Male, Female,yea, *Hermaphroditicke* eyes,
And those bring all your helpes, and perspicills,
To see me at best aduantage, and augment
My forme as I come forth, for I doe feele
I will be one, worth looking after,shortly.
Now,by and by,that's shortly. * 't strikes! One,two,
Three,foure, fiue,six.Inough, inough,deare watch,
Thy pulse hath beate inough. Now sleepe, and rest;
Would thou couldst make the time to doe so too:
I'll winde thee vp no more. The houre is come
So long expected! There, there, * drop my wardship,
My pupill age, and vassalage together.
And Liberty, come throw thy selfe about me,
In a rich suite, cloake, hat, and band, for now
I'le sue out no mans Liuery, but miny owne,
I stand on my owne feete, so much a yeere,
Right,round,and sound,the Lord of mine owne ground,
And (to ryme to it) threescore thousand Pound!
*Not come? Not yet? Taylor thou art a vermine,
Worse then the same thou prosecut'st, and prick'st
In subtill seame—(Go too, I say no more)

Thus

** His Shooe-maker has pull'd on a new payre of bootes; and hee walks in his Gowne, wastcoate, and trouses, expecting his* Taylor.
** He drawes foorth his watch,and sets it on the Table.*
** He throws off his gowne*
** He goes to the doore, and lookes.*

52 Ben Jonson (1573? –1637)
The Workes of Benjamin Jonson
London: Printed [by John Beale, John Dawson 2, Bernard Alsop and Thomas Fawcet] for Richard Meighen [Thomas Walkley and Robert Allot], 1640 [i.e. 1641]
STC 14754 Copy 4, p. 6–7

BEN JONSON'S PLAY, *THE STAPLE OF NEWS,* written a few years after the introduction of corantos to England, pokes fun at the news industry and particularly those who wasted their money buying news sheets. The publisher, Nathaniel Butter, is lampooned as Cymbal, the manager of the *News Staple,* a parody of the early corantos. The Gossips who sit on stage make a number of jokes at Butter's expense, while the industry as a whole is pilloried as a purveyor of untruths and tittle-tattle.

Viator Who art thou Ladie that aloft art ſet
In state Maiestique this faire ſpredding tree
Vpon thine head a Towre-like Coronet,
The Worldes whole Compaſse resting on thy knee.
Opinio I am OPINION who the world do swaie
Wherefore, I beare it, on my head that Towre
Is BABELS; meaning my confuſed waie
The Tree so shaken, my unſetled Bowre.
Viator What meaneth that Chameleon on thy fist
That can aſsume all Cullors saving white.
Opinio OPINION thus can everie waie shee liſt.
Transforme her self save into TRVTH, the right
Viator And Ladie what's the Fruite, which from thy Tree
Is shaken of with everie little wind
Like Bookes and papers this amuſeth mee
Beside thou ſeemest (veiled) to bee blind
Opinio Tis true I cannot as cleare IVDGMENTS see
Through self CONCEIT and haughtie PRIDE of Mind
The fruite thoſe idle bookes and libells bee
In everie streete, on everie stall you find

Viator. Cannot OPINION remedie the ſame
Opinio Ah no then should I periſh in the throng
Oth giddie Vulgar, without feare or ſhame
Who cenſure all thinges, bee they right or wrong
Viator But Ladie deare whence came at first this fruite
Or why doth WISEDOME ſuffer it to grow
And whats the reaſon its farre reaching roote
Is waterd by a sillie Foole below
Opinio Becauſe that FOLLIE giveth life to theſe
I but retaile the fruites of idle Aire
Sith now all Humors utter what they pleaſe
Toth loathing loading of each Mart and Faire.
Viator And why thoſe saplings from the roote that riſe
In such abundance of OPINIONS tree
Opinio Cauſe one Opinion many doth deviſe
And propagate, till infinite they bee
Viator. Adieu sweete Ladie till againe wee meete
Opinio But when shall that againe bee, *Viator* Ladie ſaie
Opinio Opinions found in everie houſe and streete
And going ever, never in her waie

VIRO CLA.^MO DR FRANCISCO PRVIEANO D: MEDICO, OMNIVM BONARVM AR: tium et Elegantiarum Fautori et Admiratori summo. D. D. D. *Henricus Peachamus*.

are to be Sould by Tho: Bankes, at the top of Bridewell staires

53 Henry Peacham (1576?–1643?)
The world is ruled & governed by opinion
London, 1641
P949.5

THE BLINDED FIGURE OF OPINION in the tree is no longer able to recognize truth. A man looks on in wonder at the proliferation of such pamphlets. England in 1641 was on the brink of civil war and the bookstores were overflowing with "opinions found in every house." Peacham's poem which accompanies the illustration laments this sad state of affairs: "The fruit of those idle books and libels be, In every street, in every stall you find."

(1)

THE CHARACTER OF A LONDON DIURNALL.

A *Diurnall* is a puny Chronicle, ſcarce pinfeath'd with the wings of time: It is an Hiſtory in *Sippets*; the Engliſh *Iliads* in a Nut-ſhell; the *Apocryphall* Parliaments booke of *Maccabees* in ſingle ſheets. It would tyre a Welsh-pedegree, to reckon how many aps 'tis remov'd from an Annall: for it is of that Extract; only of the yonger Houſe, like a ſhrimp to a Lobſter. The *originall ſinner* in this kind was Dutch, *Galliobelgicus* the *Protoplaſt*; and the *moderne Mercuries* but *Hans-enKelders*. The Counteſſe of *Zealand* was brought to Bed of an Almanack; as many Children, as dayes in the yeare. It may be the *Legiſlative Lady* is of that Lynage; ſo ſhee ſpawnes the *Diurnalls*, and they at *Weſtminſter* take them in Adoption, by the names of *Scoticus*, *Civicus*, *Britanicus*. In the Frontiſpice of the old *Beldame-Diurnall*, like the Contents of the Chapter, ſits the Houſe of Commons, judging the twelve Tribes of *Iſrael*. You may call them, the Kingdomes Anotomy before the weekely Kalender: for ſuch is a *Diurnall*, the day of the moneth, with what weather in the Common-wealth. 'Tis taken for the Pulſe of the Body-Politique; and the Emperick-Divines of the Aſſembly, thoſe ſpirituall *Dragooners*, thumbe it accordingly. Indeed it is a pretty *Synopſis*; and thoſe grave *Rabbyes* (though in point of Divinity) trade in no larger Authors. The Country-Carryer, when hee

54 John Cleveland (1613–1658)
The Character of a London Diurnall
[London], 1644
C4661, p. 1

JOHN CLEVELAND, A POET AND PROMINENT ROYALIST, virulently attacked London newspapers in this satire. Not without some justification, he accused them of gross exaggeration and outright lies. News traveled quickly and Cleveland's pamphlet was directly answered by three pamphlets and ridiculed in many London newspapers. Cleveland's satire was a huge success; a least four editions were published in 1645 and the 1647 edition contained his satirical poems as well.

55 Replica Renaissance press, ©Enche Tjin, Bucknell University.

DURING THE SUMMER OF 2008, George Waltman (Director of Bucknell University's Project Development Laboratory) built a working replica of a Gutenberg-style printing press for the Folger Shakespeare Library. The replica, a small-scale version of the type of press used throughout the Renaissance for most printed materials, including newspapers, is based upon a design by three mechanical engineering students at Bucknell, Shannon Cooney, Patrick Kunze, and Aaron Tajima, who developed it for their senior design project in 2000-01. The faculty advisor was Professor Thomas Rich. The Folger acquired the Waltman replica for the exhibition, *Breaking News: Renaissance Journalism and the Birth of the Newspaper*, and for future educational activities.

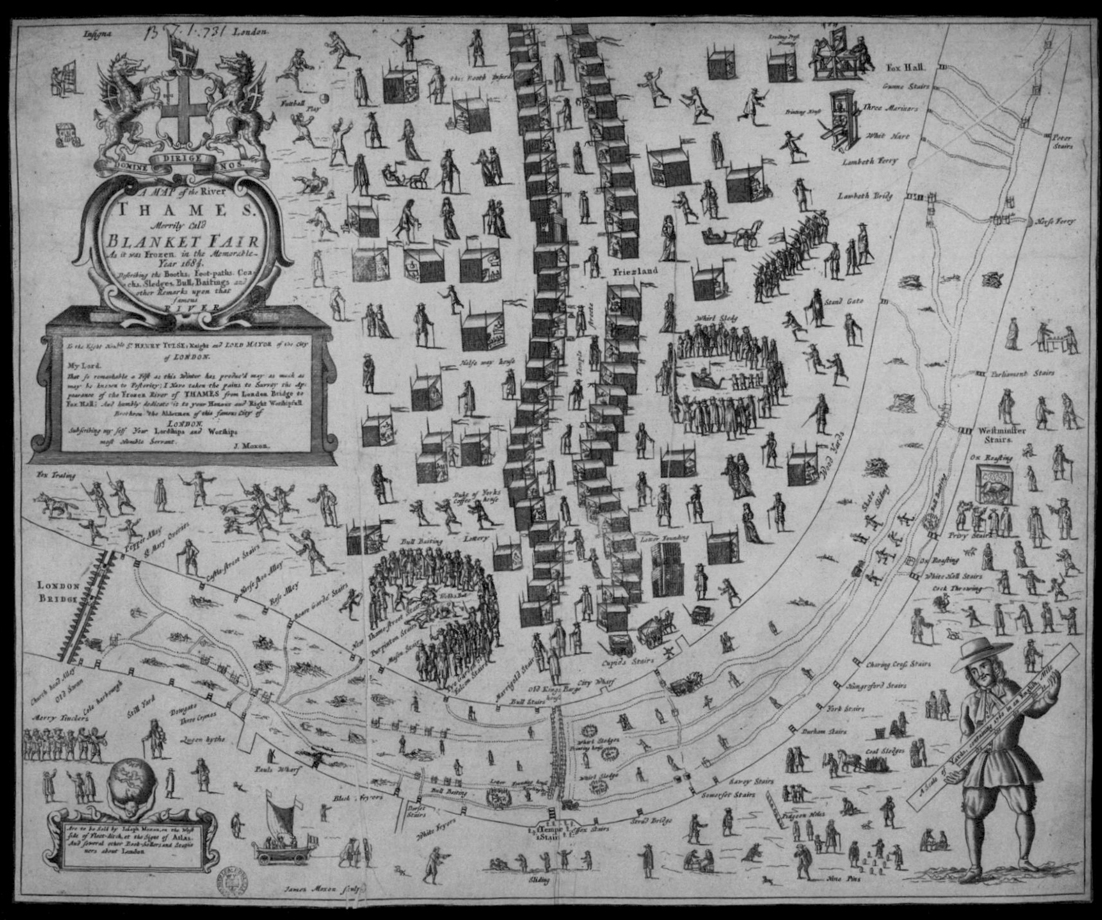

56A Joseph Moxon (1627–1691)
A Map of the River Thames
[London]: To be sold by Joseph Moxon, on the west side of Fleet-ditch, at the signe of the Atlas. And several other book-sellers and stationers about London., [1684?]
Gough Maps 21
Courtesy of the Bodleian Library

DURING THE EXTREME WINTER OF 1686–1687, when the Thames River froze over, the ice became a microcosm of entertainment in London. Joseph Moxon, a printer who specialized in mathematics and maps, captured the activities of a frost fair on the frozen river. Fairgoers could buy lottery tickets, patronize a coffeehouse, take a ride on a "whirl sledge," attend a bull-baiting, and even watch a printing press in action (Cat. No.56B).

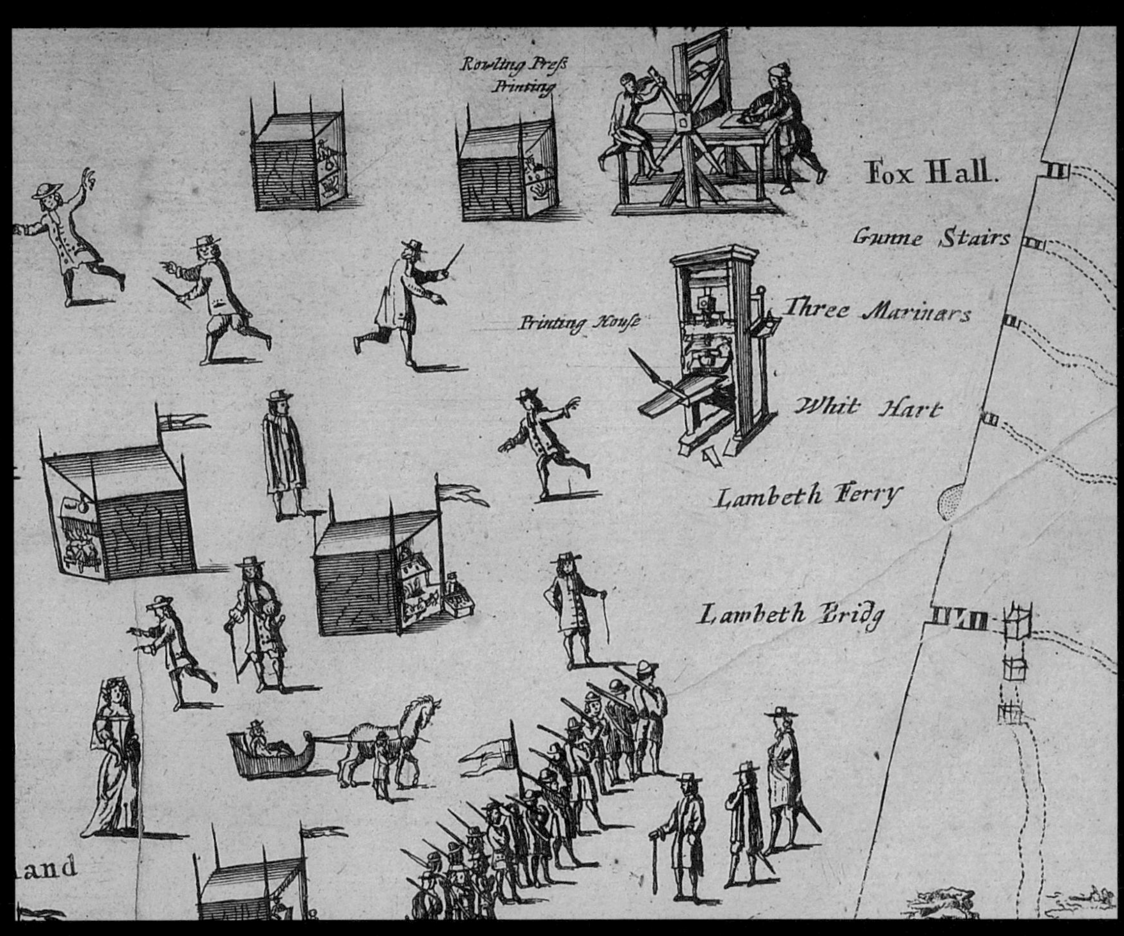

56B Joseph Moxon (1627–1691)
A Map of the River Thames
[London]: To be sold by Joseph Moxon, on the west side of Fleet-ditch, at the signe of the Atlas. And several other book-sellers and stationers about London., [1684?]
Gough Maps 21
Courtesy of the Bodleian Library

JOURNALISTS COME IN MANY SHAPES AND SIZES, and during the seventeenth century, the profession included an extremely colorful cast of characters. Some emerged from obscure backgrounds, and have left little trace beyond the newspapers they produced, while others drifted in and out of the field from other humble trades and professions, fired by both profit and political zeal. Those that are most readily identified tended not to be professional newspapermen, but were instead poets and clerics with proven literary talents.

Considerations and Proposals
In Order to the
Regulation
OF THE
PRESS:
TOGETHER WITH
Diverse *Instances* of *Treasonous*, and *Seditious Pamphlets*, Proving the *Necessity* thereof.

BY
ROGER L'ESTRANGE.

LONDON, Printed by *A.C. June* 3d. *M.DC.LXIII.*

57 Sir Roger L'Estrange (1616–1704)
Considerations and Proposals in Order to the Regulation of the Press
London: Printed by A.C., June 3d, 1663
234- 021q, title page

LIKE MANY OF THOSE WHO WERE ROYALISTS during the Civil Wars, L'Estrange had profound concerns regarding the collapse of censorship, arguing that pamphlets and newspapers had made "the multitude too familiar with the actions and counsels of their superiors, too pragmatic and censorious," and had given them "not only an itch but a colourable right and license to be meddling with the government." He served as "surveyor" of the press, and official licenser from 1662–79, and from 1685–8. In this tract, L'Estrange advocated severe punishments for seditious printing, including "death, mutilation, imprisonment, banishment, corporal pains, disgrace, pecuniary mulcts."

58A *The Observator*, 1 (April 13, 1681)
London: Printed for Henry Brome, 1681
O109.5(2d) vol. 1, title page

FOR ALL HIS HATRED OF THE PRESS, L'Estrange also clearly understood the potential benefits of journalism if strictly controlled and operated in the interests of the government. He was granted a newspaper monopoly in 1663 and wrote *The Intelligencer* until that publication was usurped by the *Gazette* in 1666. He later returned with *The Observator* (1681–1687). The latter, which appeared four times a week, became the preeminent Tory journal of its day, and its first issue contained L'Estrange's famous justification for government propaganda: "tis the press that has made 'em mad, and the press must set 'em right again."

58B *The Observator*, 1 (April 13, 1681)
London: Printed for Henry Brome, 1681
O109.5(2d) vol. 1, frontispiece

Portrait of Sir Roger L'Estrange.

(17) Numb. 3.

Mercurius Elencticus.

Communicating the unparallell'd Proceedings at Westminster, the Head Quarters, and other places; discovering their Designes, reproving their Crimes, and advising the Kingdome.

From *Friday* Novemb. 12. till *Friday* Novemb. 19. 1647.

Ridentem dicere verum quid vetat?

TIs *Martin-masse* indeed; a very seasonable time to kill Beeves, but a most unlucky moneth to destroy Kings in. *Faux* and his fellowes in the Powder Treason found it fatall; and *Fairfax* his Agitators very infortunate; particularly in their most Treasonable and damned designe of dissolving the English Monarchy in the Blood of our Gracious King *Charles* this present *November*, 1647. I shall forbeare to mention the manner of it, because it hath beene severall times Printed, and by this time dispersed to every Corner of the Kingdom. Let it suffice us, that it pleased God to deliver Him out of their Bloody hands; and that He is safely arrived in the Isle of *Wight*, where He hath cast Himselfe into the hands of Lieutenant Generall *Hammond* the Governour thereof, from whom He hath assurance of safety and Protection; *Hammond* (indeed) is a Man that hath usually trod in the Circle of a Civill life, and is observ'd not to have admitted of such dangerous Principles, nor beene so violent, either against the Cause or Person of the King, or others of his Fraternitie. And now if he be but any whit season'd with the sound Principles of his Learned and Loyall Kinsman (Dr. *Hammond*) he may render himselfe Honourable to the whole Kingdome; and make *Fairfax* asham'd of his Villany; who is now ready to hang himselfe to thinke how Childishly and basely he hath deported himselfe in the businesse. The Members at *Westminster* would be thought inno-

C cent

59 *Mercurius Elencticus*, 3 (November 12–19, 1647)
London, 1647
M1765.5 No. 3, p. 17

MERCURIUS ELENCTICUS WAS ONE OF THE LEADING ROYALIST NEWSPAPERS of the late 1640s, along with *Mercurius Pragmaticus* and *Mercurius Melancholicus*. Like them, it was extremely well-informed, capable of producing caustic prose and vitriolic pen-portraits of leading parliamentarians. Its author, George Wharton, was also fond of using poetry in order to attack politicians and journalists alike; he used the paper to pursue his personal rivalry with those astrologers who opposed the royalist cause such as William Lilly and John Booker.

Calendarium Ecclesiasticum:
OR,
A NEW ALMANACK
After the
OLD FASHION,
For the Commune yeare of Man's
Creation ——5606.
Redemption— 1657.
Being the First from the BISSEXTILE.

To which is added,
GESTA BRITANNORUM:
OR,
A briefe CHRONOLOGIE for 56. yeares last past, viz. from the yeare 1600. (in which the late K. Charls was born) until the present 1657.

By George Wharton.

Nos aliam ex aliis.

LONDON,
Printed by John Grismond. 1 6 5 7.

60 George Wharton (1617–1681)
Calendarium Ecclesiasticum
London: By J. Grismond, 1657
A2657.8, title page

ALTHOUGH HE WROTE NEWSPAPERS DURING THE 1640S, George Wharton's primary interest lay elsewhere, and he is better known as one of the preeminent astrologers of his age. Such men were trained in mathematics and astronomy and were often well-respected among the country's elite. Their almanacs, including the *Calendarium Ecclesiasticum*, were enormously popular. Like other astrologers, Wharton put his skills to political use during the Civil Wars, serving in the royalist army as well as working as a prognosticator and propagandist.

(78)

beene a Faſt held in ſome part of *London,* to pray againſt Accommodation, which held from ſeven a clocke in the morning untill nine at night, and that ſome Ladies of quality ſate out all the time.

From *Briſtoll* it was ſignified, that the Citizens are not pleaſed with Colonell *Eſſex*, the Governour of the Citie at this time for the two Houſes of Parliament, who having killed one of his men for demanding pay, and finding that the Citizens had ſent their Coroner to take a view of the dead body, and cauſe an Inqueſt to paſſe upon him, beat them away, and not onely would not ſuffer them to doe it, but cauſed a Proclamation to be forthwith made, which hath much diſpleaſed them. But there's another thing which doth more diſpleaſe them, then the rough carriage of their pretended Governour; which is, that thoſe parts of *Wales* which buy the moſt part of their commodities in that Citie, and owe great ſummes of money to the Merchants there, have publiſhed and declared, that none of them will be reſponſall for any debts which they owe in *Briſtol*, unleſſe the Citie doe returne to the Kings obedience: A matter which concernes them much in caſe of profit, which many times workes more in ſome ſorts of men, then a caſe of conſcience.

SATURDAY. *Feb.* 11.

There came advertiſement this day, that the Rebels in *Cheſhire* having put themſelves into the Towne of *Namptwich*, and were there beſieged by the Kings Forces, with very great likelihood of prevailing; in caſe the newes of the *Ceſſation*, which began very hotly to be talked of in the Court this day, as a thing agreed upon by both Houſes for 13 dayes, occaſioneth not (before the ſame be fully and abſolutely confirmed for truth) the ſlackning of the ſiege e're the Towne be taken.

FINIS.

In the laſt weekes Diurnall pag. 64. *for Royall Name, reade Royall Navy. And in the number of the ſlaine by Sir* Ralph Hopton, *for betwixt* 20 *and* 30, *reade betwixt* 200 *and* 300.

(79)

MERCVRIVS AVLICVS,

Communicating the Intelligence and affaires of the Court, to the reſt of the KINGDOME.

The ſeventh VVeeke.

SUNDAY. *Febr.* 12.

His day His Majeſtie cauſed a Letter to be written to the high Sheriffe and Juſtices of the Peace of the County of *Glouceſter*: In which His Majeſtie taking notice how deeply that County had ingaged it ſelfe in the Rebellion raiſed againſt Him, and that notwithſtanding His gracious offers of Pardon, they had ſo obſtinately ſtood out againſt His Authority, that He was forced to ſend a conſiderable part of His Army to reduce them to obedience; doth further for the reparation of Himſelfe, and the ſecurity and protection of his good ſubjects there, require the ſaid Sheriffe and Juſtices of the Peace to call together the people of that County at ſuch convenient times and ſeaſons as to them ſeemed beſt, and to demand (beſides the monethly contribution which was impoſed on all proportionably) their free and voluntary aſſiſtance for the ſupport of His Eſtate, and their owne preſervation: wherein His Majeſtie expected that ſuch as had beene moſt active in maintaining the former troubles, ſhould (for the

N better

61 *The Mercurius Aulicus, 7* (February 12–18, 1643) Oxford: Printed by Henry Hall, 1643 235- 953q, pp. 78–79

WHEN THE ROYALIST PARTY OF CHARLES I sought to establish a newspaper shortly after the outbreak of the Civil Wars, the secretary of state, Sir Edward Nicholas, summoned Peter Heylyn to Oxford, "to take directions for some special and important service... to write the Weekly Occurrences." Heylyn may only have accepted this employment reluctantly, and was probably more than happy to give up the position only months later. That he was succeeded by Sir John Berkenhead, whose prose style better suited the requirements of journalism, indicates how rapidly newspapers developed during this period.

NEWSPAPERS FROM THE SEVENTEENTH CENTURY may look very different from those of today, but there are more similarities than might be imagined. Journalists owe much to the innovations in formatting made by their predecessors. A number of modern press features can be traced back to early experiments in journalism: standard features of our own newspapers, such as layout, content, arrangement, and regularity were first introduced over three hundred years ago.

THE Numb.7.

LONDON POST:

Faithfully Communicating His

Intelligence of the Proceedings of Parliament, and many other Memorable Paſſages certified by Letters and Advertiſements,

From Lime. Barnſtable. Coome. Bathe. Monmouth. Beachley. VVye. Namtwich. Briſtoll. Oxford. Bazing. Banbury. Leverpoole. Pomfret. Carlile. Newcaſtle.

The taking of Monmouth *Caſtle, by the Victorious and Vigilant Colonell* Maſſey, *with all their Armes, Ordnance and Ammunition. His fine Exploit and Stratagem of War, in ſurpriſing and defeating Captain* Kirle, *with all his Troop. Colonell* Chiſnall, *the Governour of* Latham-houſe, *ſubmitting to the Parliament. The Earl of* Kalander *returned from* Scotland *unto the ſiege of* Newcaſtle; *And the great hope of the ſpeedy Reducing of that place. Colonell* Butler *committed to the Tower. His Majeſties Advance; and the preſent Affaires of the* Weſt *certified in Letters from his* Excellence, *and from Sir* William VValler. *Sir* VVilliam VValler, *his Noble reſolution*: Cumberland *and* VVeſtmerland *quit of the Enemy, the Garriſon only of* Carlile *excepted.*

Publiſhed by Authority: And Printed for G.B. October, 1. 1644.

I T hath alwayes been the Care and Buſineſſe of this Pen to poſſeſſe the Readers with Truth, and to deliver no Intelligence unto them, but what hath been confirmed by great and grave Authority. And I doe here religiouſly proteſt, that it hath been a greater taske unto me, to pick out Newes to pleaſe the people, and to deſcend to their capacity, then to compile a Story to be preferred to the judgement, and Protection of the greateſt States-men in the World.

The Curtaine being drawn, and the moſt labour'd Scene of the War (if you regard either the Acts or Actors) being diſcovered to be in the *Weſt*, Wee will begin our Intelligence this week with the Narration of the ſad Occurrences in that place. You need

G not

62 *The London Post*, 7 (October 1, 1644) [London]: Printed by G[eorge] B[ishop], 1644 248- 435q, title page

ONE OF THE EARLIEST TITLES TO BEAR THE NAME "POST," this newspaper was produced by a leading publisher of civil war journalism, George Bishop. It was written by Parliament's recently-appointed licenser of newspapers, John Rushworth, who would soon become secretary to the army, with the assistance of his deputy, Gilbert Mabbott. This journal was innovative not merely because of its title, but also because it provided headlines on its front page.

63 *Mercurius Rusticus: or, the Countrys Complaint*
[Oxford], 1646
R2448, title page

NEWS EVENTS WERE REGULARLY RECYCLED during the Civil Wars and nowhere more dramatically than in this volume. Compiled of stories from a royalist newspaper, *Mercurius Rusticus* (the name of which came from a Roman historian cited by Tacitus), it was written by the royal chaplain, Dr. Bruno Ryves. Ryves specialized in recounting the brutality of parliamentarian soldiers towards royalists. Here the title page contains an illustrated index that refers to particular news stories inside, including the first pitched battle of the Civil War, Edgehill in 1642.

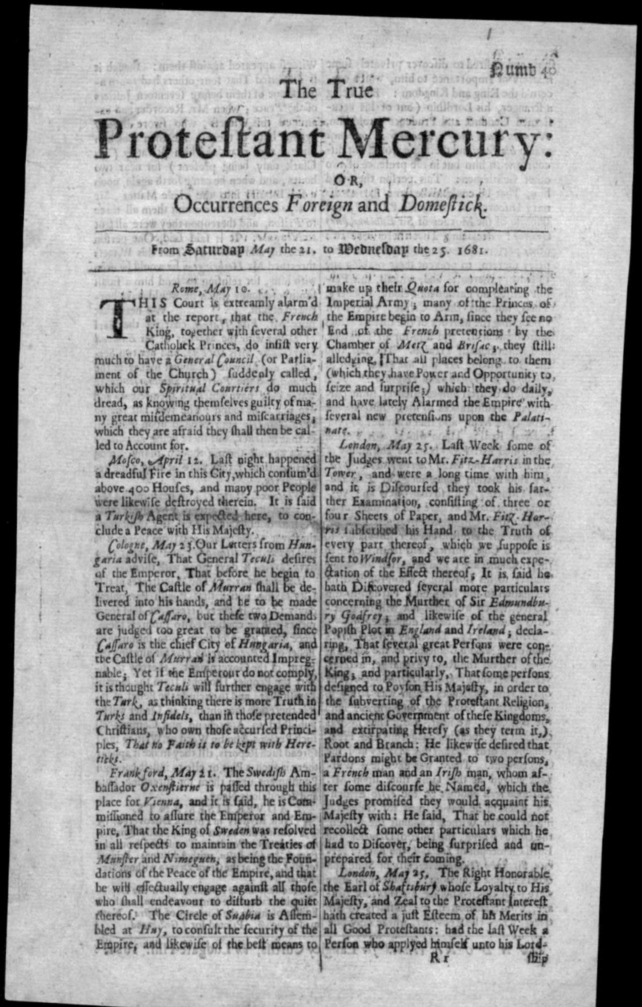

64 *The True Protestant Mercury*, 40 (May 21–25, 1681)
London: Printed for H.T. & L.V. and sold by Langley Curtis ..., 1680–1682
243- 549, title page

NEWSPAPER FORMATS CHANGED DRAMATICALLY after 1660, shifting away from the smaller quarto size towards the larger folio and including columns. They also appeared more frequently, particularly during the attempt to prevent Charles II's Catholic brother, the future James II, from inheriting the throne. This paper was published twice a week by the Whig publisher, Langley Curtis and his wife Jane, and was written by Henry Care, until being closed by the government in 1682. A sometime pornographer, who was repeatedly charged with seditious libel, Care subsequently abandoned his hostility to James II. He defended the Catholic king in print, motivated by a genuine passion for religious toleration.

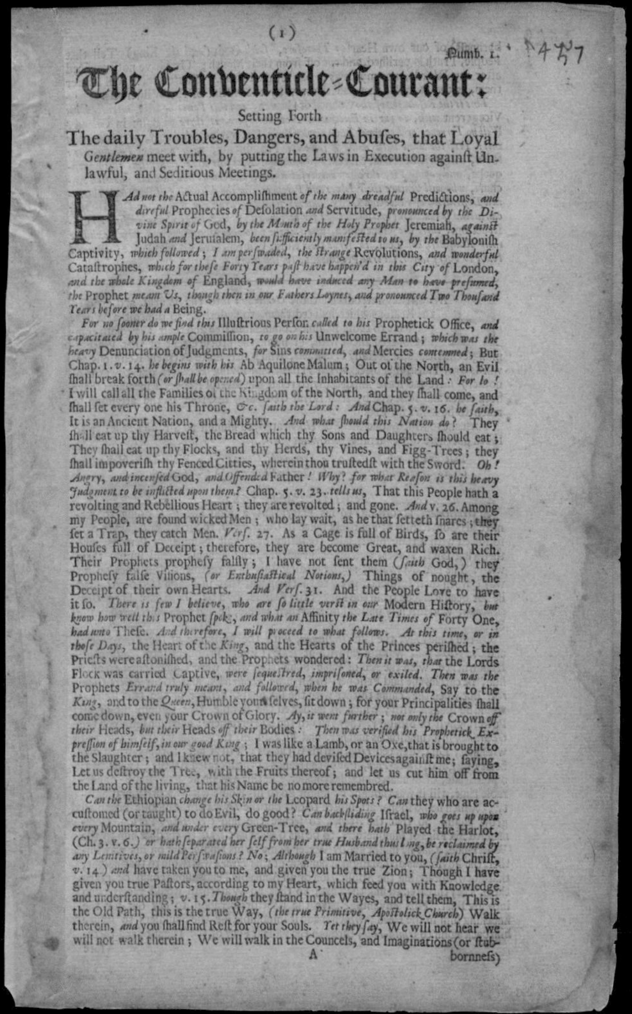

(1)

Numb. 1.

The Conventicle-Courant:

Setting Forth

The daily Troubles, Dangers, and Abuſes, that Loyal *Gentlemen* meet with, by putting the Laws in Execution againſt Unlawful, and Seditious Meetings.

HAd not the Actual Accompliſhment *of the many dreadful* Predictions, *and direful* Prophecies *of* Deſolation *and* Servitude, *pronounced by the Divine Spirit of* God, *by the Mouth of the Holy Prophet* Jeremiah, *againſt* Judah *and* Jeruſalem, *been ſufficiently manifeſted to us, by the* Babyloniſh Captivity, *which followed; I am perſwaded, the ſtrange* Revolutions, *and wonderful* Cataſtrophes, *which for theſe Forty Years paſt have happen'd in this City of* London, *and the whole Kingdom of* England, *would have induced any Man to have preſumed, the* Prophet *mean Us, though then in our Fathers Loynes, and pronounced Two Thouſand Years before we had a* Being.

For no ſooner do we find this Illuſtrious Perſon *called to his* Prophetick Office, *and capacitated by his ample* Commiſſion, *to go on his* Unwelcome Errand; *which was the heavy* Denunciation of Judgments, *for* Sins *committed, and* Mercies *contemned*; But Chap. 1. *v.* 14. *he begins with his* Ab Aquilone Malum; Out of the North, an Evil ſhall break forth *(or ſhall be opened)* upon all the Inhabitants of the Land: *For lo!* I will call all the Families of the Kingdom of the North, and they ſhall come, and ſhall ſet every one his Throne, *&c. ſaith the Lord: And* Chap. 5. *v.* 16. *he ſaith*, It is an Ancient Nation, and a Mighty. *And what ſhould this Nation do?* They ſhall eat up thy Harveſt, the Bread which thy Sons and Daughters ſhould eat; They ſhall eat up thy Flocks, and thy Herds, thy Vines, and Figg-Trees; they ſhall impoveriſh thy Fenced Citties, wherein thou truſtedſt with the Sword. *Oh! Angry, and incenſed* God, *and Offended* Father! *Why? for what Reaſon is this heavy Judgment to be inflicted upon them?* Chap. 5. *v.* 23. *tells us*, That this People hath a revolting and Rebellious Heart; they are revolted; and gone. *And* v. 26. Among my People, are found wicked Men; who lay wait, as he that ſetteth ſnares; they ſet a Trap, they catch Men. *Verſ.* 27. As a Cage is full of Birds, ſo are their Houſes full of Deceipt; therefore, they are become Great, and waxen Rich. Their Prophets propheſy falſly; I have not ſent them (*ſaith* God,) they Propheſy falſe Viſions, *(or Enthuſiaſtical Notions,)* Things of nought, the Deceipt of their own Hearts. *And Verſ.* 31. And the People Love to have it ſo. *There is few I believe, who are ſo little verſt in our* Modern Hiſtory, *but know how well this* Prophet *ſpoke, and what an* Affinity *the Late Times of* Forty One, *had unto* Theſe. *And therefore, I will proceed to what follows. At this time, or in thoſe Days*, the Heart of the *King*, and the Hearts of the Princes periſhed; the Prieſts were aſtoniſhed, and the Prophets wondered: *Then it was, that* the Lords Flock was carried Captive, *were ſequeſtred, impriſoned, or exiled. Then was the* Prophets *Errand truly meant, and followed, when he was Commanded*, Say to the *King*, and to the *Queen*, Humble your ſelves, ſit down; for your Principalities ſhall come down, even your Crown of Glory. *Ay, it went further; not only the* Crown *off their* Heads, *but their* Heads *off their* Bodies: *Then was verified his Prophetick Expreſſion of himſelf, in our good King*; I was like a Lamb, or an Oxe, that is brought to the Slaughter; and I knew not, that they had deviſed Devices againſt me; ſaying, Let us deſtroy the Tree, with the Fruits thereof; and let us cut him off from the Land of the living, that his Name be no more remembred.

Can the Ethiopian *change his Skin or the* Leopard *his Spots? Can* they who are accuſtomed (or taught) to do Evil, do good? *Can backſliding* Iſrael, *who goes up upon every* Mountain, *and under every* Green-Tree, *and there hath* Played the Harlot, (Ch. 3. v. 6.) *or hath ſeparated her ſelf from her true Husband thus long, be reclaimed by any Lenitives, or mild Perſwaſions? No; Although* I am Married to you, (*ſaith* Chriſt, *v.* 14.) *and* have taken you to me, and given you the true Zion; Though I have given you true Paſtors, according to my Heart, which feed you with Knowledge and underſtanding; *v.* 15. *Though* they ſtand in the Wayes, and tell them, This is the Old Path, this is the true Way, *(the true Primitive, Apoſtolick Church)* Walk therein, *and* you ſhall find Reſt for your Souls. *Yet they ſay*, We will not hear we will not walk therein; We will walk in the Councels, and Imaginations (or ſtubbornneſs)

A

65 *The Conventicle-Courant*, 1 (July 14, 1682)
London: Printed by the assigns of John Hilton, 1682
C5978h no. 1

THIS SHORT-LIVED PAPER WAS WRITTEN in order to recount the deeds of the notorious "Hilton gang." The group sought out and prosecuted religious dissenters in a reign of terror that lasted for four years. The word "courant" in the title, which was later adopted by James Franklin in Boston in 1721, was another innovation introduced during the Restoration. The title survives to this day in the oldest surviving American newspaper, *The Hartford Courant*, founded in 1764. Moreover the latter, like *The Washington Post*, demonstrates another similarity to *The Conventicle-Courant*: the use of otherwise outdated gothic typeface for the title.

DAWKS's News-Letter.

Sr London August 3. 699.

Last night we received an Holland Mail, with some of these particulars following.

Lemberg, July 31. The Bassa Capigi, Treasurer General to the Grand Seignior, arrived at Caminieck on the 6th. instant, and gave Orders to the Governour to prepare to March out with his Garrison, and evacuate that Fortress to the Poles; whereupon the Turks have already begun to pack up their Baggage. The Hospodar of Walachia is also arrived upon the Frontiers, and is laying a Bridge over the Dniester, for the more convenient carrying of the Baggage. The Field Marshal of the Crown has sent to acquaint the King herewith.

Warsaw, July 18. The Diet is now like to have a good Issue, the King having Declared that he will maintain the Liberties of the People; that his Saxon Troops were all on their March homewards; That he will keep no Regiments by his Person, but only a Guard of 1200 Men at his own Charge, all of them Poles and Lithuanians: That if the Saxons do not March out of the Kingdom within the time limited, or return again on any Pretence whatsoever, without consent of the Republick, it shall be lawful for the Nobility to Assemble on Horseback without his Order, and Treat them as Publick Enemies. And in return hereof the Diet have obliged themselves to secure his Majesties Person with their utmost Power; that they will Severely Punish all that Act or but Speak against him: That all Libels against him shall be Burnt by the Hand of the Hangman; and the Authors of them serv'd in the same manner, if they can be apprehended. His Majesty will hold a Diet in Saxony in September; and its said he will bring his Queen hither with him when he returns.

Hamburg, August 4. Dr. Meyer, the Minister having Printed his Latin Oration upon the Marriage of the King of the Romans, on Cloth of Silver and Gold, and edg'd every Leaf of it with Point of Venice, which altogether cost this City 500 Crowns, he sent the same to the Emperour and King of the Romans, who have thereupon made the Doctor a Palsgrave, and given him his Patent free.

Hague, August 8. They write from Nieuenheusen in the County of Benthem, that 300 Neuburgers came to put the Countrey under Military Execution, for not submitting to the Popish Count; but that a Body of Dutch Soldiers advancing, who were sent by the States to support the Protestant Count, put the Neuburgers to flight, having kill'd a Lieutenant and wounded three others. Letters from Hungary say, that General Nehm, who was impower'd to be present at adjusting the Frontiers, falling into some Difference with the Bassa of Temeswaer, Struck him Dead from his Horse; whereupon some other Turkish Officers taking up the Quarrel, there were 30 or 40 Men Killed on both sides; however the Commissioners went on with adjusting the Frontiers. Admiral Aylmer with his Squadron is Sail'd from Messina to Leghorn: The French Gallies shunn'd meeting him, because they knew he would oblige them to Strike. A Million of Crowns has been collected at Rome by way of Alms, for the Irish Papists as is given out. The refreshing Rains we have had of late, have in some manner dissipated the Fevers which raged in this Country, especially at Amsterdam; where People suffered very

66 Ichabod Dawks (1661–1731)
Dawks's Newsletter
(August 3, 1699)
London, 1699
Courtesy of the British Library

THE RISE OF PRINTED NEWS did not displace traditional formats entirely, and official hostility towards journalism after 1660 encouraged the revival of commercial manuscript newsletters, which often contained much more interesting news. *Dawks's Newsletter*, which ran from 1696 until 1716, was printed to look like a hand-written letter, and left space for additional comments by those customers who intended passing on their copies to friends outside London. Appearing three times a week by quarterly subscription, it could also claim to be the first evening newspaper.

(309)

Numb. 19.

Mercurius Politicus.

Comprising the Summe of all Intelligence, with the Affairs, and Designs now on foot, in the three Nations of *England*, *Ireland*, and *Scotland*.

In defence of the Common-wealth, and for Information of the People.

——*Ità vertere Seria Ludo.* {Hor. de Ar.Poet.

From *Thursday*, October 10. to *Thursday*, October 17. 1650.

EE have shewn how the *supreme Power*, resides in the *Peoples Representatives*, without, and against both *King*, and *House of Lords*: The main *Quere* further is, *Whether this present Assembly of Parliament be a complete House, and have a just Title to the Legislative, and supreme Power?* This may be made apparent by viewing the present constitution of the House, and by clearing of mistakes which are entertained concerning the *Breach of Priviledge*, and the Force which is conceived to have been used against the *House*.

For, whereas divers look upon the present constitution of the *House*, as defective in Authority, because they want their full number; and many that are *Members*, excluded wrongfully, to the Breach of *Priviledges*, which the *Covenant* obliges them to maintaine; They may be pleased to consider, that the number of 40. to all intents and purposes, hath

Pp always

67 *Mercurius Politicus*, 19 (October 10–17, 1650)
London: Printed by Matthew Simmons, 1650
Case J 5454. 569
Courtesy of the Newberry Library

DESPITE HIS REPUTATION AS A SIDE-CHANGING HACK, Marchamont Nedham was one of the most important republican writers of the seventeenth century. His most important innovation was the newspaper editorial. He pioneered journalistic comment before 1650, but perfected the art in *Politicus*, not least in a series of short essays which were later collected into a book that would influence John Adams' defense of the American Constitution.

ADVERTISEMENTS.

THese are to satisfie all persons, that Thomas Hinde's famous and never-failing Cordial Drink, formerly made by him in Charterhouse-yard, and since by his wife, (who are both dead) is now made and sold by me Jacob Hinde (Brother to the said Thoma Hinde) Picture drawer, next door to the Fountain-Tavern within Aldersgate, who hath the true Receipt thereof under the said Thomas Hinde's own hand. Now being there are so many false pretenders to this inestimable Jewel, I have ordered it to be sold by Mr. William Jackson, a Pewterer, at the Pewter-Platter over against the Kings-head-Inn in the Borrough of Southwork, and by Mr. Thomas Tonge a Grocer, at the Lion and Sugar-loaf over against Charing-cros, on the left hand going to White-hall, and no where else in London.

THe Communicants Catechism, for the full Information of all true Believers.

AS NEWSPAPERS BECAME MORE ESTABLISHED, and their authors more professional, it was increasingly common for them to sell advertisements as a means of raising money. These ads promoted a variety of products, services, and cultural events, and provided a forum for personal notices. Both informative and entertaining, they shed important light upon the culture of the time, the impact of commercial expansion and the development of capitalism.

(12)

Advertiſements of Books newly publiſhed.

☞ There is newly come forth a learned Book, entituled An Apology for the Diſcipline of the Antient Church Intended eſpecially for that of our Mother the Church of England, in Anſwer to the Admonitory Letter lately publiſhed. By *William Nicolſon*, Archdeacon of *Brecon*. Sold by *William Leake* at the Crown in Fleetſtreet, betwixt the two Temple Gates.

Φιλαδελφία, or the Grand Characteriſtick, whereby a man may be known to be Chriſts Diſciple. Delivered in a Sermon at St. *Pauls* before the Gentlemen of *Wiltſhire*, *Novemb.* 10. 1658. It being the day of their yearly Feaſt. By *Tho. Peirce*, Rector of *Brington*. Printed for *R. Royſton.* and are to be ſold by *John Courtney* Bookſeller in *Salisbury*.

The unparallel'd Monarch, or the Portraiture of a Matchleſs Prince, expreſt in ſome ſhadows of his Highneſs my Lord Protector.

Dilucidatio Articulorum controverſorum fidei inter Chriſtianos Reformatos, *Lutheranos*, *Calvinianos*, & *Arminianos*, quâ luculenter patet hos omnes in eſſentiâ doctrinæ controverſæ convenire, & unam eandemque veritatem modo duntaxat diverſo Fidei analogiæ nullatenus repugnantia concipere. Per *Lucam Morin* in almâ Monſpelienſium Medicorum Univerſitate Doctorem Medicum. Both ſold at the Three Pigeons in *Pauls* Churchyard.

A Treatiſe, entituled *Trigonometria Britannica* in Engliſh, with a Table of Logarithms to a hundred thouſand: The like not extant. Sold by *G. Hurlock* at *Magnus* Church corner, *J. Kirton* at the Kings Arms, and *T. Pierrepont* at the Sun in *Pauls* Churchyard, and *W. Fiſher* at the Poſtern near Tower-hill.

Murrels two Books of Cookery, containing many choice Receipts for dreſſing all manner of Fleſh, Fiſh, or Fowl, and for making Sauces for each Diſh after the beſt Engliſh and French manners; whereunto is added many choice experiments in Preſerving, Conſerving, and Candying, the beſt extant. Sold by *Robert Horn* at the Turks-head in Cornhil, near the Royal Exchange.

Mount *Ebal* Levell'd, or Redemption from the Curſe by Jeſus Chriſt, maintained, and practically improved. By the Reverend Mr. *Elk. Wales*, Miniſter of the Word at *Pudzey* in *Yorkſhire*.

A Treatiſe of Self-denial, wherein the neceſſity and excellency of it is demonſtrated, with ſeveral Directions for the practice of it. By *Theophilus Polwheile*, Teacher of the Church at *Tiverton* in *Devon*.

A Copy of the Covenant of Grace, with a diſcovery of ſeveral falſe pretenders to that eternal Inheritance, and of the right Heir thereunto, with ſuch ſafe inſtructions as will enable him to clear his Title, and to make it unqueſtionable. By *Robert Bidwel*, Miniſter of Gods Word, &c. All three ſold by T. *Johnſon* at the Key in St. *Pauls* Churchyard.

☞ A brief Chronology of the moſt remarkable Paſſages and Tranſactions, which occurred ſince his late Renowned Highneſs, *Oliver* Lord Protector was Inveſted with the Government of the Commonwealth of England, Scotland, and Ireland, &c. With the manner of his Death, and the deſcription of his lying in State at Somerſet-Houſe, ſet forth with a Braſs cut, and printed in a large ſheet of one ſide. Sold by *Edward Thomas* at the *Adam* and *Eve* in *Little Britain*, and at other Bookſellers ſhops.

Ad-

(13)

Advertiſements.

TAke notice that thoſe famous *Lozenges* or Pectorals, ſo generally known and approved for the Cure of *Conſumptions*, *Coughs*, *Aſthmaes*, and all Diſeaſes incident to the *Lungs*, are made by, and to be had onely of Mr. *Edmond Buckworth*, at his Houſe in *Katherine*'s Street, near the Tower, next door to the ſign of the George. This is publiſhed to prevent the Deſigns of divers Pretenders, who counterfeit the ſame about the City of *London*, to the prejudice and diſparagement of the ſaid Gentleman, and the abuſe of the people. For more convenience to thoſe that live remote in the City, quantities of them ſealed up with his Coat of Arms, are left conſtantly with Mr. *Richard Lownds* a Bookſeller, at the White Lyon in St. *Pauls* Churchyard, near the Little North-door.

WHereas *Penelope*, the Wife of *Eraſmus Deligne* of *Harlaxton*, in the County of *Lincoln*, Eſq; hath voluntarily deſerted her ſaid Husband, and accepted of a certain Annual allowance from him for Alimoney. He the ſaid *Eraſmus Deligne* doth therefore hereby publiſh and declare to all manner of perſons, as well Tradeſmen as others, reſiding within the Dominions and Territories of his Highneſs *Richard* Lord Protector, &c. not to Credit or Truſt the ſaid *Penelope Deligne* with any Wares, Merchandiſes, or other Commodities whatſoever. Foraſmuch as the ſaid *Eraſmus Deligne* by the Laws of this Nation is not, ſo from henceforth he will not be liable to the payment or other ſatisfaction of any ſuch perſon or perſons, for any ſuch Wares, Merchandiſes, or Commodities; nor for any other Debts which the ſaid *Penelope Deligne*, or any other perſon or perſons employed by her, ſhall contract on her behalf. Dated and publiſhed this Thirteenth day of *November*, 1658.

Eraſmus Deligne.

TUeſday, *Novemb.* 15. 1658. Stoln out of the Stable of *Matthew Hardy* Eſq; of *Lambeth*-houſe, one black Gelding, about thirteen hands high; no white but onely Saddle-ſpots; all his paces, very handſome made, branded on the near ſhoulder and the further buttock with *W. K.* on the near Buttock with *M.* about ſeven years old. Whoſoever gives notice to the place aboveſaid of this Gelding, and a bay Gelding loſt the ſeventh of *October*, ſhall have Five pounds for their pains, as a reward.

STraid the Twelfth of *November*, 1658. from *Mortlack* one of Mr. *William Ruſhouts* Field, a little black Nag about 12 or 13 hand high, he hath a ſtar in his forehead, and a mark of a ring and croſs on the ſhoulder, and a bit in the right eye-lid. If any give notice of him to Mr *Ruſhouts* in Fan-Church ſtreet, over againſt the Church, or to his Houſe at *Mortlack*, ſhall have forty ſhillings for their reward.

From Paris, Nov. 18. S. N.

We hear from Bruſſels of the ſecond of this month, that the 28 of the laſt, Marſhal Tureine had tranſported his Army over the Scheld, and marched towards Geerdberghe and Grammont, which places he hath taken and plundered; ſince that he hath alſo taken Aleſt, a ſmall Town in the midway between Gaunt and Bruſſels, which was but meanly fortifyed,

but

68 *Mercurius Politicus*, 442 (November 11–18, 1658)
London: Printed by Thomas Newcomb, 1650
Case J 5454. 569, pp. 12–13
Courtesy of the Newberry Library

NEDHAM DID NOT INVENT NEWSPAPER ADVERTISING, but he certainly took it to a new level in the 1650s, contributing to his image as a mercenary who sought profit alone. Here his paper promoted new books, including early biographies of the recently deceased Oliver Cromwell, as well as medicinal lozenges, and also featured an advertisement offering a reward for the recovery of a stolen horse. Most intriguing, however, is Erasmus Deligne's notice to tradesmen that he would no longer pay the bills amassed by his wife, by whom he had recently been "deserted," and to whom he already paid alimony.

W R

Not Acted theſe 16 Years.

T the New THEATRE,

in Little Lincolns-Inn Fields,

morrow being Thurſday the 28th of

October, will be Reviv'd, A Play call'd,

TROILUS and CRESIDA;

OR,

Truth Found too Late.

NO PERSON TO STAND ON THE STAGE.

Nor any Money to be after Return'd the Curtain is Drawn up.

By His Majeſties Servants. VIVAT REX.

69 London. Lincoln's Inn Fields
Playbill
October 28, [1697]
Bd.w. Z.e.37

ADVERTISEMENTS WERE NOT ONLY INSERTED INTO NEWSPAPERS but also produced as single sheets that could be displayed publicly, handed out, or even scattered about the streets. Printing ensured that numerous copies could be produced quickly and cheaply, and that events such as theatrical performances could be promoted at short notice. Playbills like this one, advertising a 1697 revival of John Dryden's adaptation of Shakespeare's *Troilus and Cressida*, are incredibly rare.

he might (if he had had the honeſt luck to have been abroad, and taken ſo much pains as was by others) have been certified of the contrary, and as likewiſe have conſidered, that the ſaid *Mary Preſton* did not fall ſick till the *Thurſday* after ſhe had made the diſcovery, ſhe having ſeen the Apparition about *Sunday* before, and was at the time of her relating it as much *compos mentis*,, as the *Intelligencer* was when he threw away his Guineys; and moreover, there was preſent a Juſtice of the Peace when the relation was made by Mr. *Clough*, and Mr. *Lane* and his Wife, *&c.* which are all ready to aſſert the truth thereof.

Yeſterday (being the 25 inſtant) about 6 of the clock in the morning, an Apprentice in *Fleet-ſtreet*, oppoſite to the end of *Fetter-lane*, cut his own throat to the wind-pipe; the Maid-ſervant of the houſe being ſent up ſtairs to call him, finding the door ſhut where he was, looked through the key-hole, and perceiving him all bloody, with the Pen knife ſticking in his throat, cried out for help, upon which, others of the family going up ſtairs, broke open the door, and found him weltring in his blood; they immediately ſent for a Chyrurgeon, who came and ſowed up the wound; but it is thought he will hardly recover, the wound being ſo deſperate.

The Youth was of a melancholly temper, and was tempted, as is reported, by the Devil to make away with himſelf, who appeared to him in ſeveral ſhapes.

Laſt night *Sir Thomas Davies*, one of the Aldermen of the City of *London*, who deceaſed on *Saturday* laſt) was interred in *St. Sepulchres* Church, the Lieutenancy hath not as yet appointed who ſhall be Colonell of the *Orange* Regiment in his ſtead.

Ovids Epiſtles, lately tranſlated into *Engliſh* by the perſons following

The Epiſtle of *Sapho* to *Phaon*, by *Sir Car. Scroop*, Baronet.

Canace to *Macareus*, by Mr. *Dryden.*
Phillis to *Demophoon.* by Mr. *Potley.*
The ſame again. by Mr. *Edward Floyd.*
Hypermneſtra to *Linus*, by Mr. *Wright.*
Ariadne to *Theſeus*, by an unknown hand.
Hermione to *Oreſtes*, by Mr. *Poultny.*
Leander to *Hero*, and the Anſwer, by Mr. *Tate.*
Laodamia to *Proteſilaus*, by Mr. *Flatman.*
Oenone to *Paris*, by Mis. *Behn.*
Paris to *Hellen*, by Mr. *Duke.*
Hellen to *Paris*, by the Earl of *Mulgrave.*
Penelope to *Ulyſſes*, by Mr. *Rymer.*
Hypſipyle to *Jaſon*, by Mr. *Settle.*
Medea to *Jaſon*, by Mr. *Tate.*
Dido to *Æneas*, by Mr. *Dryden.*
The ſame again, by another hand.
Briſeis to *Achilles*, by Mr. *Caryl*
Deianyra to *Hercules*, by a Perſon of Quality.
Phedra to *Hypolitus*, by Mr. *Ottway.*
Acontius to *Cydippe*, by Mr. *Duke.*
Cydippe to *Acontius*, by Mr. *Butler.*

To this Book is prefix'd a Preface, giving ſome account of the Life and VVritings of *Ovid*, and a Diſcourſe of Poetical Tranſlations in general; by Mr. *Dryden. Sold by* Jacob Tonſon, *at the* Judges Head *in* Chancery-lane *near* Fleet-ſtreet.

The account of the Bill of Mortality for the City of *London* runs thus:

Chriſtn.	*Males* 158	*Females* 121	*In all* 279		
Buried.	*Males* 168	*Females* 159	*In all* 327	*Pl.* 00	

Decreaſed in the Burials this week 00

ADVERTISEMENTS.

These are to ſatisfie all perſons, that Thomas Hinde's *famous and never-failing Cordial Drink, formerly made by him in* Charterhouſe-yard, *and ſince by his Wife, (who are both dead) is now made and ſold by me* Jacob Hinde (*Brother to the ſaid* Thomas Hinde) *Picture drawer, next door to the* Fountain-Tavern *within* Alderſgate, *who hath the true Receipt thereof under the ſaid* Thomas Hinde's *own hand. Now being there are ſo many falſe pretenders to this ineſtimable Jewel, I have ordered it to be ſold by Mr.* William Jackſon, *a Pewterer, at the* Pewter-Platter *over againſt the* Kings-head-Inn *in the Borrough of* Southwork. *and by Mr.* Thomas Tonge *a Grocer, at the* Lion and Sugar-loaf *over againſt* Charing-croſs, *on the left hand going to* White-hall, *and no where elſe in* London.

The Communicants Catechiſm, for the full Information of all true Believers.

The Vermin-killer, being a very neceſſary Family-Book, containing Exact Rules and directions for the Artificial killing and deſtroying of all manner of Vermin, &c. Rats *and* Mice, Moles, Piſmires, Flyes, Fleas *and* Lice Adders Snakes Weaſles Catterpillars Buggs Froggs, *&c. Whereunto is added the Art of taking of all ſorts of* Fiſh *and* Foul, *with many other Obſervations never before extant. Both Sold by* Samuel Lee *at the* Feathers *near the* Poſt-Office *in* Lumbard-ſtreet.

A Sermon Preached at the French Church in the Savoy, *which was Accuſed for Hereitical; Printed in French, and Engliſhed, and Dedicated to the Biſhop of* London, *by* L. D. E. D.

Mercy Triumphant, *the Kingdome of Chriſt, Enlarged, beyond the Narrow bounds wont to be ſet unto it, by* E. L. *Miniſter of the Goſpel; Being an Antidote againſt a late Book of Dr.* Du Moulins, *called* Moral Reflections on the number of the Elect; *wherein he aſſerts that it is not probable, that one of a Million ſince* Adam *can be ſaved. Both Printed for* W. Crook *without* Temple Barr *at the* Green Dragon,

The ſo well approved Drink, called Dr. Butler's Ale, *the vertue or operation of which is effectual in cleanſing the Stomach, helping Digeſtion, and provoking Urin; it alſo preſerveth the Lungs, being good againſt the Diſeaſes of the ſame, as Conſumptive Coughs, Ptiſicks, wind,* &c. *The which Drink is with much care and faithfulneſs rightly prepared made, and ſold by* Decimus Stockall, *at the* Dolphin *in* Bloomsbury Fiſh-market, *Price* 3 d. per Quart.

Next door to the Popes Head Tavern *in* Moor-fields, *is to be ſeen that much admirable Rarity, by the name of the* Indian Water-works; *being with much coſt and induſtry brought at length to perfection, by a very Famous and Ingenious Artiſt; and improv'd with ſeveral additions. This rare and Incomparable piece of Workmanſhip, is to be ſeen daily from next* Eaſter Monday, *and ſo to continue all the Year.* VIVAT REX.

The moſt infallible Cure for the Fiſtula *in any part of the body, by application onely of a few Drops, by an approved Doctor, as ſeveral can teſtifie, ſome having been cured by once dreſſing. Alſo he ſafely cures any* Piles *or* Ulcers, *and all* Venereal Diſeaſes, *and the* Scurvy, *with ſpeed, whether old or new; he ſhews what danger any are in* gratis. *At his Chamber over againſt the* Meuſe *by* Charing-croſs, *a Sadlers houſe, next the* Hat and Feather. *His hours to be ſpoke with are from* 12 *to* 4 *in the afternoon.*

London, Printed by *Nath. Thompſon*, next the *Croſs-Keys* in *Fetter-lane.* An. Dom. 1680.

70A *True Domestick Intelligence*, 76 (March 23–26, 1680)
London: Printed by Nathaniel Thompson, 1680
T2689a Bd.w. P3831a Copy 2

THE EMERGENCE OF LONDON as a wealthy commercial powerhouse in the late seventeenth century is mirrored in newspaper advertisements. This edition reveals not just learned sermons, but also guidebooks for the extermination of vermin, quack medical cures for any number of ailments, and a variety of drinks, such as "Dr Butler's Ale" and Hinde's "famous and never-failing cordial drink," which were claimed to have remarkable properties. It also contains the first known illustrated advertisement, for a mysterious spectacle known as the "Indian water-works," which could be "seen daily" in London (Cat. No. 70B).

NExt door to the Popes Head Tavern *in* Moor-fields, *is to be ſeen that much admirable Rarity, by the name of the* Indian Water-works; *being with much coſt and induſtry brought at length to perfection, by a very Famous and Ingenious Artiſt; and improv'd with ſeveral additions. This rare and Incomparable piece of Workmanſhip, is to be ſeen daily from next* Eaſter Monday, *and ſo to continue all the Year.* VIVAT REX.

70B *True Domestick Intelligence,* 76 (March 23–26, 1680)
London: Printed by Nathaniel Thompson, 1680
T2689a Bd.w. P3831a Copy 2

We are desired to give notice, That a young man about 28 yeares of age, called *Iohn Thacker*, servant to *Walter Blithe* a Grazier, hath been missing from about this City of *London* ever since Thursday sevennight last, and supposed that some misfortune may befall him, He is a low man, strong set, of a brown complexion with pale yellowish thin haire, gray eyed, his hand a little freckled, in Grayish apparrell, having about him severall weighty Accompts of Cattel sould, and should have a good quantity of Silver and Gold about him. Whosoever can bring notice to the three Legs in *Fleetstreet London*, or the Star in *Coventry*, of his Person, Accompts, or Moneys, shall be exceeding wel rewarded for his pains and costs bestowed, answerable to the distance of place, from what part soever. *Grammaticall Cards*, In which are compendiously comprised all the Rules of Grammer. Made by *Baptist Pendleton*, sold at his house neer S. *Dunstans* in the East.

71 *A Perfect Diurnall*, 55 (December 23–30, 1650) London: Printed by F. Leach and E. Griffin, in the Old Baily, 1650 P1486.5, p. 732

***A PERFECT DIURNALL* WAS ONE OF THE FIRST NEWSPAPERS** to experiment with advertisements, which were initially dominated by announcements regarding the publication of new books of a serious and scholarly nature. Fairly quickly, however, these were supplemented by notices for lost and stolen property, from valuable artworks to rustled horses. This one, evidently inserted in haste after the edition had been typeset, gives a detailed description of a missing person, evidently a servant who had absconded with his master's money, and offered an unspecified reward.

and may do what you pleaſe, for all ſuch Obligations are mutual, and 'tis always underſtood (tho' it were not expreſt) that both ſides are bound or free; for there's no one can marry another againſt their Wills. We know of no other Method to be us'd, but this Venture or a ſingle Life, which you're at liberty to chooſe, as you think either more eligible.

Queſt. 4. *This laſt Execution-day, after Prayers ſaid, and Pſalm ſung, one of the Condemned Perſons hanged himſelf, by lifting up his Leggs, ſo that ſeemingly he was dead before the Cart was drove away: Pray your Opinion, (tho' he was inevitably to dye, yet this Act being voluntary, and not the Act of the Law) if he is not guilty of Self-murder?*

Anſw. 'Twas judg'd by ſeveral Perſons there, that 'twas the Fear and Apprehenſion of Death that overcame his Spirits, and made him faint away, and not any voluntary Act of his own.

Queſt. 5. *I being juſtly inform'd that there is Nine Gentlemen that have an Employment of* 800 l. per An. *each, moſt in* London, *know that Seven of the ſaid Nine do daily promote the* French *King's Intereſt, by putting into Employment and Protecting ſuch as drink King* James's *Health, and all againſt the Government, what ought to be done in ſuch a Caſe?*

Anſw. You or your Informer are Oblig'd as you will Anſwer it to God Almighty or the Publick Good, to give Notice of it to the Magiſtrate, for the prevention of ſuch ill conſequences as may be too reaſonably fear'd from the influence of ſuch Perſons.

Queſt. 6. *Your Opinion in this Caſe is deſired — A Perſon marrying a Wife in the Month of* February, 84. *and lived with him 'till* May, 89. *in very good order, and of a ſuddain left him, without any provocation, and hath been abſent ever ſince; he deſires, being much troubled in mind about it, how he may anſwer for her, to know what is become of her, he being willing to diſcharge his Duty to her before God and Man: I pray your Advice in this matter as ſoon as poſſible?*

Anſw. Put her in the *Gazette*, and Promiſe ſhe ſhall be well treated if ſhe will return to you; and if it has the Effect, be ſure you be as good as your word.

Queſt. 7. A. *and* B. *both in one Concern mutually agree, that whatever was gained by either, ſhould be equally divided; it happened that* B. *meets with a conſiderable Advantage, but refuſes to give* A. *the ſhare that was due to him, pretending it was wholly owing to his Care; they ſtill continue to act in the ſame Stations, and* A. *has an opportunity to repay himſelf, and* B. *not know it: The Queſtion is, Whether he may lawfully in any part pay himſelf, without the others knowledge?*

Anſw. Since ye have both agreed to divide what was got by either, you are Oblig'd to your Agreement, altho' he has been unjuſt to you; but either there are ſuch Articles drawn up betwixt you, or not, if there be, you have relief by 'em; if there be not, you have acted imprudently, to enter a Partnerſhip without them: A good Man won't refuſe to be bound to do a thing which he purpoſes, and an ill Man ought to be bound for his Partner's ſecurity.

Queſt. 8. *A Man marries a Wife, whoſe Father under Hand and Seal before Witneſs promiſes to give a conſiderable Fortune to his Daughter, but after Marriage refuſes to be as good as his Word; the Father and Son are Obliged for ſome time to continue in Joint-Buſineſs, and the Father leaves the Management to the Son: Now the Queſtion is, Whether the Son may not upon the paſſing the Accounts help himſelf to ſome part of what is his juſt due, (tho' not near a fourth part) when he has no other way to get any part that is owing, and this way he may have ſome relief, if he gives the Father no Notice?*

Anſw. You ſhou'd not act underhand in this Caſe: Your Father's Promiſe under Hand and Seal, before Witneſſes, is as good Security for the Portion as you need; ſo that there's no need of indirect means in the Caſe, tho' if there were no other remedy, they ought not to be embraced.

Queſt. 9. *I have but one Son, and he is an extraordinary lewd liver, now is it lawful for me to diſinherit this ſaid Son from my Eſtate, which lyes in my power to do, and give it to one of my Relations, if he do not mend his Life?*

Anſw. It wou'd be a very hard thing to give away the Eſtate out of the Family, ſince his Children if he marries may be better, and it wou'd be ſevere to diſinherit them for his ſake; tho' on the other hand, 'tis not only lawful to diſinherit ſuch a Perſon, but ſinful to leave him an Eſtate to maintain his Luſts and Follies: Now ('tis our private Opinion, and you may act as you pleaſe) there might be yet a better Expedient found out, *viz.* To leave him only a Competent Maintenance for his Life, but to ſettle the Eſtate out of his diſpoſal for his Children, if he has any; if not, to what other Intents and Purpoſes you think fitting.

⁂ That Gentleman that has been ſo kind as to offer a Draught of St. *Luke*'s Genealogy, reconcil'd with that of St. *Matthew*'s, is deſired to ſend it, and we will inſert it for the Service of the Church, ſome Atheiſtical Perſons having made dangerous Cavils about it.

Advertiſements.

This Morning is Publiſhed

☞ T*He Second Edition of* The ſecond SPIRA, *well Atteſted.* Price Six Pence. *Printed for* John Dunton *at the* Raven *in the* Poultrey. LICENSED and ENTERED according to Order.

☞ T*He Fourth Edition of* The New Martyrology, *or Bloody Aſſizes*, &c. Containing ſeveral Speeches, *Letters*, *Elegies*, and *New Diſcoveries* (ſent out of the *WEST*) ne're Printed before.

☞ T*He* TRYALS *of ſeveral* WITCHES lately Executed in *New-England*, and of ſeveral remarkable Curioſities therein Occurring. By *Cotton Mather.* Publiſhed by the Special Command of the Governour. Both Printed for *John Dunton* at the *Raven* in the *Poultrey.*

AT the *Rotterdam* Coffee-houſe by the *Cuſtom-Houſe* in *Thames-ſtreet*, and at a Cutlers Shop over againſt the *Mermaid* Tavern in *Cornhill*, is ſold an Infallible Cure for an AGUE, if any Perſon tryes it, and it proves ineffectual, their Money ſhall be return'd.

AN Excellent SNUFF to Prevent and Cure the Tooth-Ach. This *Snuff*, which if taken as common *Snuff*, when you have the Tooth-Ach, gives you preſent Eaſe whilſt you are taking it, and if taken three or four times in the Week, prevents your ever having of it again. It is Sold at theſe places following: At the *Rainbow* Coffe-houſe at the end of *St. Martins-Lane*, at the *Italian* Coffee-Houſe in *Katharine-ſtreet*, *Covent-Garden*; at *Tom*'s Coffee-houſe at *Ludgate*; at the *Rainbow* Coffee-houſe in *Cornhill*, near the *Exchange*; at *Richard*'s Coffee-houſe at *Temple-Bar*, at the Bookſellers in *George-yard* in *Cornhill*, going into *Lombard ſtreet*. This *Snuff* is ſold for 1 *s.* each Paper, and 2 *s.* the Box, Sealed with a Coat of Arms.

D*Affy's Elixir Salutis*, rightly Prepared by *Charles Trubſhaw* at the two Blue Poſts in *Saliſbury-Court*, is to be had at Mr. *John Dunton's* at the *Raven* in the *Poultrey.* Price 2 *s.* 6 *d.*

LONDON, Printed for John Dunton at the *Raven* in the *Poultrey*, 1693.

72 *The Athenian Mercury*, 11 (January 17, 1693)
London: Printed for John Dunton, 1693
A4111a Copy 1

PUBLISHERS OF NEWSPAPERS OFTEN USED ADVERTISING SPACE in order to promote their own works. The *Athenian Mercury*, which was designed to answer readers' queries on any subject, was run by the leading Whig bookseller and publisher, John Dunton. Here, among advertisements, Dunton promoted his book about the trials of Whig rebels at the so-called "bloody assizes," the trials presided over by the brutal Judge Jeffreys, as well as a book about the Salem witch trials by the New England minister, Cotton Mather, whom Dunton had befriended on a visit to Boston in 1686.

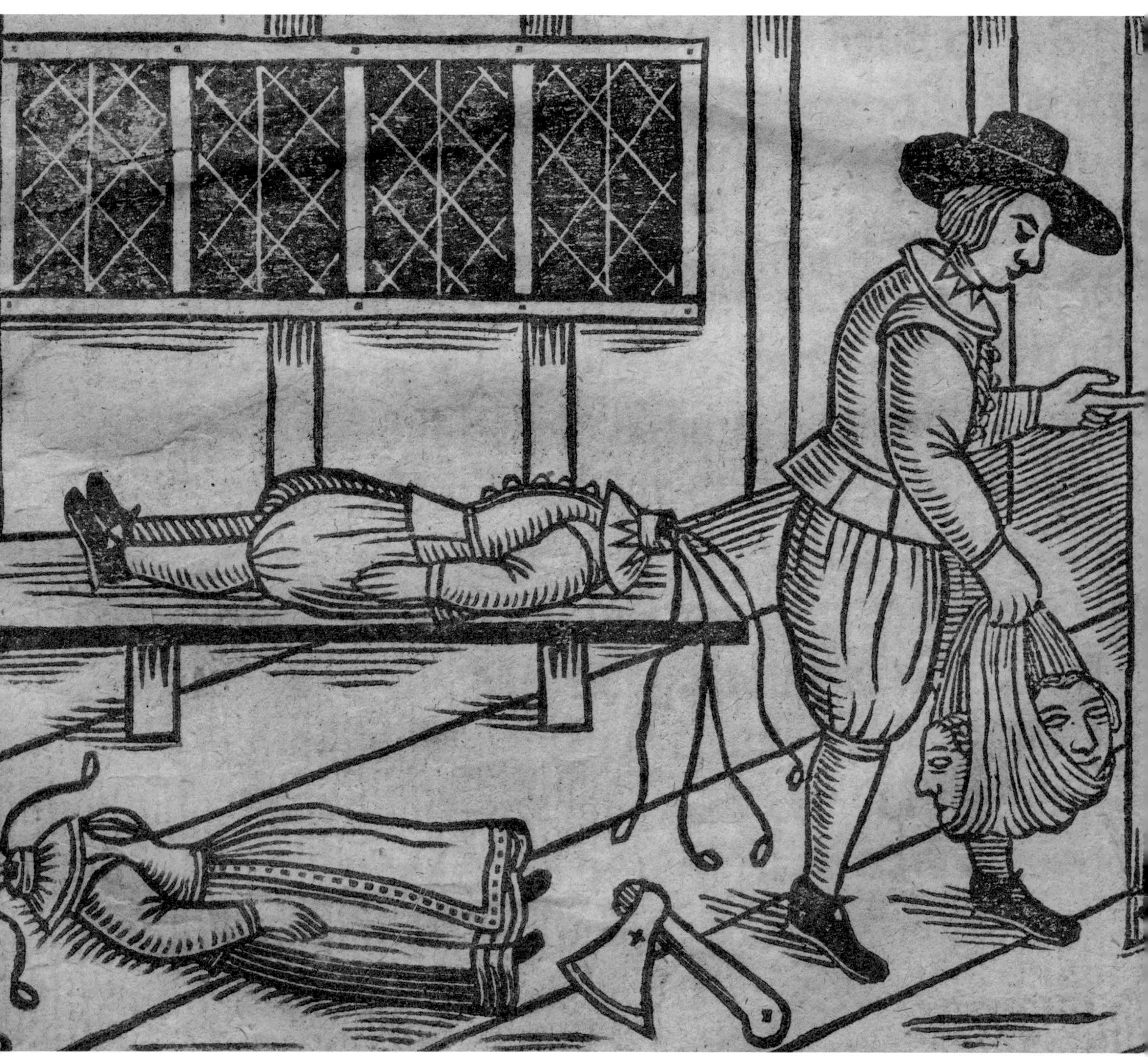

JOURNALISTS WERE NOT ENTIRELY PREOCCUPIED by the concerns of the political elite, and a high proportion of news coverage involved what later became known as "tabloid" journalism. Both press and public were fascinated by crime and disorder, and the stories they read and reported revealed fears about the dangers of moral decay. By examining these extraordinary tales from the lives of ordinary people, it is possible to observe just how willing contemporaries were to invest such events with political and religious meaning and significance.

A

TrueRelation of a moſt
deſperate Murder, committed vpon
the Body of Sir IOHN TINDALL
Knight, one of the Maiſters of the
Chancery;
Who with a Piſtoll charged with 3. bullets, was ſlaine
going into his Chamber within *Lincolnes-Inne*, the 12.
day of Nouember, by one *Iohn Barterham* Gent:
Which *Barterham* afterwards hanged himſelfe in the
Kinges-Bench in *Southwarke*, on Sunday being the
17. day following. 1*616*.

LONDON
Printed by *Edw: All-de*, for *L. L.* dwelling in *Pauls* Church-yard,
at the ſigne of the Tygers head. 1617.

73 *A True Relation of a Most Desperate Murder*
London: Printed by Edw. All-de for L.L dwelling in Paul's Church-yard at the signe of the Tygers Head, 1617
STC 24435, title page

ALTHOUGH CRIME WAS COMMON in the seventeenth century, murder was rare. This explains the popularity of pamphlets describing unusually violent incidents, often with dramatic woodcut illustrations of the crimes they described. Here is a true story about the killing of a prominent lawyer by a disgruntled litigant, the criminal's capture and trial, and subsequent suicide in prison. The author's purpose was to warn others of the need to resolve grievances through legal means, and of God's judgment upon wrongdoers.

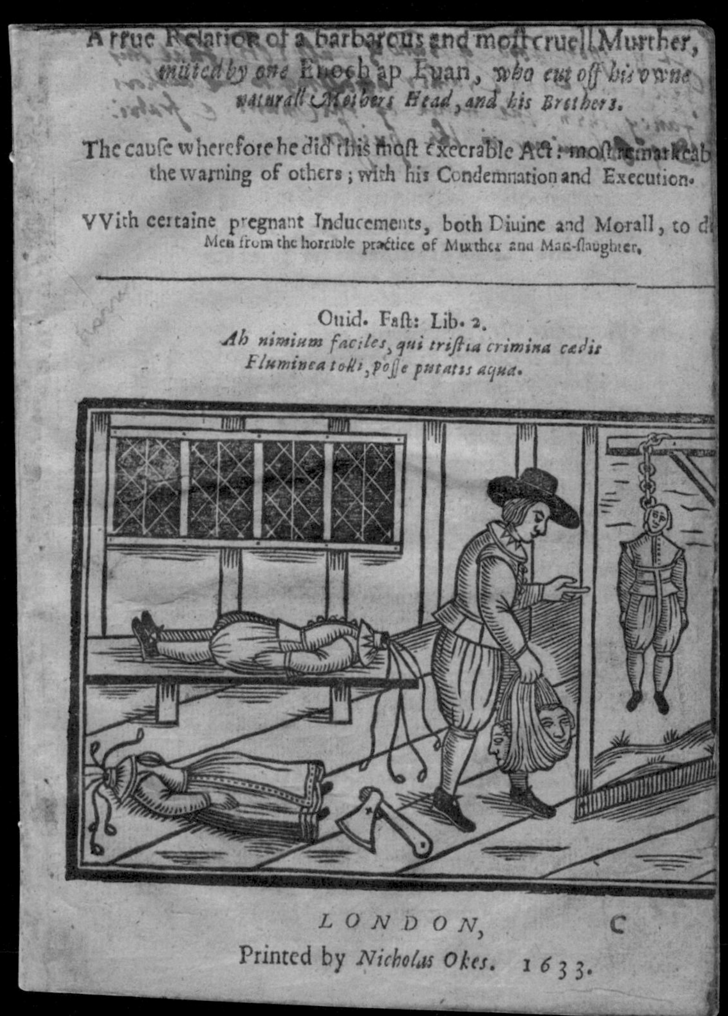

A true Relation of a barbarous and most cruell Murther, mitted by one Enoch ap Euan, who cut off his owne naturall Mothers Head, and his Brothers.

The cause wherefore he did this most execrable Act: most remarkab the warning of others; with his Condemnation and Execution.

VVith certaine pregnant Inducements, both Diuine and Morall, to d Men from the horrible practice of Murther and Man-slaughter.

Ouid. Fast: Lib. 2.
Ah nimium faciles, qui tristia crimina cædis
Fluminea tolli, posse putatis aqua.

LONDON, C
Printed by *Nicholas Okes.* 1633.

74 *A True Relation of a Barbarous and Most Cruell Murther*
London: Printed by Nicholas Okes, 1633
STC 10582, title page

MURDER PAMPHLETS REPRESENTED MUCH MORE than merely sensational reporting of terrible deeds. They provided a chance to preach and moralize, in part by highlighting the repentance of individual criminals. On some occasions the significance of such crimes went much further, as with this story of Enoch ap Evans' savage beheading of both his mother and brother. The crime apparently occurred following a family argument over religious beliefs and practices, and Enoch's case was quickly exploited, in a range of tracts and treatises, by those who drew a connection between his Puritanism and his criminal behavior.

Bloody Newes from Dover. 18

BEING A True

RELATION

OF

The great and bloudy Murder, committed by *Mary Champion* (an Anabaptist) who cut off her Childs head, being 7. weekes old, and held it to her husband to baptize. Also another great murder committed in the North, by a Scottish Commander, for which Fact he was executed.

Printed in the Yeare of Discovery, *Feb.* 13. 1647.

75 *Bloody Newes from Dover*
London: Printed in the yeare of discovery, February 13, 1647
G.389A.327
Courtesy of the Boston Public Library

CRIME REPORTING ARGUABLY BECAME EVEN MORE IMPORTANT during the Civil Wars, as controversy raged regarding the dangers resulting from religious division and the emergence of new sects. Radical Puritans were demonized for challenging authority through outrageous behavior, as with this gruesome story of a woman who murdered her baby rather than let it be baptized by her Presbyterian husband. She was reported to have said "now go and baptise it, if you will, you must christen the head without a body." The culprit apparently repented in prison, after being tormented by visions of headless infants.

76 Nehemiah Wallington (1598–1658)
"An extract of the passages of my life or the booke of all my writting books"
Manuscript journal, 1654
V.a.436, p. 151

THAT MURDER PAMPHLETS WERE POPULAR is evident from this notebook belonging to a Puritan London woodturner, Nehemiah Wallington. Wallington was addicted to all sorts of cheap pamphlets and newspapers, which he likened to "so many theeves that had stole away my mony before I was aware of them," and regularly mentioned them in his many notebooks. An enemy of religious groups such as the Baptists, he clearly understood the moral of the story contained in *Bloody Newes from Dover*, which he recounts near the bottom of p. 151.

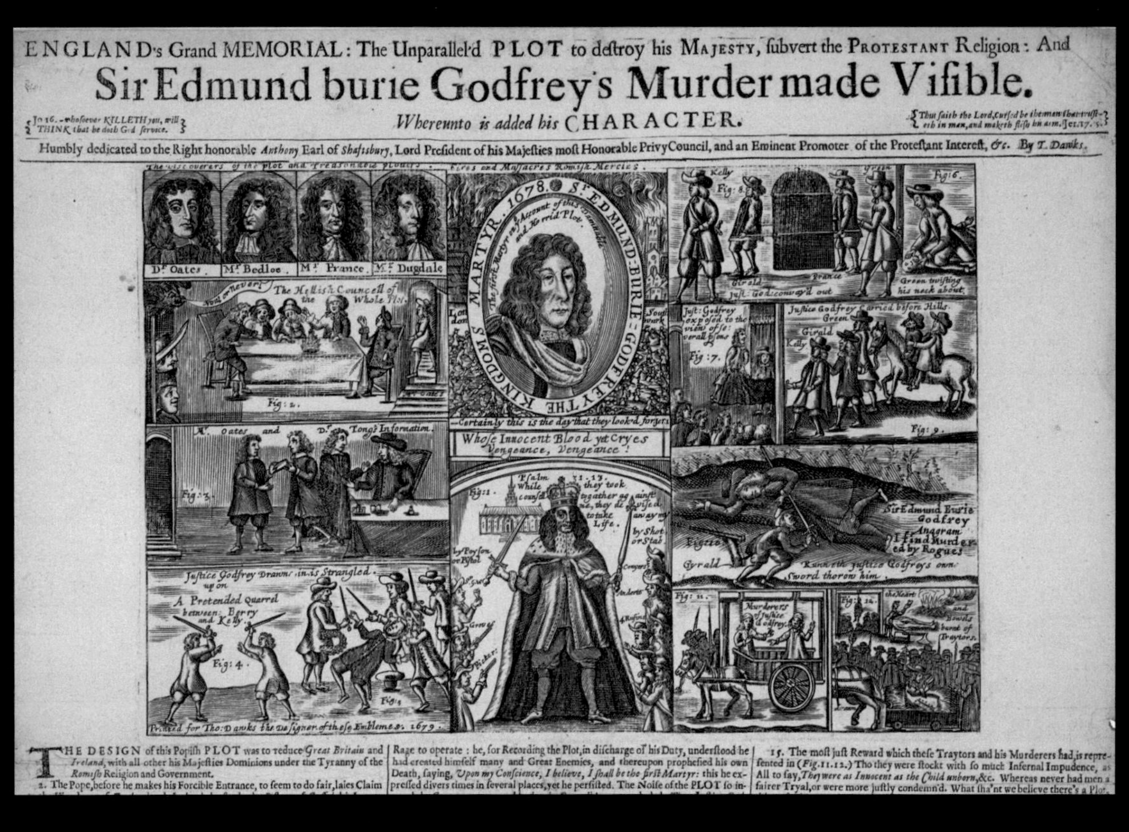

77 *England's Grand Memorial*
London: Printed by Th. Dawks, 1679
262- 606b

SOME CRIMES WERE OVERTLY POLITICAL IN NATURE, and, as a result, scandalized the entire nation when they became known. One of the greatest examples was the murder of Sir Edmund Berry Godfrey, the magistrate who nervously and half-heartedly investigated claims of a "popish plot" in 1678. The discovery of his strangled and stabbed body was quickly exploited by those Whigs who were critical of the Crown, who claimed that he had been killed by Catholic conspirators, and who sought to turn Godfrey into a Protestant martyr, especially through broadsides such as *England's Grand Memorial.*

Numb.49.

THE

True Domestick Intelligence,

OR, News both from

CITY & COUNTRY.

Publiſhed to prevent False Reports.

Tueſday, December 23. 1679.

LAſt *Friday* night, Mrs. *Celliers* was had before the Council, and, as it is ſaid, made a large diſcovery of what ſhe knew concerning the Plot; ſhe confeſs'd, that *Jane* the Prieſt had ſeveral ſums of Money which ſhe knew of to carry on their deſigns.

The Roads are ſo infeſted with Robbers, that the Carriers are cautious of carrying Goods of any conſiderable value, unleſs the Owners will ſtand to the loſs of them.

Mr. *Dryden* (the Kings Poet Laureat) coming out of a Coffee-houſe on *Thurſday* night laſt, was ſet upon by three men, who did beat him ſo ſeverely, that 'tis thought he will hardly recover it.

Upon *Friday* laſt were executed ſeven perſons, *viz.* five Men and two Women, one of them, named *Parker*, a Watch-maker by Trade, ſuffering for Coining falſe Guinneys. The day before his Execution he was viſited by two men of his acquaintance, whom he accuſed to be guilty of the ſame crime; upon which they were ſecured, in order to their further examination.

Captain *Richardſon*, Keeper of his Majeſties Gaol of *Newgate*, uſed many endeavours to draw a Confeſſion from *Dean*, (another of the Criminals that were executed) in relation to the murther of *Dell*'s Father in Law, Brother in Law, and Wife, (this *Dell*, being likewiſe one of thoſe that were executed, was accuſed of theſe murders, but died for another crime) the preſumptions being very ſtrong against them, (though acquitted as to thoſe accuſations) but *Dean* would not acknowledge particulars, but in general, that *Dell* had drawn him in to his own ruine.

Sir *Edward* —— Envoy Extraordinary in *Sweden*, being on his way home, Sir *John Robinſon* officiates as Secretary till the arrival of *Phillip Warwick* Eſq. who ſucceeds Sir *Edward*.

The Patent is paſſing for making the Earl of *Cheſterfield* Juſtice in Eyre of the Foreſts.

The active men about Petitions begin to decline the proſecution of that buſineſs, finding themſelves not ſo well back'd as they expected.

The Liſt of the Catholicks which was taken and preſented to the Houſe of Commons at their laſt ſitting, was ſince given to the Lord Chancellor, and read the 19 inſtant at the Council-Table, who will inſpect it.

The Juſtices of Middleſex have a Commiſſion to ſearch all Priviledged Places, as alſo to command out of any Forreigners houſes any of his Majeſties Subjects in order to proceed againſt them.

The Gentleman that was tried at the *Kings-Bench-Bar* the next day after the Term ended, for killing another Gentleman at *Whitehall-gate*, and found guilty of Man-ſlaughter, was on *Thurſday* laſt to have been tried in the Verge of *Weſtminſter-hall* for ſtriking in the Kings Court (which crime is puniſhable with the loſs of the hand that ſtrikes) but ſome difficulties ariſing, is put off till the Seſſions at the *Old Baily*.

On *Wedneſday* laſt was a hearing to be before the Council, about a difference between a Captain of a Privateer, and the other Sea-men, about a Prize taken in the *Dutch* War, the Captain having (as the Sea-men ſay) wronged them of their part.

The Lord *Culpepper* having ſtaid on ſhoar beyond the time for which the Commiſſioners of the Admiralty had ordered Victuals for the Veſſel that was to tranſport him to *Virginia*, the Veſſel went off to Sea without him; his Lordſhip is at preſent at *Graveſend*, and hath ſent to the Lords of the Admiralty to deſire them to recall the ſaid Veſſel, or order him another.

His Majeſty hath thought fit to revoke his Letters Patents conſtituting the Duke of *Monmouth*

78 *True Domestick Intelligence*, 49 (December 23, 1679)
London: Printed by Nathaniel Thompson, 1679
T2689a(49) Bd.w. P3831a
Copy 2

CRIME, POLITICS AND CELEBRITY proved to be a heady mixture in the news reporting of the late seventeenth century. This Tory newspaper probably sought to foster the impression that moral decay and political dissent were closely connected. It reports on highways which were "infested with robbers," on the activities of those seeking to foment opposition to Charles II's Catholic heir, and on the brutal assault upon the celebrated poet and playwright, John Dryden, which had recently taken place in Covent Garden. After the attack the poet laureate was left fighting for his life.

PEOPLE IN SEVENTEENTH-CENTURY ENGLAND were captivated by stories about unusual or sensational events. From stormy weather to conjoined twins, murder, atrocities, and supernatural tales, these "news" pamphlets provided both entertainment and education. Beware of the devil, avoid temptation and be a good Christian and all will be well … or so they believed.

The VVonders of this windie winter.

By terrible ſtormes and tempeſts, to the loſſe of liues and goods of many thouſands of men, women and children.

The like by Sea and Land, hath not beene ſeene, nor heard of in this age of the World.

LONDON.

Imprinted by *G. Eld*, for *John Wright*, and are to bee ſold at his Shop neere

79 *The Wonders of this Windie Winter*
London: Printed by G. Eld for John Wright and are to bee sold at his shop in Christ-Church dore, [1613]
STC 25949, title page

THROUGH THE "NOSTRILS OF GOD," as this pamphlet concludes, England was devastated by stormy weather during the winter of 1612–1613. But why? Unlike the complex scientific calculations which meteorologists undertake to predict the weather, the author found the answer in the sinful behavior of the people. God's punishment for immoral conduct included hundreds of ships lost, whole villages flooded, and goods swept away. Not only could the buyers of this pamphlet read the news from all over England on the weather, but they could learn how the next winter could be milder if they spent more time in religious devotion.

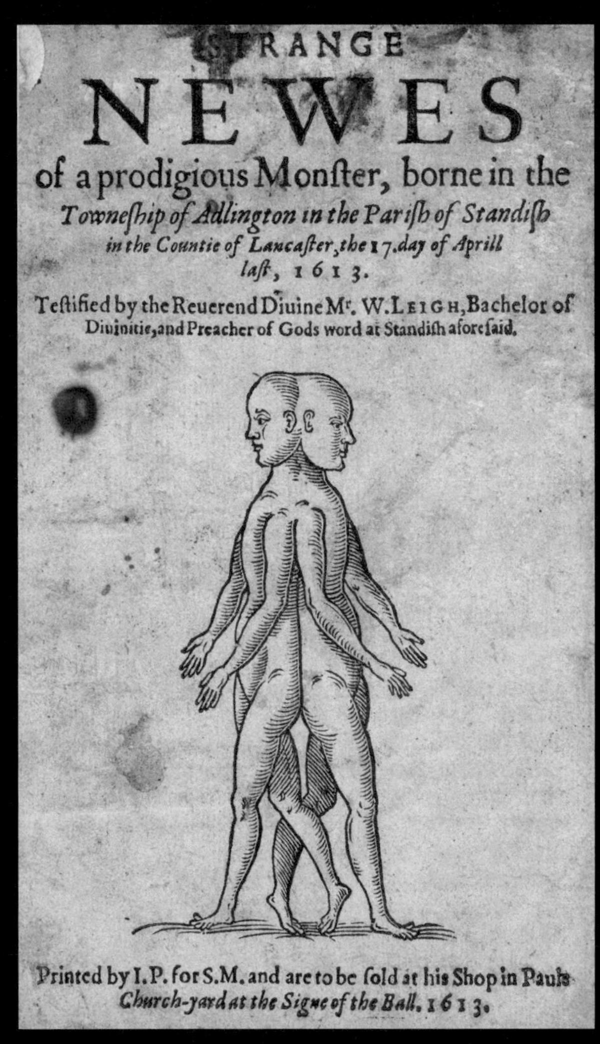

STRANGE

NEWES

of a prodigious Monſter, borne in the
Towneſhip of Adlington in the Pariſh of Standiſh
in the Countie of Lancaſter, the 17. *day of Aprill*
laſt, 1613.

Teſtified by the Reuerend Diuine Mr. W. Leigh, Bachelor of Diuinitie, and Preacher of Gods word at Standiſh aforeſaid.

Printed by I. P. for S. M. and are to be ſold at his Shop in Pauls
Church-yard at the Signe of the Ball, 1613.

80 *Strange Newes of a Prodigious Monster*
London: Printed by I. P[indley] for S. M [an] and are to be sold at his shop in Pauls Church-yard at the signe of the Ball, 1613
STC 15428 Bd.w. STC 20863/5, title page

UNUSUAL OCCURRENCES AND PHYSICAL ABNORMALITIES, such as the birth of conjoined twins, always provided rich fodder for sensational and popular news stories. In this case, expert testimony was also sought to authenticate and provide veracity of the event. The title page prominently notes a preacher with a Bachelor of Divinity could attest to the accuracy of the news.

The Diseases and Casualties this Week.

Aged	14
Cancer	1
Canker	1
Childbed	5
Chrisomes	2
Consumption	61
Convulsion	62
Dropsie	9
Drowned 8, one at S. John at Hackney, one at S. Giles in the fields, one at S. Katharine Tower, one at S. Mary Islington, one at St. Paul Shadwel, one at S.Martin in the fields, and two at Stepny	8
Evil	2
Feaver	43
Flox and Small pox	12
Flux	1
French-pox	1
Griping in the guts	57
Jaundies	2
Impostume	1
Infants	3
Kill'd 2, one at S.Martin in the fields, and one by an accidental fall from a Wharf at at S. Martin Vintrey	2
Overlaid	2
Quinsie	1
Rickets	5
Rising of the Lights	1
Spotted Feaver	9
Stilborn	13
Stone	1
Stopping in the Stomach	4
Suddenly	1
Surfeit	8
Teeth	29
Thrush	1
Tissick	1
Ulcer	1
Wind	1

Christned: Males—96, Females—131, In all—227

Buried: Males—189, Females—176, In all—365. Plague—0

Increased in the Burials this week—29

Parishes clear of the Plague—132 Parishes infected—0

The Assize of Bread set forth by Order of the Lord Mayor and Court of Aldermen.
A penny Wheaten Loaf to contain Ten Ounces and an half, and three half-penny White Loaves the like weight. And Houshold Bread made of Wheat to contain double the weight of White Bread.

81 Worshipful Company of Parish Clerks
Diseases and Casualties this Week (July 6–13, 1680)
[London: Printed for the Parish Clerks by the printer to the city of London]
252- 869q

THE WEEKLY REPORT OF THE NUMBER OF DEATHS IN LONDON—and their causes—attests to a widespread fascination with mortality. Not every death seems explicable through science: two perished by "evil," "suddenly" accounted for one poor soul, and an astonishing nineteen people died as a result of problems with their teeth. Quick to capitalize on the interest in death, the sheet provided a prime opportunity for the London authorities to advertise their new policies on bread production.

The Cry and Reuenge of Blood.

Expreſsing the Nature and haynouſ-
neſſe of wilfull Murther.

Exemplified
In a moſt lamentable Hiſtory thereof, com-
mitted at Halſworth *in* High Suffolk, *and*

Lately Conuicted at Bury Aſsize, 1620.

LONDON,
Printed by NICHOLAS OKES, for *Iohn*
Wright, dwelling in *Pie-corner* 1620.

82 Thomas Cooper
The Cry and Reuenge of Blood
London: Printed by Nicholas Okes for John Wright dwelling in Pie-corner, 1620
STC 5698 Copy 2, title page

TRUE CRIME STORIES, especially tales of murder instigated by the devil, were the stuff of bestselling pamphlets. Descriptive, lengthy titles and vivid illustrations were blazoned on the title page. Publication usually immediately followed the trial, after all the details had been revealed and the punishment (execution) carried out. This book is dedicated to Sir Henry Mountague, the trial judge, and lavishly praises his godly behavior in sentencing the murderers to death.

The Ranters Ranting:

WITH

The apprehending, examinations, and confession of *John Collins*, *I. Shakespear*, *Tho. Wiberton*, and five more which are to answer the next Sessions. And severall songs or catches, which were sung at their meetings. Also their several kinds of mirth, and dancing. Their blasphemous opinions. Their belief concerning heaven and hell. And the reason why one of the same opinion cut off the heads of his own mother and brother. Set forth for the further discovery of this ungodly crew.

LONDON
Printed by *B. Alsop*, 1650.

83 John Reading
The Ranters Ranting
London: Printed by B. Alsop, 1650
R450, title page

MANY RADICAL SOCIAL AND RELIGIOUS GROUPS sprang up in the turbulent times in England after the Civil Wars of the 1640s and the execution of the monarch in 1649. One such group, the Ranters, who were much feared and reviled, was alleged to have believed in shedding their clothes, free love and wife-swapping as well as many other "ungodly" practices. This pamphlet gives prominent status to their myriad sins, including public nudity, gluttony and dancing.

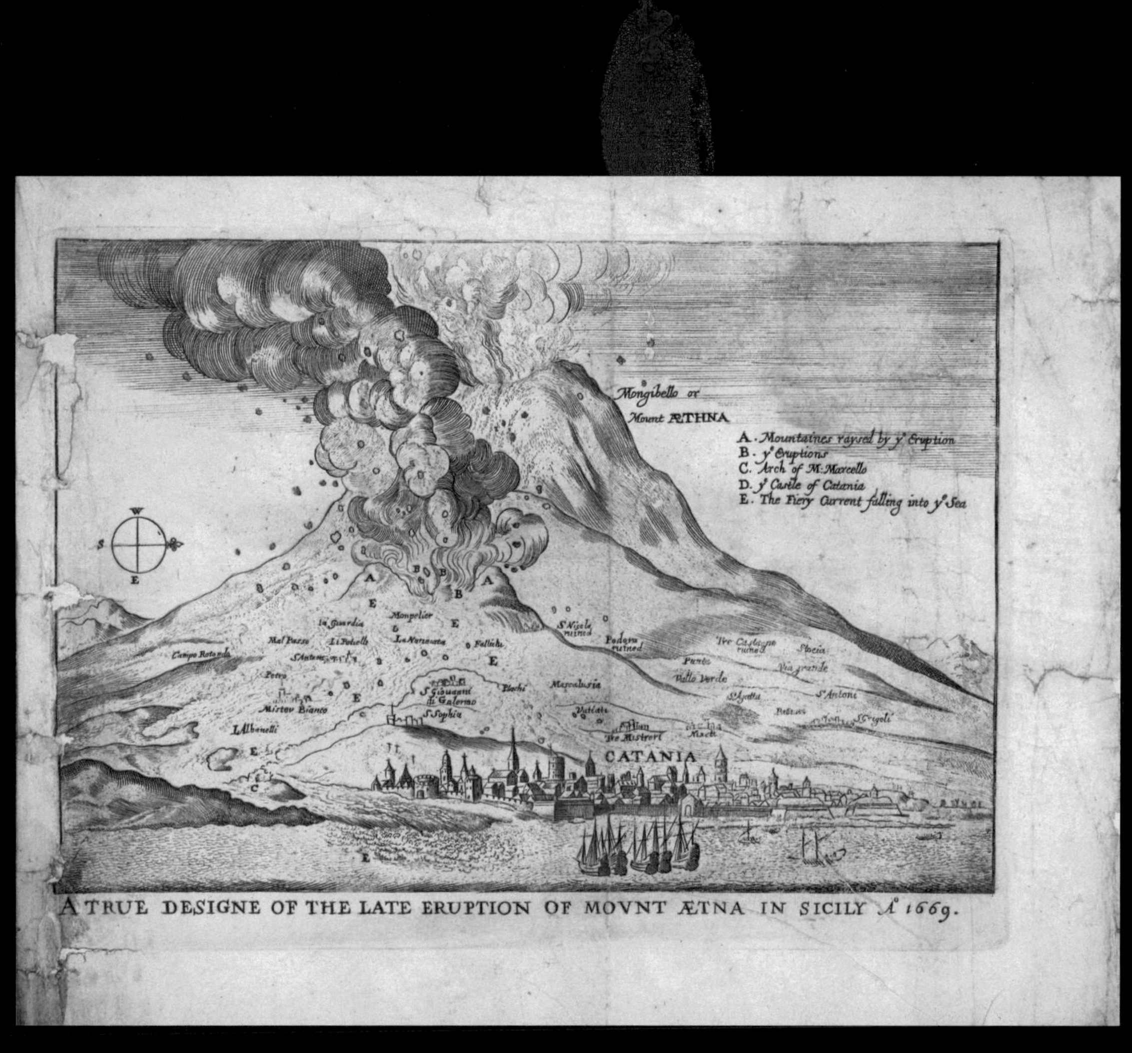

84 Heneage Finch, third Earl of Winchilsea (1627/8–1689)
True and Exact Relation of the Late Prodigious Earthquake
[London]: Printed by T. Newcomb in the Savoy, 1669
135- 331q, btw. pp. 30–31

HENEAGE FINCH WAS THE ENGLISH AMBASSADOR in Constantinople (Istanbul) during the 1660s. On a voyage home in 1669, he stopped off in Sicily to see the lava flows caused by the devastating eruption of Mount Etna and jotted down his impressions. Of course, natural disasters always made good news. After Winchilsea hastily completed his eyewitness account, it went through a number of printings in quick succession.

The TATLER.

The London Gazette.

Proteſtant Mercury.

The SPECTATOR.

THE FINAL PHASE OF THE RENAISSANCE witnessed rapid change within the newspaper industry, and the period after the collapse of censorship in 1679 saw the appearance of titles and trends which would shape the modern newspaper. It is to this period that we owe the idea of the topical magazine, as well as the very first attempt to produce the daily newspaper.

The Impartial Protestant Mercury

From Tuesday, *September* 20. to Friday *September* 23. 1681.

85 *The Impartial Protestant Mercury*, 44 (September 20–23, 1681)
London: Printed for Richard Janeway, 1681
I87.5, title page

THE CROWN'S NEWSPAPER MONOPOLY broke down temporarily during the campaign to exclude the Catholic Duke of York from the royal succession, thereby enabling a range of highly political papers to emerge. This Whig title offered a counterweight to the *Gazette*, to which its contemporary reader here compares its coverage. On this occasion, the *Mercury* provided a vivid picture of political tension on the streets of London, defended religious non-conformists, and supported Titus Oates' allegations regarding the existence of a "popish plot."

Numb. 85.

The London Gazette.

Publiſhed by Authority.

From Monday, Septemb. 3. to Monday, Septemb. 10. 1666.

White-hall, Sept. 8.

THe ordinary courſe of this Paper having been interrupted by a ſad and lamentable accident of Fire lately hapned in the City of *London:* It hath been thought fit for ſatisfying the minds of ſo many of His Majeſties good Subjects, who muſt needs be concerned for the Iſſue of ſo great an accident, to give this ſhort, but true Accompt of it.

On the ſecond inſtant at one of the clock in the Morning there hapned to break out a ſad & deplorable Fire, in *Pudding-lane* neer *New Fiſhſtreet*, which falling out at that hour of the night, and in a quarter of the Town ſo cloſe built with wooden pitched houſes, ſpread it ſelf ſo far before day, and with ſuch diſtraction to the Inhabitants and Neighbours, that care was not taken for the timely preventing the further diffuſion of it by pulling down houſes, as ought to have been; ſo that this lamentable Fire in a ſhort time became too big to be maſtered by any Engines or working neer it. It fell out moſt unhappily too, That a violent Eaſterly wind fomented it, and kept it burning all that day, and the night following ſpreading it ſelf up to *Grace-church*-ſtreet, and downwards from *Cannon-ſtreet* to the Water-ſide as far as the *Three Crans in the Vintrey*.

The people in all parts about it diſtracted by the vaſtneſs of it, and their particular care to carry away their Goods, many attempts were made to prevent the ſpreading of it, by pulling down Houſes, and making great Intervals, but all in vain, the Fire ſeiſing upon the Timber and Rubbiſh, and ſo continuing it ſelf, even through thoſe ſpaces, and raging in a bright Flame all Monday and Tueſday, notwithſtanding His Majeſties own, and His Royal Highneſs's indefatigable and perſonal pains to apply all poſſible remedies to prevent it, calling upon and helping the people with their Guards; and a great number of Nobility and Gentry unweariedly aſſiſting therein, for which they were requited with a thouſand bleſſings from the poor diſtreſſed people. By the favour of God the Wind ſlackned a little on Tueſday night, and the Flames meeting with Brick-buildings at the Temple, by little and little it was obſerved to loſe its force on that ſide, ſo that on Wedneſday morning we began to hope well, and his Royal Highneſs never diſpairing or ſlackning his perſonal care wrought ſo well that day, aſſiſted in ſome parts by the Lords of the Councel before and behind it, that a ſtop was put to it at the *Temple Church*, neer *Holborn-bridge*, *Pie-corner*, *Alderſgate*, *Cripple-gate*, neer the lower end of *Colemanſtreet*, at the end of *Baſing hall ſtreet*, by the *Poſtern*, at the upper end of *Biſhopſgate ſtreet*, and *Leadenhall-ſtreet*, at the *Standard* in *Cornhill*, at the Church in *Fanchurch ſtreet*, neer *Clothworkers-hall* in *Mincing-lane*, at the middle of *Mark-lane*, and at the *Tower dock*.

On thurſday by the bleſſing of God it was wholy beat down and extinguiſhed; but ſo as that Evening it unhappily burſt out again afreſh at the *Temple*, by the falling of ſome ſparks (as is ſuppoſed) upon a Pile of Wooden buildings, But his Royal Highneſs, who watched there that whole night in Perſon, by the great labours and diligence uſed, and eſpecially by applying Powder to blow up the Houſes about it, before day moſt happily maſtered it.

Divers Strangers, Dutch and French, were, during the fire, apprehended, upon ſuſpition that they contributed miſchievouſly to it, who are all impriſoned, and Informations prepared to make a ſevere inquiſition thereupon by my Lord Chief Juſtice *Keeling*, aſſiſted by ſome of the Lords of the Privy Councel, and ſome principal Members of the City; notwithſtanding which ſuſpicions, the manner of the burning all along in a Train, and ſo blowen forwards in all its way by ſtrong winds, makes us conclude the whole was an effect of an unhappy chance, or to ſpeak better, the heavy hand of God upon us for our ſins, ſhowing us the terrour of his Judgment in thus raiſing the fire, and immediately after, his miraculous and never enough to be acknowledged Mercy in putting a ſtop to it when we were in the laſt deſpair, and that all attempts for the quenching it, however induſtriouſly purſued, ſeemed inſufficient. His Majeſty then ſat hourly in Councel, and ever ſince hath continued making rounds about the City in all parts of it where the danger and miſcheif was greateſt, till this morning that he hath ſent his Grace the Duke of *Albemarle*, whom he hath called for to aſſiſt him in this great occaſion, to put his happy and ſucceſsful hand to the finiſhing this memorable deliverance.

About the Tower the ſeaſonable orders given for plucking down Houſes to ſecure the Magazins of Powder, was more eſpecially ſucceſsful, that part being up the Wind, notwithſtanding which it came almoſt to the very Gates of it, ſo as by this early proviſion, the ſeveral ſtores of War lodged in the Tower were entirely ſaved: And we have further this infinite cauſe particularly to give God thanks that the fire did not happen in any of thoſe places where his Majeſties Naval ſtores are kept, ſo as tho it hath pleaſed God to viſit us with his own hand, he hath not, by disfurniſhing us with the means of carrying on the War, ſubjected us to our enemies.

It muſt be obſerved, that this fire happened in a part of the Town, where tho the Commodities were not very rich, yet they were ſo bulky that they could not well be removed, ſo that the Inhabitants of that part where it firſt began have ſuſtained very great loſs, but by the beſt enquiry we can make, the other parts of the Town, where the Commodities were of greater value, took the Alarm ſo early, that they ſaved moſt of their Goods of value, which poſſibly may have diminiſhed the loſs, tho ſome think, that if the whole induſtry of the Inhabitants had been applyed to the ſtopping of the fire, and not to the ſaving of their particular Goods, the ſucceſs might have been much better, not only to the publick, but to many of them in their own particulars.

Through this ſad Accident it is eaſie to be imagined how many perſons were neceſſitated to remove themſelves and Goods into the open fields, where they were forced to continue ſome time, which could not but work compaſſion in the beholders; but his Majeſties care was moſt ſignal in this occaſion, who, beſides his perſonal pains, was frequent in conſulting all wayes for relieving thoſe diſtreſſed perſons, which produced ſo good effect, aſwell by his *Majeſties* Proclamations, and the Orders iſſued to the Neighbour Juſtices of the Peace to encourage the ſending in proviſions to the Markets, which are publickly known, as by other directions, that when his Majeſty, fearing leſt other Orders might not yet have been ſufficient, had commanded the Victualler of his Navy to ſend bread into *Moore-fields* for the relief of the poor, which for the more ſpeedy ſupply he ſent in Bisket out of the Sea ſtores; it was found that the Markets had

Qqqq been

86A *The London Gazette*, 85
(September 3–10, 1666)
London: Printed by Thomas
Newcomb, 1666
L2895a vol. 1, title page

ORIGINALLY BEGUN AS THE *OXFORD GAZETTE* IN 1665, when the royal court left London in order to avoid an terrible outbreak of the plague, this was an official newspaper run by under-secretary of state Joseph Williamson, and written by a series of leading journalists and authors. Renamed and relocated in 1666, it here described the Great Fire of London that had just devastated the capital (Cat. No. 86B). The *Gazette* has been "published by authority" and run uninterrupted ever since, as the official newspaper of record regarding Parliament, the law courts, and royal family.

White-hall, Sept. 8.

THe ordinary courſe of this Paper having been interrupted by a ſad and lamentable accident of Fire lately hapned in the City of *London*: It hath been thought fit for ſatisfying the minds of ſo many of His Majeſties good Subjects, who muſt needs be concerned for the Iſſue of ſo great an accident, to give this ſhort, but true Accompt of it.

On the ſecond inſtant at one of the clock in the Morning there hapned to break out a ſad & deplorable Fire, in *Pudding-lane* neer *New Fiſhſtreet*, which falling out at that hour of the night, and in a quarter of the Town ſo cloſe built with wooden pitched houſes, ſpread it ſelf ſo far before day, and with ſuch diſtraction to the Inhabitants and Neighbours, that care was not taken for the timely preventing the further diffuſion of it by pulling down houſes, as ought to have been; ſo that this lamentable Fire in a ſhort time became too big to be maſtered by any Engines or working neer it. It fell out moſt unhappily too, That a violent Eaſterly wind fomented it, and kept it burning all that day, and the night following ſpreading it ſelf up to *Grace-church*-ſtreet, and downwards from *Cannon-ſtreet* to the Water-ſide as far as the *Three Cranes in the Vintrey*.

86B *The London Gazette*, 85
(September 3–10, 1666)
London: Printed by Thomas Newcomb, 1666
L2895a vol. 1, title page

87 *The Tatler* (July 1710)
London, 1710
PR 1365 T2, no. 193 Cage

THE EARLY EIGHTEENTH CENTURY WITNESSED the emergence of new kinds of serial publications, whose titles are familiar today. The first of these, *The Tatler*, was founded in 1709 by Richard Steele, the sometimes playwright, member of Parliament and former editor of the *London Gazette*, along with his close friend, Joseph Addison. Together they adopted the pseudonym "Isaac Bickerstaff" in order to provide satirical and moral essays, as well as theater criticism, three times a week.

NUMB. 1

The SPECTATOR.

Non fumum ex fulgore, sed ex fumo dare lucem
Cogitat, ut speciosa dehinc miracula promat. Hor.

To be Continued every Day.

Thursday, March 1. 1711.

I Have obſerved, that a Reader ſeldom peruſes a Book with Pleaſure 'till he knows whether the Writer of it be a black or a fair Man, of a mild or cholerick Diſpoſition, Married or a Batchelor, with other Particulars of the like nature, that conduce very much to the right Underſtanding of an Author. To gratify this Curioſity, which is ſo natural to a Reader, I deſign this Paper, and my next, as Prefatory Diſcourſes to my following Writings, and ſhall give ſome Account in them of the ſeveral Perſons that are engaged in this Work. As the chief Trouble of Compiling, Digeſting and Correcting will fall to my Share, I muſt do my ſelf the Juſtice to open the Work with my own Hiſtory.

I was born to a ſmall Hereditary Eſtate, which I find, by the Writings of the Family, was bounded by the ſame Hedges and Ditches in *William* the Conqueror's Time that it is at preſent, and has been delivered down from Father to Son whole and entire, without the Loſs or Acquiſition of a ſingle Field or Meadow, during the Space of ſix hundred Years. There goes a Story in the Family, that when my Mother was gone with Child of me about three Months, ſhe dreamt that ſhe was brought to Bed of a Judge: Whether this might proceed from a Law-Suit which was then depending in the Family, or my Father's being a Juſtice of the Peace, I cannot determine; for I am not ſo vain as to think it preſaged any Dignity that I ſhould arrive at in my future Life, though that was the Interpretation which the Neighbourhood put upon it. The Gravity of my Behaviour at my very firſt Appearance in the World, and all the Time that I ſucked, ſeemed to favour my Mother's Dream: For, as ſhe has often told me, I threw away my Rattle before I was two Months old, and would not make uſe of my Coral 'till they had taken away the Bells from it.

As for the reſt of my Infancy, there being nothing in it remarkable, I ſhall paſs it over in Silence. I find, that, during my Nonage, I had the Reputation of a very ſullen Youth, but was always a Favourite of my School-Maſter, who uſed to ſay, *that my Parts were ſolid and would wear well.* I had not been long at the Univerſity, before I diſtinguiſhed my ſelf by a moſt profound Silence: For, during the Space of eight Years, excepting in the publick Exerciſes of the College, I ſcarce uttered the Quantity of an hundred Words; and indeed do not remember that I ever ſpoke three Sentences together in my whole Life. Whilſt I was in this Learned Body I applied my ſelf with ſo much Diligence to my Studies, that there are very few celebrated Books, either in the Learned or the Modern Tongues, which I am not acquainted with.

Upon the Death of my Father I was reſolved to travel into Foreign Countries, and therefore left the Univerſity, with the Character of an odd unaccountable Fellow, that had a great deal of Learning, if I would but ſhow it. An inſatiable Thirſt after Knowledge carried me into all the Countries of *Europe*, where there was any thing new or ſtrange to be ſeen; nay, to ſuch a Degree was my Curioſity raiſed, that having read the Controverſies of ſome great Men concerning the Antiquities of *Egypt*, I made a Voyage to *Grand Cairo*, on purpoſe to take the Meaſure of a Pyramid; and as ſoon as I had ſet my ſelf right in that Particular, returned to my Native Country with great Satisfaction.

I have paſſed my latter Years in this City, where I am frequently ſeen in moſt publick Places, tho' there are not above half a dozen of my ſelect Friends that know me; of whom my next Paper ſhall give a more particular Account. There is no Place of publick Reſort, wherein I do not often make my Appearance; ſometimes I am ſeen thruſting my Head into a Round of Politicians at *Will's*, and liſtning with great Attention to the Narratives that are made in thoſe little Circular Audiences. Sometimes I ſmoak a Pipe at *Child's*; and whilſt I ſeem attentive to nothing but the *Poſt-Man*, over-hear the Converſation of every Table in the Room. I appear on *Sunday* Nights at St. *James's* Coffee-Houſe, and ſometimes join the little Committee of Politicks in the Inner-Room, as one who comes there to hear and improve. My Face is likewiſe very well known at the *Grecian*, the *Cocoa-Tree*, and in the Theaters both of *Drury-Lane*, and the *Hay-Market*. I have been taken for a Merchant

upon

88 *The Spectator*, 1 (1711)
London, 1711
, title page

AFTER THE CLOSURE OF *THE TATLER* by the Tory government, Addison and Steele quickly re-emerged with a daily journal, and another immensely successful title that is familiar to modern readers. In this first issue, Addison promised to "observe" rather than comment, and to maintain "an exact neutrality between the Whigs and Tories." As a regular visitor to London's coffeehouses, he boasted about his ability to provide gossip that had been gleaned by "thrusting my head into a round of politicians."

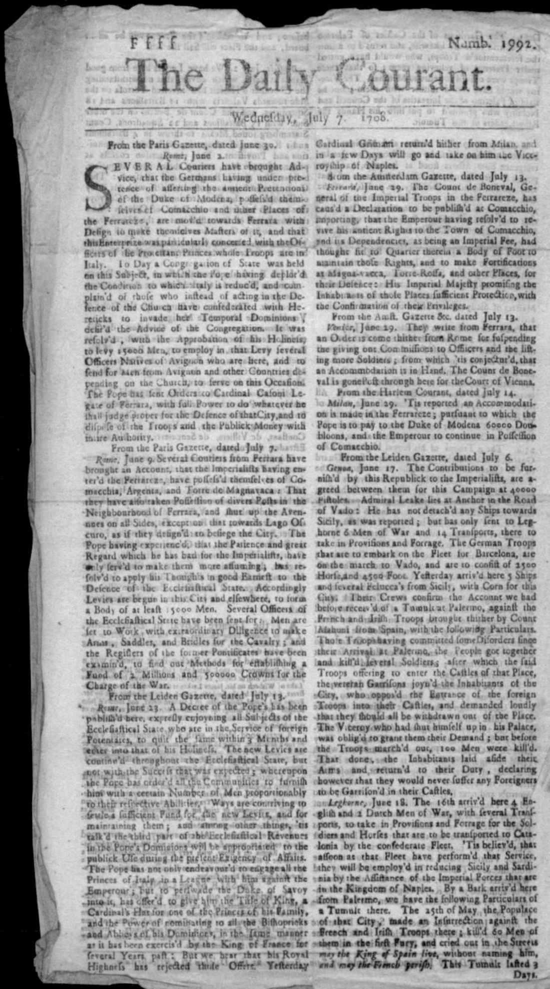

89 *The Daily Courant*, 1992
(July 7, 1708)
London, 1708
187- 474q, title page

MARCH 1702 SAW THE LAUNCH OF THE FIRST REGULAR DAILY national newspaper from a room above a tavern in Fleet Street. Run by Samuel Buckley, who later wrote the *London Gazette*, it eventually came under the political and financial control of the government, and survived until 1735. It generally provided stories culled from European newspapers, although this issue also advertised a performance of "The London Cuckolds" at the Theatre Royal in Drury Lane.

GOOD

NEWVES FROM

VIRGINIA.

SENT TO THE COVNSELL
and Company of VIRGINIA, reſident
in England.

FROM ALEXANDER WHITAKER, THE
Miniſter of HENRICO in
Virginia.

WHEREIN ALSO IS A NARRATION
of the preſent State of that Countrey, and
our Colonies there.

Peruſed and publiſhed by direction
from that Counſell.

NEWS ABOUT AMERICA BECAME INCREASINGLY POPULAR during the seventeenth century. Stories of the wide open fertile land and the opportunities for colonization flourished alongside contradictory accounts of both friendly and hostile Native Americans. *Publick Occurrences*—the first American newspaper—was printed in the late seventeenth century, although it was quickly suppressed by the colonial government. It was not until 1704 that the *Boston News-Letter* became America's first continuous newspaper.

GOOD

NEWES FROM

VIRGINIA.

SENT TO THE COVNSELL and Company of VIRGINIA, resident in England.

FROM ALEXANDER WHITAKER, THE Minister of HENRICO in Virginia.

WHEREIN ALSO IS A NARRATION of the present State of that Countrey, and our Colonies there.

Perused and published by direction from that Counsell.

And a Preface prefixed of some matters touching that Plantation, very requisite to be made knowne.

AT LONDON,
Imprinted by Felix Kyngston for WILLIAM WELBY, and are to be sold at his Shop in Pauls Church-yard at the signe of the Swanne 1613.

90 Alexander Whitaker (1585–1617)
Good Newes from Virginia
London: Imprinted by Felix Kyngston for William Welby and are to be sold at his shop in Paul's Church-yard at the signe of the Swanne, 1613
F229 .W57 English Print Copy 1
Courtesy of the Library of Congress

ALEXANDER WHITAKER TRAVELED TO VIRGINIA IN 1611 and became the minister at the newly established settlement of Henrico. In England, people were eager to read the news from America and the Virginia Company published this pamphlet, written in the form of a letter, in which Whitaker attacked the hold of Native American priests over their people. However, he also saw hope for their eventual conversion to Christianity and he achieved success the following year with the conversion of Pocahontas.

1

Newes from *America*, or a late and experimentall diſcoverie of *New England*.

I Shall not ſpend time (for my other occaſions will not permit) to write largely of every particular, but ſhall as briefly as I may performe theſe two things, firſt give a true narration, of the warre-like proceedings that hath been in *New England* theſe two years laſt paſt. Secondly, I ſhall diſcover to the Reader divers places in *New England*, that would afford ſpeciall accommodations to ſuch perſons as will plant upon them, I had not time to doe either of theſe as they deſerved, but wanting time to doe it as the nature of the thing required; I ſhall according to my abilitie begin with a Relation of our warre-like proceedings, and will inter-weave the ſpeciall places fit for *New Plantations*, with their deſcription, as I ſhall find occaſion in the following diſcourſe, but I ſhall according to my promiſe begin with a true relation of the new

A 3 *England*

91 John Underhill
(c. 1608–1672)
Newes from America
London: Printed by I. D[awson] for Peter Cole, and are to be sold at the signe of the Glove in Corne-hill neere the Royall Exchange, 1638.
E83.63 .U55 English Print Copy 1
Courtesy of the Library of Congress

IN 1630, JOHN UNDERHILL EMIGRATED TO AMERICA and became a captain in the militia of the Massachusetts Bay Colony. In 1636, he led an attack on a fortified Pequot village in which many hundreds were killed. Underhill published news of his military success in this pamphlet that also extolled the virtues of the land of New England for plantation. Inside the pamphlet, a vivid depiction of the battle highlights the power of the gun over the bow and arrow and the fact that many Pequot seem to have been slaughtered.

Numb. 1.

PUBLICK OCCURRENCES

Both *FORREIGN* and *DOMESTICK*.

Boſton, Thurſday *Sept.* 25*th*. 1690.

IT is deſigned, that the Countrey ſhall be furniſhed once a moneth (or if any Glut of Occurrences happen, oftener,) with an Account of ſuch conſiderable things as have arrived unto our Notice.

In order hereunto, the Publiſher will take what pains he can to obtain a Faithful Relation *of all ſuch things; and will particularly make himſelf beholden to ſuch Perſons in* Boſton *whom he knows to have been for their own uſe the diligent Obſervers of ſuch matters.*

That which is herein propoſed, is, Firſt, *That* Memorable Occurrents *of* Divine Providence *may not be neglected or forgotten, as they too often are.* Secondly, *That people every where may better underſtand the Circumſtances of Publique Affairs, both abroad and at home; which may not only direct their* Thoughts *at all times, but at ſome times alſo to aſſiſt their* Buſineſſes *and* Negotiations.

Thirdly, *That ſome thing may be done towards the* Curing, *or at leaſt the* Charming *of that* Spirit of Lying, *which prevails amongſt us, whe efore nothing ſhall be entered, but what we have reaſon to believe is true, repairing to the beſt fountains for our Information. And when there appears* any material miſtake *in any thing that is collected, it ſhall be* corrected *in the* next.

Moreover, the Publiſher of theſe Occurrences *is willing to engage, that whereas, there are many* Falſe Reports, *maliciouſly made, and ſpread among us, if any well-minded perſon will be at the pains to trace any ſuch* falſe Report *ſo far as to find out and Convict the* Firſt Raiſer *of it, he will in this Paper (unleſs juſt Advice be given to the contrary) expoſe the Name of ſuch perſon, as* A malicious Raiſer of a falſe Report. *It is ſuppos'd that none will diſlike this Propoſal, but ſuch as intend to be guilty of ſo villanous a Crime.*

THE Chriſtianized *Indians* in ſome parts of *Plimouth*, have newly appointed a day of Thanksgiving to God for his Mercy in ſupplying their extream and pinching Neceſſities under their late want of Corn, & for His giving them now a proſpect of a very *Comfortable Harveſt*. Their Example may be worth Mentioning.

'Tis obſerved by the Husbandmen, that altho' the With-draw of ſo great a ſtrength from them, as what is in the Forces lately gone for *Canada*; made them think it almoſt impoſſible for them to get well through the Affairs of their Husbandry at this time of the year, yet the Seaſon has been ſo unuſually favourable that they ſcarce find any want of the many hundreds of hands, that are gone from them; which is looked upon as a Merciful Providence

While the barbarous *Indians* were lurking about *Chelmsford*, there were miſſing about the beginning of this month a couple of Children belonging to a man of that Town, one of them aged about eleven, the other aged about nine years, both of them ſuppoſed to be fallen into the hands of the *Indians*.

A very *Tragical Accident* happened at *Water-Town*, the beginning of this Month, an *Old man*, that was of ſomewhat a Silent and Moroſe Temper, but one that had long Enjoyed the reputation of a *Sober* and a *Pious Man*, having newly buried his Wife, The Devil took advantage of the Melancholy which he thereupon fell into, his Wives diſcretion and induſtry had long been the ſupport of his Family, and he ſeemed hurried with an impertinent fear that he ſhould now come to want before he dyed, though he had very careful friends to look after him who kept a ſtrict eye upon him, leaſt he ſhould do himſelf any harm. But one evening eſcaping from them into the Cow-houſe, they there quickly followed him found him *hanging by a Rope*, which they had uſed to tye their *Calves* withal, he was dead with his feet near touching the Ground.

Epidemical *Fevers* and *Agues* grow very common, in ſome parts of the Country, whereof, tho' many dye not, yet they are ſorely unfitted for their imployments; but in ſome parts a more *malignant Fever* ſeems to prevail in ſuch ſort that it uſually goes thro' a Family where it comes, and proves *Mortal* unto many.

The *Small-pox* which has been raging in *Boſton*, after a manner very Extraordinary is now very much abated. It is thought that far more have been ſick of it then were viſited with it, when it raged ſo much twelve years ago, nevertheleſs it has not been ſo Mortal, The number of them that have

92A *Publick Occurrences Both Forreign and Domestick*, 1 (September 25, 1690)
Boston: Printed by R. Pierce for Benjamin Harris at the London Coffee-House, 1690
CO 5/855, item 121
Courtesy of the National Archives

THE FIRST NEWSPAPER PUBLISHED IN AMERICA, *Publick Occurrences*, appeared in Boston on September 25, 1690. The publisher, Benjamin Harris, had fled to America after a lengthy and highly provocative career printing newspapers in England. Shortly after his arrival in 1686 he set up the London Coffee House and established a printing press. *Publick Occurrences* was marketed as a periodical which would appear monthly with foreign and domestic news, snippets about God's intervention in human affairs and items of business interest (Cat. No 92B). However, the first issue was also to be the last. The Governor and Council of Massachusetts quickly issued a broadside to suppress the unlicensed paper. They found some "reflections of a very high nature"—a scandalous implication. The report that Louis XIV of France had slept with his daughter-in-law and another item which questioned the worth of Native American allies ensured its suppression.

IT is designed, that the Countrey shall be furnished once a moneth (or if any Glut of Occurrences happen, oftener,) with an Account of such considerable things as have arrived unto our Notice.

In order hereunto, the Publisher will take what pains he can to obtain a Faithful Relation of all such things; and will particularly make himself beholden to such Persons in Boston whom he knows to have been for their own use the diligent Observers of such matters.

That which is herein proposed, is, First, That Memorable Occurrents of Divine Providence may not be neglected or forgotten, as they too often are. Secondly, That people every where may better understand the Circumstances of Publique Affairs, both abroad and at home; which may not only direct their Thoughts at all times, but at some times also to assist their Businesses and Negotiations.

Thirdly, That some thing may be done towards the Curing, or at least the Charming of that Spirit of Lying, which prevails amongst us, wherefore nothing shall be entered, but what we have reason to believe is true, repairing to the best fountains for our Information. And when there appears any material mistake in any thing that is collected, it shall be corrected in the next.

Moreover, the Publisher of these Occurrences is willing to engage, that whereas, there are many False Reports, maliciously made, and spread among us, if any well-minded person will be at the pains to trace any such false Report so far as to find out and Convict the First Raiser of it, he will in this Paper (unless just Advice be given to to the contrary) expose the Name of such person, as A malicious Raiser of a false Report. It is suppos'd that none will dislike this Proposal, but such as intend to be guilty of so villanous a Crime.

92B *Publick Occurrences Both Forreign and Domestick*, 1 (September 25, 1690)
Boston: Printed by R. Pierce for Benjamin Harris at the London Coffee-House, 1690
CO 5/855, item 121
Courtesy of the National Archives

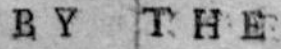

BY THE

GOVERNOUR & COUNCIL

WHEREAS *ſome have lately preſumed to Print and Diſperſe a Pamphlet, Entituled*, Publick Occurrences, both Foreign and Domeſtick: Boſton, Thurſday, *Septemb.* 25*th*. 1690. *Without the leaſt Privity or Countenance of Authority.*

The Governour and Council having had the peruſal of the ſaid Pamphlet, and finding that therein is contained Reflections of a very high nature: As alſo ſundry doubtful and uncertain Reports, do hereby manifeſt and declare their high Reſentment and Diſallowance of ſaid Pamphlet, and Order that the ſame be Suppreſſed and called in; ſtrictly forbidding any perſon or perſons for the future to Set forth any thing in Print without Licence firſt obtained from thoſe that are or ſhall be appointed by the Government to grant the ſame.

By Order of the Governour & Council.

Iſaac Addington, Secr.

Boſton, September 29*th*. 1690.

93 *By the Governour & Council. A Proclamation Suppressing Publick Occurrences.*
Boston: September 29, 1690
BDSDS 1690
Courtesy of the American Antiquarian Society

N. E. Numb. 1

The Boſton News-Letter.

Publiſhed by Authority.

From Monday April 17. to Monday April 24. 1704.

London Flying-Poſt from *Decemb.* 2*d.* to 4*th.* 1703.

LEtters from *Scotland* bring us the Copy of a Sheet lately Printed there, Intituled, *A ſeaſonable Alarm for* Scotland. *In a Letter from a Gentleman in the City, to his Friend in the Country, concerning the preſent Danger of the Kingdom and of the Proteſtant Religion.*

This Letter takes Notice, That Papiſts ſwarm in that Nation, that they traffick more avowedly than formerly, and that of late many Scores of Prieſts & Jeſuites are come thither from France, and gone to the North, to the Highlands & other places of the Country. That the Miniſters of the Highlands and North gave in large Liſts of them to the Committee of the General Aſſembly, to be laid before the Privy-Council.

It likewiſe obſerves, that a great Number of other ill-affected perſons are come over from *France*, under pretence of accepting her Majeſty's Gracious Indemnity; but, in reality, to increaſe Diviſions in the Nation, and to entertain a Correſpondence with *France*: That their ill Intentions are evident from their talking big, their owning the Intereſt of the pretended King *James* VIII. their ſecret Cabals, and their buying up of Arms and Ammunition, wherever they can find them.

To this he adds the late Writinge and Actings of ſome diſaffected perſons, many of whom are for that Pretender; that ſeveral of them have declar'd they had rather embrace Popery than conform to the preſent Government; that they refuſe to pray for the Queen, but uſe the ambiguous word Soveraign, and ſome of them pray in expreſs Words for the King and Royal Family; and the charitable and generous Prince who has ſhew'd them ſo much Kindneſs. He likewiſe takes notice of Letters, not long ago found in Cypher, & directed to a Perſon lately come thither from St. *Germains*.

He ſays that the greateſt Jacobites, who will not qualifie themſelves by taking the Oaths to Her Majeſty, do now with the Papiſts and their Companions from St. *Germains* ſet up for the Liberty of the Subject, contrary to their own Principles, but meerly to keep up a Diviſion in the Nation. He adds, that they aggravate thoſe things which the People complain of, as to *England's* refuſing to allow them a freedom of Trade, &c. and do all they can to foment Diviſions betwixt the Nations, & to obſtruct a Redreſs of thoſe things complain'd of.

The Jacobites, he ſays, do all they can to perſuade the Nation that their pretended King is a Proteſtant in his Heart, tho' he dares not declare it while under the Power of *France*; that he is acquainted with the Miſtakes of his Father's Government, will govern us more according to Law, and endear himſelf to his Subjects.

They magnifie the Strength of their own Party, and the Weakneſs and Diviſions of the other, in order to facilitate and haſte their Undertaking; they argue themſelves out of their Fears, and into the higheſt aſſurance of accompliſhing their purpoſe.

From all this he infers, That they have hopes of Aſſiſtance from *France*, otherwiſe they would never be ſo impudent; and he gives Reaſons for his Apprehenſions that the *French* King may ſend Troops thither this Winter, 1. Becauſe the *Engliſh* & *Dutch* will not then be at Sea to oppoſe them. 2. He can then beſt ſpare them, the Seaſon of Action beyond Sea being over. 3. The Expectation given him of a conſiderable number to joyn them, may incourage him to the undertaking with fewer Men, if he can but ſend over a ſufficient number of Officers with Arms and Ammunition.

He endeavours in the reſt of his Letters to anſwer the fooliſh Pretences of the Pretender's being a Proteſtant, and that he will govern us according to Law. He ſays, that being bred up in the Religion and Politicks of *France*, he is by Education a ſtated Enemy to our Liberty and Religion. That the Obligations which he and his Family owe to the *French* King muſt neceſſarily make him to be wholly at his Devotion, and to follow his Example; that if he ſit upon the Throne, the three Nations muſt be oblig'd to pay the Debt which he owes the *French* King for the Education of himſelf, and for Entertaining his ſuppoſed Father and his Family. And ſince the King muſt reſtore him by his Troops, if ever he be reſtored, he will ſee to ſecure his own Debt, before thoſe Troops leave *Britain*. The Pretender being a good Proficient in the *French* and *Romiſh* Schools, he will never think himſelf ſufficiently aveng'd, but by the utter Ruine of his Proteſtant Subjects, both as Hereticks and Traitors. The late Queen, his pretended Mother, who in cold Blood when ſhe was Queen of *Britain*, advis'd to turn the Weſt of *Scotland* into a hunting Field, will be then for doing ſo by the greateſt part of the Nation; and, no doubt, is at Pains to have her pretended Son educated to her own Mind: Therefore, he ſays, it were a great Madneſs in the Nation to take a Prince bred up in the horrid School of Ingratitude, Perſecution and Cruelty, and filled with Rage and Envy. The *Jacobites*, he ſays, both in *Scotland* and at St. *Germains*, are impatient under their preſent Straits, and knowing their Circumſtances cannot be much worſe than they are, at preſent, are the more inclinable to the Undertaking. He adds, That the *French* King knows there cannot be a more effectual way for himſelf to arrive at the Univerſal Monarchy, and to ruine the Proteſtant Intereſt, than by ſetting up the Pretender upon the Throne of Great *Britain*, he will in all probability attempt it; and tho' he ſhould be perſuaded that the Deſign would miſcarry in the cloſe, yet he cannot but reap ſome Advantage by imbroiling the three Nations.

From all this the Author concludes it to be the Intereſt of the Nation, to provide for Self defence; and ſays, that as many have already taken the Alarm, and are furniſhing themſelves with Arms and Ammunition, he hopes the Government will not only allow it, but encourage it, ſince the Nation ought all to appear as one Man in the Defence

94 *The Boston News-Letter*, 1 (April 17–24, 1704)
Boston: John Campbell, 1704
News–Apr. 17-24, 1704
Courtesy of the American Antiquarian Society

THE FIRST CONTINUOUSLY PUBLISHED NEWSPAPER IN AMERICA, the *Boston News-Letter*, started on April 24, 1704. Its editor was John Campbell, the postmaster of Boston. It appeared weekly as a single-sheet printed on both sides. In the first issue Campbell reprinted news from England, taken directly from two English newspapers, the *London Gazette* and the *Flying Post.* In addition, the first issue featured a column of local news focusing upon shipping as well as a report of an "excellent sermon" preached at the Old South Church in Boston. It continued publication until 1776.

Joyners — — — 95
nholders — — — 101
ronmongers — — —103
Leatherſellers —— — 105
Merchant Taylors — 109
Mercers — — — 118
Muſicians — — — 122
Maſons — — — 123
Painterſtainers — — 124
Plumbers — — — 127
Poulterers — — — 129
Pewterers — — — 130
Plaiſterers — — — 133
Salters — — — 135
Stationers — — — 138
Skinners — — — 143
Scriveners — — — 147
Sadlers — — — 148
Tallowchandlers— — 150
Turners — — — 153
Vintners — — — 155
Upholders — — — 160
Weavers — — — 168
Waxchandlers — — 167
Glaſs-ſellers — — 170
An Alphabetical Liſt of the

Apothecaries.	*Heathcote*	*Aſhhurſt*	*Bateman*	*Ward*
Mic. Armſtead				
Si. Andrews	—	—	—	—
John Acklam	—	—	—	—
John Broughton	—	—	—	—
David Boncheret	—	—	—	—
Edward Baker	—	—	—	—
Joſ. Biſcoe	—	—	—	—
John Blackſtone	—			
Tho. Bromfield				
Peregrine Browne	—	—	—	—
Sam. Birch				
Daniel Baxter				
John Biſcoe	—	—	—	—
William Browning	—	—	—	—
Nathaniel Brook	—	—	—	—
George Bew				
Richard Chapman				
Robert Catterell	—	—	—	—
Samuel Chapman			—	—
Francis Conde	—	—	—	—
Joſeph Cruttendon	—	—	—	—
Thomas Drury	—	—		

NATIONAL ELECTIONS ONCE TOOK PLACE without extensive media coverage and in the absence of well-oiled party machines. However, this is an area where the seventeenth century witnessed key experiments and innovations. Integral to the upheavals of the period were issues regarding who should be able to vote, and what power the electorate ought to have over their representatives. A range of pamphlets and prints were produced in order to influence voters, provide them with information regarding politicians, and record the proceedings at elections.

(1)

Some Advertiſements for the new Election of Burgeſſes for the Houſe of COMMONS.

Anno 1645.

IN this great and weightie buſineſſe of electing fit perſons to fill up the much-decayed Houſe of Commons, I will beſtow upon my dear Countrey an Admonition for rectifying their judgements: My Admonition will be two-fold. Vpon the firſt I will not inſiſt, becauſe it is ſufficiently treated of by * Mr. *Withers*. It is againſt electing ſuch men whom Fooles admire for their *Wealth*. The ſecond part, is againſt chooſing ſuch men, whom Fooles admire for their *Wit*, *Lawyers*. This Vice muſt be thorowly handled.

* *Vox Pacifica.*

* When Rome was in her integritie, the great men ſtudied the Lawes, and pleaded the cauſe of the poore without fee, *Jure Clientelæ*: Everie eminent man having many hundreds, nay, ſome thouſands of poore men under their protection, for whom they did, *reſpondere de jure*, make defence in Law. This was a mutuall Obligation of common charitie; and theſe unfeed Patrons were juſtly ſtiled, *Sacerdotes Juſtitiæ*, Prieſts of *Themis* the Goddeſſe of juſtice. But afterwards, *Cum abundantes divitiæ deſiderium invexere per luxum atque libidinem pereundi perdendique omnia*: When abundant wealth brought in luxurie to afflict the manners of the Common-wealth, they grew into corruption with the times, took fees, and became *viles rabulæ*, Hackney Petty-foggers, and Huckſters of the Law.

* *Dion. Halicarn. l. 2. Livius l. 1. Plutarch. in Romulo. The like was uſed amongſt the Theſſalians, who called theſe kind of Clients, Peneſtæ. And amongſt the Athenians, who called them Thetæ. Lazius Comment. Reipub. Rom. lib. 12. c. 3. Dempſter. Antiquitatum Rom. lib. 1. c. 16, 17. Car. Sigon. de Antiquo Jure Civium Rom.*

Now, though our Lawyers were never in that ſtate of innocencie, to practiſe without Fee, yet were they never in that height of corruption, and unlimited way of gain, they are now in. I have heard old men ſay, they remembred when Lawyers at the beginning of a Term, would ſtand at a pillar

A in

95 *Some Advertisements for the New Election of Burgesses for the House of Commons* [London, 1645] 178- 721q, title page

AS THE SEVENTEENTH CENTURY PROGRESSED, parliamentary elections were increasingly dominated by political divisions rather than gentlemanly agreements. One result of this change was the increased need to win over the electorate by force of argument. This short tract, perhaps distributed freely among electors, is among the earliest surviving pieces of electoral propaganda. It did not favor individual candidates, however, but merely made general recommendations, notably that voters should avoid choosing men from the propertied elite, or professional lawyers.

(1)

Englands Remembrancers.

O R,

A word in ſeaſon to all Engliſh men about their Elections of the members for the approaching Parliament.

Dear Chriſtian friends and Countrey-men

E have all reaſon to complain, and ſay, this day is a day of trouble, rebuke, and blaſphemy; our country that was great among the nations is now become vile, all her friends have dealt treacherouſly with her, they are become her enemies; how is the profeſſion of holineſſe (by the unrighteouſneſſe amongſt us) blaſted with the names of hypocriſie, falſeneſſe, ambition and covetouſneſſe? how is the glory and ſtrength of our nation ſpoiled, and the bloud of many thouſands poured forth in waſt like water? how is the treaſure exhauſted, trade and commerce deſtroyed? and how are all our rights, liberties and properties invaded, and ſubverted by arbitrary powers and force of armes? who can ſay his life or eſtate is ſecured for a moment, if the jealouſie, envy, pride, luſt or covetouſneſſe of ſome in power pleaſe to command it? and how is deſtruction threatned daily by forreign enemies? ſurely the day of the Lord is very great and terrible againſt us, and yet there is mercy with him that he might be feared, for in his abundant goodneſſe he ſeems to open a door of hope, and to give us all leave by our Deputies to adviſe the means of our ſafety and peace; and the preſent writts for election of our repreſentatives being the product of divine providence, and we are confident not long ſince, beyond the thoughts of thoſe that ſent them forth, may be juſtly looked upon as the voice of God to you all ſaying; gather the people, call a ſolemn Aſſembly, go and reaſon together, for in the multitude of councell there is ſafety. Dear Chriſtians, it is by the choice of your Deputies only, that the whole body politick of this nation can conſult together for their preſervation by this means only you may all ſpeak your minds, one to another and every one to the whole nation; it is the naturall way to ſettle your Government, and provide for your common good, and in your preſent caſe,

A there

96 *Englands Remembrancers*
[London, 1656]
144- 687q, title page

WITHOUT NAMING SPECIFIC CANDIDATES, this controversial tract pursued a very clear political agenda: opposing the regime of Oliver Cromwell, and advocating a policy of religious toleration. By scattering copies about the streets in a number of towns and cities, and by encouraging voters to organize meetings in order to discuss individual candidates and issues, its authors and publishers caused serious concern within the government. As a result, a concerted effort—ultimately unsuccessful—was made to locate and punish those involved.

A

SPEECH

Made at

Nottingham,

April 2. 1660.

At the Election of

Arthur Stanhope Eſquire,

and

Collonel *John Huchinſon*,

Their Burgeſſes to ſerve in the next Parliament.

LONDON,

Printed for *H. B.* 1660.

97 Charles Howard (1610–1681)
A Speech Made at Nottingham
London: For H.B., 1660
185- 960q, title page

PRINT HELPED TO TRANSFORM THE RELATIONSHIP between the public and their representatives, not least by increasing the possibilities for holding politicians to account. In part this involved making public the advice and instructions given to officials upon their election, as with this pamphlet containing the exhortation delivered to Nottingham's two members of Parliament in 1660. The tract attempted to heal the divisions of the recent Civil Wars, defend the Church of England, and protect the local interests of the town.

THE

FANATICK RAMPANT

OR AN

ELECTION

AT

CAMBRIDGE.

ONE day I heard a zealous ſhout
I then lookt up and loe the rout
of Saints were come to town.
Who by their Hats right gravely ſet.
And Collar-bands I gueſs were met
to cry the Biſhops down.

But ſee how groſly I did err.
For they came only to prepare
againſt that Godly buſtle.
And therefore did moſt fervently
With carnal Throats extended cry,
a *Ruſſel*, yea, a *Ruſſel*.

Some cry'd a *Ruſſel*, ſome again
Miſtook the Name and cry'd *Amen*.
ſome with erected fiſt
Cry'd O, we find by Revelation
That this is he muſt heal the Nation
and hamſtring Antichriſt.

At length there comes me a Freeholder
With head inclin'd to the left ſhouder
and Circumciſed hair. (vel
VVho with his ſnout all wet with ſni-
and looks enough to ſcare a Devil
Did thus begin his Prayer.

Lord, if thou dos't thy Saints regard
Look on the keepers of thy Heard
Even on thy choſen *Ruſſel*.
See but what honour we have done him
And then, thou needs muſt powre upon
Thy bleſſings by the Buſhel. (him

Thy tender flock (Lord) hel'e not pound
but doth regard the Poor.
Lord he hath done more for my Wife
Than er'e I did in all my life,
O bleſſed Senator.

Do thou in time his Worſhip bring
To be, to be, a Lordiſh thing.
as was his noble Kin. ——
Thou ſeeſt how he alone doth ſtand,
And hates the great ones of the Land.
O well doth he begin.

Then give him grace Lord not to ceaſe
Till he hath broke the Cord of Peace,
That Girdle of the VVhore.
That we again may ſee that day.
In which we all may preach and pray.
and then il'e ask no more.

With that I ſpy'd an Image fair
High mounted in his ſtately Chair.
I think to mock the Pope.
Down Brethren, to the Gallowes gang.
Said I, he ſhall not burn but hang
though I pay for the Rope.

98 *The Fanatick Rampant, or an Election at Cambridge*
[London], 1679
254- 498q, title page

THE TWO GENERAL ELECTIONS IN 1679 were particularly controversial, as Whigs campaigned to alter the line of royal succession in order to prevent the Catholic Duke of York from taking the throne. In this tense atmosphere, print became a powerful means of attacking and mocking individual candidates, as in this "Tory" libel, which conveys the sometimes rowdy nature of elections, and which may have helped to ensure the defeat of one prominent Whig, Gerard Russell. Ballads such as these were a common method of distributing news, particularly on controversial or salacious subjects.

(2)

Q. 9. Who sent Mr. *Buckly* to Goal for Discovering Sir *E. S's* Letter, wherein he promised a pair of Organs for the Town of *Tornes*. Notwithstanding *S.* owned his Letter in the House of Commons.

Q. 10. Who were they that did not call *Jack How* to an Account for Impudently affronting the King in calling Him a Felon in a full House?

Q. 11. Who kept Company with Count *Tallard* the *French* Ambassador? and whether they are fit to sit in an *English* Parliament?

Q. 12. Who Voted to make good all Deficiencys, and then took care to destroy all Parliamentary Credit?

BERKS.
Will. Jennens,
Tho. Renda,
Sym. Harcourt.

BUCKS.
Will. *Lord* Cheyney,
James Herbert,
Sir Samuel Gerrard,
John Backwell,
Sir James Etheridg.

CAMBRIDGE.
Anthony Hammond,
a Poussineer.

CHESHIRE.
Peter Shakerly.

CORNWALL.
Henry *Lord* Hide,
John Hoblyn,
Charles Godolphin,
Sydney Godolphin,
Alexander Pendarvis,
Henry Mannaton,
John Mounstevens,
Francis Scobell,
Francis Godolphin,
Sir Henry Seymour,
John Tregagle,
John Granvill,
William Beaw,
Sir Rich Vivgan,
Francis Stratford,
John Prideaux,
Sir Jos. Tredenham,
John Tredenham,
a Poussineer,

CUMBERLAND.
William Seymour,
George Fletchex.

DEVON.
Will. Courtenay,
Samuel Roll,
Sir Ed. Seymour,
Sir Bartho Shower,
Francis Gwin,
Thomas Coulson,
Charles Trelawny,
Henry Trelawny,
Thomas Northmore,
Nicholas Hooper,
Frederick Hern,
Nathaniel Hern.

DORSET.
Thomas Freke,
Tho. Strangways,
Nath. Napier,
Henry Thinn,
Charles Churchil,
Michael Harvey,
Edward Nicholas,
Thomas Chafin,
Richard Fownes.

DURHAM.
William Lambton,
Thomas Conyers.

ESSEX.
Sr. Charles Barrinton,
Sir Thomas Cooke,
William Fytch,
Sir Thomas Davall.

A

GLOU-

(3)

GLOUCESTER.
John How,
James Thyn,
Charles Cox.

HEREFORD.
Thomas Foley,
James Bridges,
Edward Harley.

HERTFORD.
Ralph Freeman,
Thomas Halsey,
——Gape,
Charles Cæsar.
——Gulston.

KENT.
Henry Lee,
Thomas Bliss,
——Mitchell.

LANCASTER.
Richard Bold,
Robert Heysham,
Thomas Leigh,
Thomas Brothecton,
William Clayton.

LEICESTER.
John Veaney,
John Wilkins.

LINCOLN.
Sir John Belles,
Edmund Boulter,
Thomas Vyner,
William Cecill,
Charles Bartie.

MIDDLESEX.
Hugh Smithson,
Warwick Lake,
Sir John Fleet.
Thomas Cross.

NORFOLK.
Sir Jacob Astley,
Robert Davey,
Thomas Blofeild,
Edmun Soam.

NORTHAMTON.
Sir Justin Isham,
Gilbert Dolbern,
Thomas Ekins.

NOTINGHAM.
——Sacheverell,
Sir Willoughby Hickman.
John Reyner.

OXON.
Sir Robert Jenkinson,
Sir Edward Norreys,
Heneage Finch,
William Bromely,
James Bertie,
Charles North,
Thomas Rowney,
Francis Norreys.

RUTLAND.
Sir Thomas Mackworth,
Richard Holford.

SALOP.
Sir Edward Acton,
Sir Thomas Powys,

SOMERSET.
Henry Portman.
Sir Francis Wart,
James Anderton.

SOUTHAMTON.
Thomas Jervoise,
Roger Mompesson,
Anthony Sturt,
William Etrick.

STAFFORD.
Thomas Foley,
Sir John Levenson Gower,
Sir Henry Gough.

SUFFOLK.
Sir Samuel Barnardiston,
Earl of Dysert,
Sir Charles Duncomb,
Sir Chtales Blois,
Sir Edmund Turner,
Sir Edmund Bacon,
Henry Johnson,
Sir John Cordell,
Sir Robert Dowers.

SURRY.
John Weston,
Sir John Parsons,
Sir Theo. Oglethorp.

SUSSEX.
John Miller,

Willi-

99 *A List of One Unanimous Club of Members of the Late Parliament*
[London], 1701
148- 350q, p. 2

THE LATE SEVENTEENTH CENTURY WITNESSED A NEW FORM of political literature: the "black list." This controversial tract represented an explicit attempt by Whigs to influence voters ahead of the election in December 1701. It catalogued those members of Parliament who had opposed the Glorious Revolution (which had brought William III to the throne), and who were allegedly conspiring with the country's enemies. It helped to ensure that at least some of these men failed to secure re-election.

(1)

Apothecaries.	*Heathcote*	*Ashhurst*	*Bateman*	*Ward*	*Withers*	*Hoare*	*Newland*	*Cass*
Mic. Armstead					—	—	—	—
Si. Andrews	—	—	—	—				
John Acklam	—	—	—	—				
John Broughton	—	—	—	—				
David Boncheret	—	—	—	—				
Edward Baker	—	—	—	—				
Jos. Biscoe	—	—	—	—				
John Blackstone	—				—	—	—	
Tho. Bromfield					—	—	—	—
Peregrine Browne	—	—	—	—				
Sam. Birch					—	—	—	—
Daniel Baxter					—	—	—	—
John Biscoe	—	—	—	—				
William Browning	—	—	—	—				
Nathaniel Brook	—	—	—	—				
George Bew					—	—	—	—
Richard Chapman					—	—	—	—
Robert Catterell	—	—	—	—				
Samuel Chapman			—	—	—	—		
Francis Conde	—	—	—	—				
Joseph Cruttendon	—	—	—	—				
Thomas Drury	—	—						
George Dare					—	—	—	—
Bellavir Davys	—	—	—	—				
Francis Dandridge					—	—	—	—
Thomas Dalton	—	—	—	—				
Arthur Emmerson					—	—	—	—
William Finch					—	—	—	—
Charles Fowler				—		—	—	—

B

(186)

Total of the POLL, as declar'd by the Sheriffs,

Sir *GILBERT HEATHCOTE*,	3185
Sir *WILLIAM ASHHURST*,	3048
Sir *JAMES BATEMAN*,	3104
JOHN WARD, Esquire,	3224
Sir *WILLIAM WITHERS*,	3629
Sir *RICHARD HOARE*,	3572
Sir *GEORGE NEWLAND*,	3385
JOHN CASS, Esquire,	3240

Then a Scrutiny was demanded; which being ended, the Sheriffs caus'd to be proclaim'd upon the *Hustings*, That they had no Reason to depart from their former Declaration; so the Election fell on the four last Worthy Gentlemen.

100 *The Poll of the Livery-Men of the City of London*
London: John Morphew, 1710
134- 644.5q, pp. 1, 186

THE EMERGENCE OF POLITICAL PARTIES made elections tense and fractious, and London's 1710 contest was particularly controversial. Some commentators alleged that mobs and the press exerted undue influence in order to ensure that the Tories took all four seats. This "poll book" revealed the votes—one for each of the available places—cast by individual voters, as well as the final outcome. It demonstrated a high turnout (around eighty percent), and a highly polarized electorate.

Terms

BROADSIDE
A single sheet, printed on one side, of folio size or larger, and meant for public display.

COMMITTEE OF BOTH KINGDOMS
The executive body set up by Parliament to run the war effort during the Civil Wars. It was comprised of members of Parliament, English peers, and leading figures from their Scottish allies.

CORANTO
A term used to refer to the first format of printed newspapers in England. A variation of *courant* (messenger), *coranto* is often used synonymously with the terms *gazette*, *newsletter*, or *newspaper*. The word *courant* is still found as part of the title of a number of newspapers.

THE CIVIL WARS
The armed struggle which took place in England, Scotland, and Ireland from 1642 to 1648 between Royalist supporters of King Charles I and those who sought to increase the power of Parliament at the expense of the Crown. It resulted in a victory for Parliament, the execution of the King in 1649, and the declaration of a republic that lasted until the restoration of the monarchy in 1660.

FOLIO
A single sheet of printer's paper, printed on both sides and folded once to create two leaves or four pages.

THE GLORIOUS REVOLUTION
The events surrounding the abdication of King James II, involving the "invasion" by the Dutch ruler, William of Orange, the husband of James II's daughter, Mary. William and Mary were offered the crown and ruled as joint monarchs (William III and Mary II). This resulted in a constitutional revolution which forever limited the power of English monarchs.

LEVELLERS
A radical group of Parliamentarians that emerged in the late 1640s. Levellers sought political reform and religious toleration. They have been seen as early advocates of democratic change, especially in their efforts to extend voting rights to more people.

LICENSE

All printed material published in England required the approval of the civil and religious authorities before it could be published. The authorization for publication was known as a license, and those who reviewed printed works and granted permissions were known as licensers of the press.

LONG PARLIAMENT

An assembly of Parliament that met from November 1640 until April 1653. This unusually long Parliament became possible once the king had lost his power to dissolve parliaments, in 1641.

MONOPOLY

A grant in the form of a patent, given by the monarch to an individual or group for the sole right to control a certain type of business or trade, such as the manufacture of soap or the importation of Madeira wine. Unfair practices in granting patents and the growth of monopolies caused widespread public discontent.

NEWSBOOK

The term *newspaper* was used only rarely before the eighteenth century. Before that time, readers would have been much more familiar with the word *newsbook*, which meant small serials or periodicals that published the latest information on the progress of a war or political affairs, such as election results or new laws.

NEWSLETTER

The generic term for manuscripts containing news. *Newsletters* could take the form of private letters within networks of family and friends, but the term was used more often to refer to those items produced more or less regularly, sometimes from within government circles and the office of the secretary of state, but also by well-informed private individuals. Consumers generally subscribed to newsletter services, which were fairly expensive but which could include updates tailored to readers' personal interests.

PAMPHLET

In the publishing trade, *pamphlets* were printed *quartos*. A quarto was a book based upon a printer's sheet folded in half twice to form four small pages. Pamphlets were no more than twelve sheets, or ninety-six pages, long based upon the maximum number of pages that could be crudely stitched together, rather than thoroughly sewn as in bookmaking. More generally, the term *pamphlet* was used to describe small publications, not meant to last for a long time, that dealt with the news of the day and opinions about controversial subjects.

PARLIAMENTARIAN

Those people identified with Parliament during the 1640s, in opposition to the Royalists, and who sought to place limits upon the power of the monarch.

POPISH PLOT

Popish plot was a term used repeatedly throughout the late sixteenth and seventeenth centuries, to refer to a widely held belief that the Pope and his agents wished to overthrow the Protestant monarchy and return England to Roman Catholicism. The term also refers to events in 1678, when false accusations about a conspiracy against Charles II led to demands for a law to be passed that would prevent any Catholic (specifically, Charles II's brother, James, Duke of York) from inheriting the throne.

PRIVY COUNCIL

The select government advisory body, similar to a modern "cabinet," whose members were appointed by the monarch.

PROTECTORATE

The period between 1653 and 1659, when Oliver Cromwell assumed the position of Lord Protector, with powers broadly similar to those of a king.

REGICIDES

The name given to the fifty-nine soldiers and members of Parliament who signed the warrant condemning Charles I to death, following his trial in January 1649. The word comes from the Latin, and means "king killer."

REPUBLIC

The period of constitutional experimentation between 1649 to 1660, characterized by rule without a monarch.

RESTORATION

The process leading to Charles II's assumption of the English throne in 1660, after eleven years of *republican* government. The term also refers to the period of Stuart monarchy between 1660 and 1688.

ROYALIST

A supporter of Charles I and his cause during the Civil Wars (1642–1649), and one who, after the king's execution in 1649, worked on behalf of his son, the future Charles II.

STAR CHAMBER

A law court presided over by royal judges and privy councilors, which had wide powers of discretion. It was used by the early Stuart kings to clamp down on opposition to royal policies. In 1632, it banned the publication of news serials in England and was widely seen as an arbitrary and unjust tool of the monarchy. The *Star Chamber* was abolished by Parliament in 1641.

STATIONERS COMPANY

The London company which oversaw the regulation of the profession and the interests of its members, who were independent publishers, printers, and booksellers. In addition to controlling admission to the trade, the Company maintained the Stationers' Register, which listed new publications and the names of those who were entitled to print them.

TORY

Originally a term for Irish and Scottish bandits and robbers, *Tory* became a nickname for ideological descendents of civil war Royalists and hard-line supporters of Charles II and his younger brother, the Duke of York, who became James II in 1685. By the end of the seventeenth century, the label commonly described those who were determined to uphold order and authority in both church and state, although they had not yet been organized into a political party.

WHIG

Another term which began as a term of abuse for the Scots, in particular for those Presbyterians opposed the Royalist cause in the 1640s and 1650s, *Whig* became a nickname for critics of Charles II's government after 1660, who tried to prevent the Catholic Duke of York from succeeding to the throne. Like the Tories, Whigs gradually became something approaching a formal political party.

JOSEPH ADDISON (1672–1719)
A distinguished poet, government official, and Member of Parliament, Addison was most famous for his work with *The Tatler* and his cofounding of the enormously popular essay periodical *The Spectator*. Addison was a leading member of the most influential literary circles of the early eighteenth century, claiming among his many friends Jonathan Swift, Alexander Pope, and Ambrose Philips.

SIR JOHN BERKENHEAD (1617–1679)
Berkenhead, a staunch Royalist in the 1640s, wrote the first official English newsbook, *Mercurius Aulicus*. His biting acerbic wit was employed to great effect in promoting the Royalist cause. He was also an established poet of some talent. After the Restoration, he received a knighthood for his service to Charles I and was elected to Parliament.

CHARLES BLOUNT (1654–1693)
A freethinker whose numerous publications attacked many of the foundations of Christian belief, Blount incurred the wrath of the establishment for his pamphlets, many of which were suppressed or ceremonially burned in public. He was one of the leading figures who argued for a free press in England and for the removal of the Licensing Act.

SAMUEL BUCKLEY
A printer and bookseller, Buckley was responsible for the success of the first daily newspaper, *The Daily Courant*. His strong, effective writing style quickly turned the newspaper into a popular hit, selling 800 copies a day and circulating throughout England.

NATHANIEL BUTTER (1583–1664) AND NICHOLAS BOURNE (CA. 1584–1660)
Butter and Bourne were booksellers who dominated the newspaper trade in the early years of the industry. Starting in 1621, they printed weekly news from abroad; despite a few brushes with the government censors, they established a highly successful serialized newspaper in England.

HENRY CARE (1646/7–1688)
A polemicist Whig writer, Care published newspapers and tracts during the reign of Charles II that attacked the monarchy and the Catholic Church. He quickly made a name for himself as a leading writer of anti-Catholic works. Tried five times for seditious libel, he was burned in effigy before he switched sides and became a supporter of the Catholic James II. He also collaborated with his former antagonist, *Sir Roger L'Estrange*, and worked tirelessly for religious liberty for all Englishmen.

JANE COE

Jane Coe developed a flourishing business after the death in 1644 of her husband, Andrew Coe, printing dozens of cheap political pamphlets and newspapers and displaying her support for radical religious and political views, particularly for the Parliamentarian army.

HENEAGE FINCH (1621–1682)

During the Civil Wars, Finch was a staunch Royalist who heavily mortgaged his estates to assist the cause. Among many offices he received after the Restoration was the post of Ambassador to Constantinople (now Istanbul), where he successfully protected English interests in the Middle East. Married four times, he fathered twenty-seven legitimate children and died heavily in debt.

GUALTER (WALTER) FROST (BAP. 1598–1652)

Frost served as a Parliamentarian intelligence officer during the early years of the *Civil War* but soon after established himself as the co-secretary of the important *Committee of Both Kingdoms.* After the *Republic* was established in 1649, he became the secretary to the Council of State, the newly created executive body, and throughout his career he combined such duties with work as a journalist and propagandist.

BENJAMIN HARRIS (CA.1647–1720)

Harris was a prolific writer who established a number of short-lived newspapers, starting with *Domestick Intelligence* in 1679. Falling foul of the government because of his bitter anti-Catholic invective, he fled to America in 1686. He established himself in the Boston book trade and published *Publick Occurrences* in 1690, the first American newspaper. He returned to England in the mid-1690s and resumed newspaper publishing.

PETER HEYLYN (1599–1662)

A clergyman in the Protestant Church of England, Heylyn rose to prominence in the 1630s as a result of his close ties to William Laud, the unpopular Archbishop of Canterbury. Heylyn wrote numerous theological and historical tracts; at the start of the *Civil Wars,* he joined King Charles I in Oxford and became the first editor of the Royalist newspaper *Mercurius Aulicus.*

SIR ROGER L'ESTRANGE (1616–1704)

L'Estrange was a Royalist pamphleteer who became the official Surveyor and Licenser of the Press shortly after the Restoration. He acted zealously as the government censor, suppressing more than 600 works within the first few years in office. A prolific pamphleteer, he also started a thrice-weekly newspaper, *The Observator,* in 1681. The paper quickly became the most effective vehicle of Tory propaganda.

GILBERT MABBOTT (BAP. 1622–CA. 1670)
A prominent Parliamentian and newsletter writer of the 1640s and 1650s, Mabbott acted as a Licenser of the Press between 1645 and 1649. He also contributed to the radical newsbook *The Moderate*, which presented the view of the *Levellers* and the more extreme elements of the Parliamentarian army.

JOHN MILTON (1608–1674)
Milton was a prodigious author whose work ranged from theological tracts to epic poetry, sonnets, numerous defenses of the Republican regime of the 1650s, and *Areopagitica*, his strident call for freedom of the press. Blind from 1652 onward, he still managed to produce some of the most famous works in English literature, *Paradise Lost* and *Samson Agonistes*.

MARCHAMONT NEDHAM (BAP. 1620–1678)
One of the more colorful and notorious journalists of the seventeenth century, Nedham remains most famous for his willingness to change political sides. He wrote on behalf of *Parliamentarians* (1642–1646), *Royalists* (1647–1649), the *Republic* and Oliver Cromwell (1650–1660), and Charles II (1676–1678). Nevertheless, historians now recognize his skill as a journalist, his opposition to Presbyterianism, and his status as one of the most important Republican thinkers of the period, whose work exerted a lasting influence long after his death.

SIR RICHARD NEWDIGATE (1644–1710)
A Warwickshire landowner, Newdigate pioneered new and often expensive improvements to his coal mines (his greatest passion) and his estates. He briefly served as a Member of Parliament and had a long career as a Justice of the Peace in his native county.

RICHARD OVERTON (FL. 1640–1663)
A radical *Leveller* writer, Overton consistently argued for freedom of conscience in religion, and his pamphlets were particularly vitriolic against Presbyterians. In his political tracts, which formed the basis of the Leveller manifesto, Overton called for the prison reform, the elimination of corruption in government, and the expansion of suffrage. Frequently, he was targeted by the authorities, had his papers seized, and was imprisoned.

HENRY PEACHAM (1578–CA. 1644)
Peacham was a teacher, writer, and illustrator, best known for his 1622 courtesy book *The Complete Gentleman*, which offered advice on the proper form of education. He is also famous for a manuscript drawing of a scene from *Titus Andronicus*, the first known illustration of a Shakespeare play. Peacham helped pioneer emblem books in England. These works were a combination of text and illustrations, which were read together to provide lessons in morality.

SAMUEL PECKE

Although relatively little is known about Pecke's life, his importance lies in apparently being able to successfully negotiate a key phase in the transition from manuscript to printed news. Having worked as a scrivener in Westminster Hall, selling copies of political speeches and other documents relating to Parliamentarian affairs, Pecke emerged as one of the pioneering newsbook editors of the early 1640s. As the editor of the *Perfect Diurnall*, he became one of the most respected and trusted journalists during the Civil Wars.

THÉOPHRASTE RENAUDOT (1586–1653)

Although he served as a physician to Louis XIII of France, Renaudot is better known as the founder of *La Gazette*, the first weekly newspaper in France, which debuted in 1631. In an eventful career, he also established the first pawnshop in Paris and served as an overseer of the poor, pioneering clinics which offered free medical advice to those unable to afford the care of physicians.

JOHN RUSHWORTH (CA.1612–1690)

An avid observer of political events, collector of newsbooks, and author, Rushworth was made official Licenser of the Press in 1644, an office that he combined with a position close to the Parliamentarian general, Sir Thomas Fairfax. He played an important part in publishing accounts under his imprint of parliamentary activity and various battles. In the 1650s, Rushworth used his notes and newsbooks to compile a multi-volume history of the *Civil Wars*. Despite his association with Parliament and the *regicides*, he prospered after the Restoration, holding numerous legal and administrative offices.

BRUNO RYVES (CA. 1596–1677)

Ryves was a royal chaplain who also served on Charles I's council of war. As part of the Royalist war effort, he produced a newsbook, *Mercurius Rusticus*, which chronicled the horrors perpetrated on the English people by the Parliamentarian forces. After the Restoration, Ryves received a number of high-ranking appointments in the Church of England, including the office of Dean of Windsor.

THOMAS SCOTT (D. 1626)

A radical Protestant writer, Scott was a prolific writer of anti-Catholic and anti-Spanish material. After the 1620 publication of *Vox Populi*, his critique of Spanish influence over James I's government, he fled to Utrecht in Holland and became a preacher. Scott continued to pour out anti-Spanish invective until he was assassinated in 1626 by a deranged English soldier.

RICHARD STEELE (BAP. 1672–1729)

Steele was an army officer, poet, dramatist, and prose writer who later founded *The Tatler*, an essay periodical. A leading member of the Kit-Kat Club, an influential political organization, Steele continually propounded Whig ideals. After he discontinued the increasingly politicized *Tatler*, he joined with Joseph Addison to produce the nonpartisan *Spectator*.

JOHN TAYLOR (1578–1653)

Known as the Water Poet because of his career as a waterman, Taylor lived an adventurous life. A prolific scribbler of both poems and prose, Taylor put his pen to use helping the Royalist cause from Oxford, writing newsbooks and attacks on Parliament. After the surrender of Oxford to Parliament in 1646, Taylor returned to London and set up shop as an alehouse keeper. He continued to write travel pamphlets, wittily describing the pitfalls of life on the road, but he was always under suspicion for being a Royalist spy.

HENRY WALKER (FL. 1638–1660)

A former ironmonger, who subsequently became a preacher, bookseller, and journalist, Walker is best known as the editor of the newsbook *Perfect Occurrences*. This lively journal, begun in 1644, championed religious nonconformity, coupled with strong support for Parliament and Oliver Cromwell. Walker was involved with numerous other news publications in the late 1640s; he became a figure much satirized and mocked by his opponents in Royalist newspapers.

GEORGE WHARTON (FL. 1617–1681)

Wharton had many prominent public careers. He was a Royalist astrologer, captain of horse in the king's army, and almanac writer before he turned to editing newspapers in the late 1640s. In *Mercurius Elenticus*, his outspoken support for Charles I won him few friends in the Parliamentarian regime, and he was imprisoned. He escaped shortly afterward and continued to publish Royalist tracts until threats from the government largely silenced his political writings.